# HEAVY JUSTICE

# HEAVY JUSTICE

## THE STATE OF INDIANA
### v.
## MICHAEL G. TYSON

# J. GREGORY GARRISON
# AND RANDY ROBERTS

A WILLIAM PATRICK BOOK

Addison-Wesley Publishing Company
Reading, Massachusetts   Menlo Park, California   New York
Don Mills, Ontario   Wokingham, England   Amsterdam   Bonn
Sydney   Singapore   Tokyo   Madrid   San Juan
Paris   Seoul   Milan   Mexico City   Taipei

Library of Congress Cataloging-in-Publication Data

Garrison, J. Gregory.
    Heavy justice : State of Indiana v. Michael G. Tyson / J. Gregory
Garrison and Randy Roberts.
        p.    cm.
    "A William Patrick book."
    Includes index.
    ISBN 0-201-62275-0
    1. Tyson, Mike, 1966– —Trials, litigation, etc.    2. Trials
(Rape)—Indiana—Indianapolis.    I. Roberts, Randy, 1951–    .
II. Title.    III. Title: State of Indiana v. Michael G. Tyson.
KF224.T97G37    1994
345.73'02532—dc20                                          94-220
[347.3052532]                                              CIP

Jacket design by Jean Seal
Text design by Ruth Kolbert
Set in 11-point New Baskerville Book by Weimer

1  2  3  4  5  6  7  8  9-MA-97969594
First printing, March 1994

*To Phyllis Jean and Suzy,*
*who know what's best and important,*
*even when we don't*

# CONTENTS

# ACKNOWLEDGMENTS

---

This country is full of gifted, aggressive, and devoted lawyers who give their best to the craft and demands of prosecution, and their skills and dedication far exceeds anything depicted in the media or on television. It is only on one of those rare occasions when the eyes of the world become focused on a novel case—for whatever reason, or for no reason at all beyond morbid curiosity—that our work and our contributions can be seen by the people we serve.

*State* v. *Tyson* was unique in the challenge and opportunities for the deputies who tried it. Asked to return to the prosecutor's table from private practice, I had the luxury of bringing no agenda to the case beyond convicting a rapist of his crimes. Without political aspirations and owing no one any favor or duty beyond doing my best, I found myself able to address the issues, the pressures, the tensions, and even the threats with a sense of humor. I knew that it would end, the press would depart, and, one day, I would be back in my office answering my phone and taking care of my own clients' business again.

So I could joke with the reporters and give them ridiculous answers to their questions, make faces at the cameras, and, when it was over and the rules permitted, speak frankly about the events and their significance. What acclaim resulted in truth owed more to the notoriety of the rapist than to the quality of my work. Surely we did a good job of prosecuting the defendant, but, just as clearly, we and thousands like us do the job every day just as well.

This is a story about trying Michael Tyson for his crimes, but it is also the story of uncommon courage and commitment by a young woman from Coventry, Rhode Island, Desiree Lynn Washington.

Many additional people deserve recognition for the result achieved in this trial, and as many for their contributions to this book. First, the cops. They do the hard work. Detective Tom Kuzmik, my "beef," worried for us all, never shirked a task, watched over me constantly in airports, taxis, on trains, and amid streets jammed with people who had no love for what I represented, and he never doubted us or the rectitude of what we were doing. Not until you have once experienced the moment when another man purposefully interposes his own body between you and the threat of harm can you know what it means. Likewise, Detective Jack Geilker, my driver and security during the trial, and my friend always, kept me from harm's way over and over. Sgts. Charlie Briley, Jeff Duhamell, Darryl Pierce, Carey Forrestal, Steve Odle, and Bill Newman were officers devoted to the work and absolutely tireless in the discharge of every duty from coffee pot cleaning to chasing down each fragmentary lead or obstacle tossed up by the defense, to protecting a bunch of lawyers who were too preoccupied to take good care of themselves.

We were surrounded by wonderful and bright young lawyers whose devotion I referred to earlier. David Dreyer, who took the case to the grand jury; George Horn, book man extraordinaire; Kim De Vane, law clerk able to work without ever sleeping; Dave Wagner, the paralegal who never said no to a task; and Erica Roach, our lawyer volunteer from the "big guys" at Ice, Miller, Donadio and Ryan—they all demonstrated singular devotion over more hours and days than I ever dreamed would be required to accomplish the mission. And although it might sound unusual for a prosecutor to admit, the reporters who covered the trial were uniformly courteous, fair, and—with only a few obvious exceptions who will remain unnamed— were careful and accurate in their work. They were respectful of the limitations on our time and on what we could say; when the result had been attained, they were generous with their accolades.

Jeffrey Modisett, the Marion County Prosecutor, placed great stock in me and our team. He never wavered, always supported, and refused to use the case to promote his own career.

My co-counsel Barbara Trathen shared equal responsibilities with me, and her work was evident throughout the trial. This is her story as much as it is mine.

Finally, on a more personal level, I had the support, confidence, and prayers of wonderful people. My parents, Jim and Mary Blanche Garrison, for their love; my brother and law partner Chris, for accepting additional duties without complaint; my friend and law partner Mike Kiefer, for the work he did on the case and his "Gipper" speech on the eve of the trial; my cousin David, for his late-night exhortations at the barn; my children, Juli, Betsy, Kate, Ashley, and Clint, for trusting Dad; and Phyllis Jean, for more than I can express.

JGG

Working on *Heavy Justice* with Greg, I too have accumulated debts. In the Marion County Prosecutor's Office, Jeffrey Modisett, David Dreyer, Barbara Trathen, Dave Wagner, and Rob Smith answered my many questions and carefully detailed their roles in this case. I always felt that they spoke honestly, and I was impressed by their courtesy and professionalism. Similarly, reporters Jack Rinehart from WRTV, R. Joseph Gelarden from the Indianapolis *Star*, and Lester Munson of *Sports Illustrated* gave me insightful interviews. Mike Kiefer helped me not only by numerous conversations and reading several drafts of the manuscript but also with his humor and enthusiasm. Jack O'Bryan offered legal advice, friendship, and a healthy suspicion about the motives of everyone, and he was responsible for bringing Greg and me together. Other people spoke with me off the record, and I thank them as well.

The staff of the history department of Purdue University, especially Judy McHenry, Julie Mantica, and Eleanor Gerns, put up with my rushed requests and helped me in more ways than I care to remember. The same was true with the people at Addison-Wesley. William Patrick's constant good humor and accomplished surgical techniques were appreciated. No author could ask for a better editor; we both know how much he improved the manuscript. Thanks also to Bill's colleague Sharon Broll who answered so many of my questions, particularly on Fridays. Copy editor Rachel Parks's careful scrutiny caught mistakes that both Bill and I missed. Senior Production Coordinator Beth Burleigh worked on the manuscript in its final stages.

My agent and friend Gerry McCauley gave his generous and kind support to the project. He has gone beyond the call of duty for me, and it is a pleasure to acknowledge my debt and offer my thanks.

At home, three people put everything I do in perspective: the twins, Kelly and Alison, and my wife, Suzy. The twins provided delightful distractions, certain as only four-year-olds can be that their latest drawings were more important than anything I might be doing with the "peuter." Suzy read drafts, corrected excesses, and agreed that the twins' assumptions were sound. I love them all.

*RWR*

# HEAVY JUSTICE

# PART ONE

PART
ONE

# SOMETHING HAPPENED

The Reverend Edward Taylor, D.D., had a gentle face and a comforting smile. In a portrait by John Forbes done in 1846 he strikes a classic nineteenth-century religious pose: hair brushed neatly to the side, wire-rimmed glasses, cross pendant, right hand on the Bible. Although his upper and lower lips are clean-shaven, he has a beard like that of either an Amish farmer or Robert Bork. The beard gives a scholarly, ascetic air to his appearance. The painting looks as if it should hang in some remote English vicarage, forever suspended in a lost world. But somehow the portrait has made its way to the United States, to the state of Indiana, to the city of Indianapolis. There it hangs in the main lobby of the Canterbury Hotel, to the right of the bellman's stand. No Canterbury employee knows who the Reverend Taylor was, or for that matter how or why his portrait came to this fine hotel. But that doesn't seem to matter. The man of God smiles sweetly at every person who enters the Canterbury and takes a sharp right turn to the registration desk.

Though no one can give any of the biographical details of the Reverend Taylor's life, his portrait serves a purpose. It reminds all who enter that they are stepping into—however briefly— a gentler environment. The Canterbury is not the Hilton, promising standardized service and quality for the masses. Rather, it offers something the Hiltons and the Hyatts and the Omnis of the world can't: human size, personal service. The hotel's motif is decidedly English. Small portraits of monarchs, hunting prints, and still lifes fill the walls. Fresh cut flowers and wood paneling provide a country house feel. High tea is served in the small atrium. Altogether, the Canterbury looks and feels as if Ralph Lauren designed it.

The Reverend Taylor's portrait was hanging at its usual spot in the early morning of July 19, 1991. Although the previous day had been hot and humid, a cool breeze had swept into Indianapolis during the night. Outside it was a pleasant, quiet night. Indianapolis, as more than one visitor has observed, is not New York City. With a few exceptions, it doesn't cater to the late-night crowd. After midnight and certainly by one o'clock, bars close down for the night, traffic vanishes from the streets, and street lights cast shadows over empty sidewalks. Inside the Canterbury, activity slows as guests turn in for the night.

At a minute or so after 2:30 A.M., six floors above the Reverend Taylor in a $550 a night suite, a young black woman emerged from number 606. At that moment Chris Low, the Canterbury's night bellman, was delivering a bowl of scallop chowder and a Swiss and mushroom burger to Dale Edwards in Room 604. Low saw Edwards glance down the hall; a smirk crossed Edwards's face. Low turned his head, following Edwards's eyes to Suite 606. The young woman had her shoes in her hands. Her hair was mussed, and she looked about as if she was lost. She appeared to be frightened. She took a step toward Room 604 and the elevators beyond, then turned abruptly and walked in the other direction.

Low had seen the woman forty-five minutes earlier when she had entered the Canterbury with Mike Tyson, the former world heavyweight boxing champion. He had held the front door for the couple. The woman walked in first, four or five feet ahead of Tyson. She was a small, attractive woman, Low noticed, wearing some sort of jacket made of shiny fabric. But Low didn't observe much else. He focused his attention on Iron Mike Tyson, a guest at the Canterbury. Tyson walked in slowly. He smiled at Low and shook his hand. For Low it was a big deal, a chance to touch greatness. *Wow*, he thought, *Tyson shook my hand*. Low then returned to his station and his night duties.

Low didn't see the woman again that night. But he did see Tyson's limousine parked in front of the hotel. He walked outside and had a short chat with the driver, who informed him that Tyson was leaving Indianapolis on a five-thirty flight. That's odd, Low thought. July 19 was only the second night of Tyson's scheduled three-night stay. Low informed the night manager, Dave Wilson, of Tyson's change in plans and then returned to his bell stand.

At about four-fifteen he heard the elevator ding as the door opened. Seconds later he saw Tyson and Dale Edwards round the corner and walk straight out of the Canterbury. The two men seemed to be in a hurry. They didn't stop to check out. Tyson had been relaxed and friendly a few hours earlier. He had walked slowly, shaken hands, and taken time to look around the lobby and atrium. Now, Low noticed, "he just booked." Fast. Through the door and into the night.

Something had happened—something that would change the lives of Mike Tyson, the woman who was in his room, and the lawyers and investigators who would be sucked into the affair.

Twenty-six hours earlier, Tyson had come out of the night into the Canterbury accompanied by three people: his bodyguard, Dale Edwards; the limousine driver, Virginia Foster; and the singer-dancer B Angie B. Low was on duty then too. He watched Tyson like so many other people had watched Tyson—in awe of a boxer so powerful and so famous that wherever he went people stopped and stared. Edwards and Foster were bag carriers, there to serve the needs of Tyson. B Angie B, dressed in a revealing outfit that screamed sex, was also there for Tyson. Low thought she looked like a hooker, and night bellmen at five-star hotels know what hookers look like. Off-white skin-tight shorts hugged her hips, clinging to her buttocks and flat stomach as tightly as a runner's spandex tights. A short white beaded blouse hung loosely from her shoulders. Her hair draped over her shoulders. Every accoutrement seemed oversize and fake: the jewelry too big, the nails too long, the makeup too thick. *Hooker,* Low thought as he watched Tyson hug and grab and paw her.

In theory, Mike Tyson had come to Indianapolis for Black Expo, an annual week-long celebration of black culture and achievement supported by a number of foundations and private individuals. Tyson had never been to Black Expo, but his manager and promoter, Don King, donated money to the event. Black Expo courted celebrities, few more than Tyson. Celebrities brought glamour and publicity to the event: in 1991 the Reverend Jesse Jackson, the soul and gospel singer Johnny Gill, General Calvin Waller, the actor Danny Glover, Craig Hodges, three-point shooting guard for the Chicago Bulls, and other black celebrities attended Black Expo. Several times during the previous years Tyson had promised to attend the event, and each time something else had come up. On the afternoon of July 17, 1991, he finally arrived. But his schedule included more than simply the celebration of black culture and achievement.

None of the celebrities rivaled Tyson. Others commanded more respect; others provided more inspiration as role models. But none turned heads and pumped up spectators like Tyson. "When Mike's around, it's like someone turned up the juice," noted one Black Expo spectator. It had been like that for years; wherever Tyson went he turned up the juice. After all, as the toughest man in the world, the very symbol of primal masculinity, he was America's guest. What Tyson wanted he got—money, cars, clothes, women. So what if he had lost the title? Who could replace Mike Tyson in America's imagination? Buster Douglas, who blew up like a balloon after winning the title and lost his first defense? Evander Holyfield, with his decency and religion and respectability? Champion or not, Iron Mike Tyson was still The One.

But journalists speculated as to how much longer Tyson could retain that status. Was the rage that made him great—the very thing that turned on the juice—limitless? Richard Hoffer of *Sports Illustrated* wondered. A month before Tyson arrived in Indianapolis Hoffer wrote, "For some time it was reassuring to think of Mike Tyson as the careful curator of his own legend, somewhat unpredictable outside the ring, yes, but entirely dedicated to the service of history within. You could count on him for violent spectacle. . . . Yet now there is increasing doubt that Tyson can sustain his reputation. . . . There is a feeling in the boxing community that Tyson has already crested, and that even if he remains above the rest of the division, he is nevertheless on his way down."

Blame abounded. Many experts blamed Don King, who after taking over Tyson's career had fired the boxer's longtime trainer, Kevin Rooney, and severed Tyson's links to his successful past. Others pointed to the enemy of all boxers: *la dolce vita.* Too much money, too much success, too much to lose. Tyson, they claimed, was no longer hungry; boxing was no longer the center of his life. Women and champagne had become more important. Still others hinted that Tyson was too old to sustain a boxing style that demanded the cruel reflexes of youth. At his best, Tyson had combined subtle defense with a relentless offense. He moved constantly forward, throwing punches in combinations while at the same time he rolled his shoulders and bobbed his head. He was as difficult to hit as he was to avoid. Now, the experts said, his jab had gone south, his combinations had given way to a Big Bang technique, and his defense had become porous. In his two recent fights against Razor Ruddock, Tyson had looked as if he had gone to the Rocky Balboa school of boxing: *You give me your best shot and I'll give you mine, and remember—keep your head still, and only one punch at a time.* In short, Tyson had lost his art. He had become, if not ordinary, then also not extraordinary.

A few authorities believed Tyson was headed for a crash. They pointed not to his performance in the ring but to a change in his prefight language. In a press conference before his most recent fight with Ruddock, Tyson promised to make his opponent his girlfriend: "I can't wait for you to kiss me with those big lips of yours." It was jailhouse talk, language that insulted both himself and his sport. "Early in his career," observed his former friend and trainer Teddy Atlas, "when he believed in himself, he said things in a controlled way, very Spartan words, honorable words. . . . He thought it was sportsman-like, glorious. But now, when he sees himself slipping, he's grabbing for something he never thought he needed before, a stick to take into the ring."

But, Atlas thought, Tyson sensed that even a stick wouldn't be enough to keep him on top. "Sometimes, if you listen to Mike, you can hear him preparing for failure. He says, 'I've been poor once, I can be poor again.' He's said that a number of times. He's not saying, I'll never lose what I've got. He's saying the opposite—I could lose everything and I could handle it. It's like he knows he's vulnerable and he's preparing for that day."

7

Such thoughts had been aired with greater frequency during the previous three years. Before his title fight with Tyson in 1988, the former champion Larry Holmes attacked Tyson's character: "He's going down in history as an SOB. If he do happen to win the fight, down the line he'll destroy himself." Tyson would end up either in jail or the victim of a violent death, Holmes said. But in 1988 it was easy to ignore Holmes's remarks and attribute them to his perpetual sour disposition. But during the next several years, other boxing authorities echoed Holmes's opinion. The day after Tyson lost the title to Buster Douglas, Mike Lupica of the *National* cheered the result of the fight. It was poetic justice for the man who "bounces women around, and gives it in the back to his friends, and turns his back on people who helped make him champion: making it seem as if dogs have more loyalty than he does." Then, like Holmes, Lupica added an eerie prediction: "There are certain terrible headlines that when you finally see them, you feel as if you had already looked at them in a newspaper before. Billy Martin was one. Mike Tyson, believe me, would be another."

But since losing the title, Mike Tyson had not self-destructed. Rather he had prospered, winning four straight fights, two by first round knockouts. On June 28, 1991, less than a month before he came to Indianapolis, he had decisioned Razor Ruddock in Las Vegas. And the same week he arrived in Indianapolis, he signed a contract to fight Evander Holyfield on November 8 at Caesar's Palace, Las Vegas. The projected gross of the fight was over $100 million, of which Tyson was guaranteed $15 million. "I can't wait," he announced. "This is the fight I wanted." It was his chance to regain the title and the respect he had lost, the chance to silence his critics.

Normally Tyson trained for ten weeks preceding a major fight. That meant that he would begin to prepare for Holyfield in late August or early September; until then he was free to enjoy himself. Having just turned twenty-five on June 30, Tyson was young and single and determined to mingle.

After the Rudduck fight he had started to date rap singer B Angie B, whose real name was Angela Roxanna Boyd Earley. Angela Boyd was born and reared in Mississippi, but after she graduated from high school she moved to Oakland, California, where she got her first job in the music business, singing backup for M. C. Hammer and working for his Bust-It Productions. It was during her first full year with Hammer, sometime in 1988, that she first met Tyson. At the time she was just a "member of the posse," nothing special, but when she and Tyson made eye contact, sparks flew. *Maybe yes, maybe no*, Angela thought. In 1988 it was no. Tyson was married to Robin Givens, and he and Angela went their separate ways. During the next few years Tyson and Givens divorced. For her part, Angela moved out of the posse and became B Angie B—as in "Be Angie B"—the opening act for Johnny Gill and other Bust-It Productions stars.

In June 1991 Angie bumped into Tyson again, this time literally. She had just finished her set at the Washington, D.C., Bud-Fest when her personal assistant, Jeffrey Houston, told her that Tyson was in the audience. Angie walked over to the boxer and bumped into him as if by accident. Tyson grabbed her arm, telling her that he had been waiting to see her again. Angie "played him to the left a little bit," pretending that she wasn't that interested. But before he left, she gave him her pager number. Later that rainy night Tyson used the number, and he and Angie spent the night together.

When Angie's bus left D.C. the next morning, Tyson was on it. He followed her on several legs of her concert tour. The next stop was Albany, Tyson's second home, and he took Angie over to Catskill to meet his stepmother, Camille Ewald. When Angie moved on to Indianapolis, Tyson arranged to meet her there. They planned to spend a few days together in Indy and then go on to Cleveland, which was the next stop on the Bust-It tour.

Tyson arrived at the Indianapolis airport from Washington, D.C., at 4:25 P.M. on July 17. He was met by a limousine dispatched by the Reverend Charles Williams, the president of Black Expo. Williams hoped that Tyson would show up at Black Expo, but no one knew exactly what the unpredictable fighter would do. It was useless to give him a schedule. As he had demonstrated time and again, he would not be bound by itineraries. He went where he wanted to go, did what he wanted to do. And since he grew bored quickly, he was constantly on the move. Williams assumed that at some point during Tyson's stay in Indianapolis the boxer would show his support for Black Expo, but he left the timing to Tyson.

Dale Edwards, a Cleveland policeman who doubled as Tyson's bodyguard, arrived with Tyson on the flight from

Washington. He was a tall, heavyset man whose primary job was, essentially, to babysit Tyson. Tyson tended to lose keys and money and such like, and of course he had a cavalier attitude toward appointments and departure times. Edwards made travel arrangements for him, paid his bills, answered phones, kept phone numbers, responded to beepers, handled keys, and overall kept a watchful eye on his employer. Edwards also served another function. While shepherding Tyson, he guarded the interests of Don King. Tyson was King's blank check, and the promoter worried about the former champion's erratic behavior. Since King couldn't always travel with Tyson, he detailed others to travel with the boxer. Though it was understood that they would be unable to control Tyson, they were instructed "to help [him] out and to contact King immediately if anything goes wrong."

Virginia Foster, president and chief driver for the Solid Gold Limousine Service, met Tyson and Edwards outside the USAir baggage terminal in Indianapolis. Dennis Hayes, a Black Expo representative, escorted the boxer and his bodyguard to Foster's white Lincoln limo. Tyson's first item of business was to find Angie. One of his friends had been shot a few days before, and he wanted to talk to Angie about it. Foster drove him to 540 West Sixty-fourth Street, the home of Angie's aunt.

By now Angie thought she loved Tyson, but she had failed to inform him about several aspects of her own past—the most important of which was that she was married. When Tyson saw Angie, he kissed her in a way that showed he thought of himself as more than a friend. When Angie saw that her cousin had witnessed the kiss, she knew it was time for a long talk with her lover. Going outside, they strolled around the neighborhood as rubbernecking drivers swerved at the last second to avoid ditches and people came out on their sidewalks to see Angie— "You know, Betty's Mississippi niece who used to spend her summers in Indy but now was a star out in California"—and Iron Mike. Their walk together was a neighborhood happening, but somehow as they caught up on each other's lives the subject of Angie's marriage never came up.

At least, not until they returned to Angie's aunt's house, whereupon Betty Bates told Angie that a neighbor had said she saw them. "She thought Mike was your husband," she said, her emphasis clear and stern. Angie thought, *Oh, my God* just as

Tyson said, "You're married, huh?" Angie covered her face and fell into his lap while Aunt Betty flounced out of the room. For the next half hour they talked in earnest, and before long the house was alive with good-natured kidding and laughing.

At about six-thirty, Foster drove Tyson, Edwards, Angie, and Jeffrey Houston across town to a Holiday Inn that Tyson would later generously describe as crappy. While Edwards napped in the limousine, Tyson and Angie spent three hours in her room. She had vivid memories of the interlude, but Tyson's memory was less clear. He later recalled being at the Holiday Inn, but couldn't remember whether he and Angie had had sex or not, and if so for how long. "We could have," he allowed. "I'm not saying for sure if we didn't or did."

His memory of the rest of the evening was clearer. Shortly after nine-thirty, he and his small entourage left the Holiday Inn for a night on the town. They were supposed to pick up Tyson's host Dennis Hayes at an entertainment hall Hayes owned, the Sutherland, but Tyson and Edwards decided to change the plan. Although Tyson was scheduled to meet Hayes, Edwards told Foster not to pick him up because he "didn't want anyone else riding in the limousine with the champ." He instructed Foster to go instead to the Seville, a nightclub on North Michigan Road.

After drive-through stops at a Wendy's for burgers and a Dairy Queen for parfaits, Team Tyson arrived at the Seville at ten-thirty. As soon as they walked through the door the deejay announced that Mike Tyson was in the club. The manager, Mark Ritchey, sent over a complimentary bottle of house champagne. Tyson acknowledged the gift but had reservations about the quality of the champagne. He then ordered three $90 bottles of Dom Perignon, which were put on his tab. For the next two hours Tyson and his friends sipped champagne and pounded down Corona beer. Angela danced with Houston, but Tyson was too shy to try his moves.

News spread fast that the fighter was at the Seville. Soon the club started to fill with people anxious to meet and shake hands with the former champion. For Tyson, the attention was both routine and unwelcome. He was uncomfortable with strangers and disliked making small talk and signing autographs. "Fans," he told one reporter, "are a pain in the ass. They all want something from you."

Half an hour or so after midnight, the group departed the Seville, leaving the $380 bar bill on the table. Although Tyson had brought somewhere between $30,000 and $50,000 in cash with him to Indianapolis, neither he nor Edwards seemed concerned about paying for things as trivial as a few drinks. As Tyson was getting into the limousine, the photographer at the Seville asked if he could take the boxer's picture. "Fuck off," Tyson replied, slamming the limo door.

From the Seville they headed downtown to another night spot, the Mirage, on Georgia and South Meridian streets. Tyson and Angie bought a couple of slices of pizza and walked around awhile before entering the club. There Tyson drank a few more Coronas and danced with Angie on the empty dance floor. Shortly after two-thirty Foster drove Tyson, Angie, and Edwards to the Canterbury Hotel, where two rooms had been reserved for Tyson. The boxer checked into Suite 606, Edwards into Room 604. While Tyson was checking in, Angie stood in the lobby talking with Edwards. "What does Mike think of me?" Angie kept asking in different ways. "Stop tripping," Edwards replied. "He likes you. Everything is going fine." Rather than return to the Holiday Inn, Angie stayed with Tyson that night.

July 18 began in a leisurely way for Angie and Tyson. They woke up around midmorning, made love, fell back to sleep for half an hour, woke up a second time, made love again, then got out of bed. Angie departed to meet with her family and prepare for that evening's performance. Tyson called Johnny Gill, the popular gospel singer who was in town for Black Expo and a concert and who had also spent the night at the Canterbury. The two old friends got together soon afterward for brunch in the hotel restaurant. After they ate they met Dennis Hayes and the Reverend Charlie Williams in the Canterbury lobby. Williams hugged both celebrities and asked Tyson if he would "like to say hi to some of the girls in the pageant." When Tyson answered yes, Williams explained his plan. Black Expo, he said, needed Tyson's help. The events, which were to begin later that day, needed publicity, and that was where the boxer came in. If he could do a couple of promotionals, it would aid the cause. Tyson agreed to lend his support, and shortly before noon he left the hotel on foot with Williams, Hayes, and the ever-present Edwards. Gill, having nothing better to do, tagged along. The first stop was the Allison Ballroom at the Omni Severin, where a rehearsal for the Miss Black America pageant was already under way.

"Look—Mike Tyson!" one of the contestants cried out as soon as Tyson and Gill walked into the ballroom. The dance number the women were rehearsing dissolved. "They went crazy," Tyson remembered. "They started getting excited, screaming. I started walking. I walked toward them. They surrounded me, jumped on me, touched me, saying hi, kissed me, hugged me, jumped; you know, they got excited." The dance instructor called to the contestants to get back in line; there would be time for meeting Tyson and having pictures taken with him after the rehearsal was over. The rehearsal continued with renewed vigor, with the contestants giving a little extra, trying to impress and hoping to be noticed by the two celebrities. The shy Gill, who was a minister's son, sat down, hoping to deflect attention, whereas Tyson soaked it up as he walked around the ballroom, complimenting and encouraging the dancers.

While the contestants were finishing the rehearsal, Tyson stopped briefly beside Gill. The two men appraised the women on the dance floor, discussing which ones had good bodies and which didn't. Gill remembered the tenor of Tyson's conversation: "It was like, 'Look at her. Look at that ass. Look at the one she's got.' " Gradually, Tyson seemed to narrow his focus to one particular contestant.

Desiree Washington was as excited as the other contestants. Representing Rhode Island in the pageant, the eighteen-year-old was the kind of young woman that parents hoped their daughters would grow up to be like—bright, outgoing, attractive, athletic, gentle-mannered, considerate. Although she had just graduated from Coventry High School the month before, her pageant résumé contained a list of impressive accomplishments: freshman class president, National Honors Society member, varsity cheerleader, member of the high school softball team, recipient of the Outstanding High School Student Award from her school. As one of thirty-four high school students chosen to represent the United States on a summer tour of the USSR in 1990, she had met with Soviet diplomats and

officials, Vice President Dan Quayle, and American business
and church leaders. And throughout her busy high school
years, she was active in church and charity affairs: Big Sister to
a three-year-old foster child, member of the Senior Teens Aid
for the Retarded program, and an usher at the Ebenezer Baptist Church in Coventry. That fall she planned to attend Providence College on a Martin Luther King Memorial scholarship.

She had seen Tyson, flanked by the Reverend Williams and
Gill, as soon as he entered the room. Her father, along with all
the other men in her family, was a Tyson fan, and Desiree was
anxious to get the boxer's autograph and maybe a picture. As
she rehearsed a line dance, Desiree watched Tyson out of the
corner of her eye. She saw him chatting with Charlie Neal, the
pageant's master of ceremonies, and looking in her direction.
Then he lifted his arm, reached out his index finger, and
pointed at her. *They're talking about me*, she thought.

A few minutes later a group of contestants set up for Tyson's
promo. They were in a straight line that stretched perhaps
thirty feet, with Tyson toward the end of the line, still talking to
Neal. Desiree heard someone say "You're a nice Christian girl,
right?" She looked around and saw Tyson. "You're a nice
Christian girl, right?" he repeated. Embarrassed, she answered, "Yeah," and gave him a nervous smile.

The promo started. The contestants danced as Tyson walked
down the line, delivering a few rap lines about beautiful women
and a dream. When he reached Desiree he stopped, hugged
her, and asked her if she wanted to go out with him. Just like
that, as if it was the most natural thing in the world—no intro-
ductions, just "Would you like to go out on a date later on?"
Embarrassed again, Desiree answered, "Sure."

"We're taping," the director of the promo said. "Let's start
over again." They rehearsed the short routine several times,
then taped it.

Afterward the contestants mobbed Tyson as he good-
naturedly signed autographs, posed for snapshots, and flirted.
Within a month, however, several contestants would insist that
Tyson's flirting was offensive, charging that he had grabbed
their breasts and buttocks. One contestant, Noemi McKenzie
from Massachusetts, said, "While we were taking pictures, he
started touching us and rubbing up against us. When he did it

to me, I felt offended. I mean, you don't touch people like that, you know? . . . [He] acted as if he had walked into a roomful of sluts." Artavia Edwards of California said that Tyson came on to her. She tried to discourage him by mentioning that she had a boyfriend, but he persisted, commenting on her pants and loose-fitting blouse, "Why did you wear something like this? I can't see what [your body] looks like." Then, Edwards said, Tyson "grabbed my butt. From then on, I stood with my hands clasped behind my back to protect myself." Another contestant said that when she posed for a picture with Tyson, he stood behind her and pressed his pelvis tight against her. He had an erection. "Mike was, basically, being Mike," Johnny Gill said later. "He was just putting the moves on some of the contestants."

Desiree herself saw nothing offensive, just a lot of hugging and smiling faces. Tyson's behavior toward her was gentlemanly; he didn't grab her or press against her or do anything objectionable, anything that would suggest that he wasn't a "nice person."

After the brief photo session Tyson again approached Desiree, who was talking with her pageant roommate Pasha Oliver. "The date's still on, isn't it?" he asked. When Desiree introduced him to Pasha, Tyson said that both women should come. There was even some talk about a double date, Tyson and Desiree and Johnny Gill and Pasha. Tyson said he would arrange everything, and before he departed he wrote down Desiree and Pasha's room number.

Tyson was in a fine mood as he and Gill left the Omni Severin in the mid-afternoon. In the company of the usually quiet, reserved singer the mercurial boxer could relax. Although neither had ever visited at the other's house, they enjoyed getting together when they met up on the road or during one of Gill's concerts. After the rehearsal, Tyson hung with Gill while the singer fulfilled his pre-concert obligations. They did an interview together on WTLC, a black radio station in Indianapolis, and later an on-camera interview for a local television station. Although the subjects of both interviews were predictable— Black Expo, the progress of the black community, and the Gill

concert that night at the Hoosier Dome—with Tyson any interview could become an adventure. In a bad mood he might say
nothing; in a good mood he might say anything. Reporters remembered the time that Tyson was given an honorary doctorate at a small black college. Tyson thanked the school, its
administrators, teachers, and students, then remarked that he
didn't know what kind of doctorate he had received but, looking out over all the "fine women" in the audience, he hoped it
was a doctorate of gynecology. "Mike's a trip," one of his
friends observed. The radio and television interviews, however,
went according to the script.

Around five o'clock the two showed up at the Convention
Center for the official opening of Black Expo. City officials and
celebrities filled the stage—the mayor of Indianapolis, William
Hudnut; Jeffrey Modisett, the prosecutor for Marion County,
Indiana; the Reverend Charlie Williams, the Reverend Jesse
Jackson, reigning Miss Black America Rosie Jones. Hudnut
gave Tyson the key to the city. Rosie Jones gave him a hug.
Tyson smiled and laughed, uninterested in the key but very interested in Miss Black America. Jones later said that as Tyson
hugged her, his "hand went somewhere I didn't expect it to.
He said, 'You're so fine.' When I said stop, he said, 'What's
wrong, you don't want to help a black man out?' " Jones's boyfriend saw what Tyson was doing and came over. Tyson looked
at him and said, "Oh, is this your woman? Are you going to
beat me up?"

The ceremony, like most ceremonies, began to drag as one
city leader after the next expressed heartfelt wishes for the success of Black Expo, and as one celebrity after the next thanked
Black Expo and the city of Indianapolis for the singular honor
of being invited. Jesse Jackson launched into one of his famous
self-help speeches advocating self-respect and racial respect.
Tyson, wearing a TOGETHER IN CHRIST button on his designer-
make, mustard-colored silk shirt, became bored. He didn't
want to make small talk with local politicians; he wanted to mingle with the Miss Black America contestants. He walked over to
where the contestants were standing in two lines, one on the
street and the other on the sidewalk. Tyson moved through the
lines, relaxed and confident, talking with the contestants, posing for yet more photographs, copping a few cheap feels. Jackson's words of inspiration faded into the deep background.

Desiree Washington tried to pay attention to the speeches, but her feet hurt from standing on the hard pavement and her body ached from the rehearsals. She was tired, but not too tired to notice Tyson. During his ramblings, Tyson approached Desiree. "There's the two look-alike twins," he said to Desiree and Pasha. The three laughed. Agreeing that she and her roommate did look alike, Desiree showed Tyson a picture of the two of them taken during the swimsuit competition. They looked identical except for the direction that they had brushed their hair. "Wow, you do look alike," Tyson said. But though he tried to pursue his conversation with the two contestants, there was too much noise and too many people demanding his attention. He did, however, ask if they were still on for that night. "Yeah, sure," Desiree answered.

Tyson moved on. Desiree saw him again toward the end of the ceremony praying with Jesse Jackson. She briefly wondered if he would really take her out. He seemed like a nice man, unaffected by his wealth and fame, "real down to earth." Others who were present saw a different side of Tyson, one that didn't seem so nice. Jackson, watching Tyson with the contestants, told a Black Expo official, "Get him the hell out of here before he hurts someone." Jeffrey Modisett had a foreboding sense that here was trouble, in the form of a man who didn't give a damn about Black Expo, Indianapolis, or anything or anybody but himself.

After the opening ceremony, Tyson joined Jesse Jackson, Charlie Williams, and a few other Black Expo officials for dinner at the Black Orchid Lounge, a soul food restaurant on North Illinois Street. While they ate fish and chops and fried chicken, Jackson and Williams worked on Tyson to enlist his services for various Black Expo events. The two ministers had known Tyson for years—Jackson had even baptized the boxer in 1988—and they had both attended a few of his fights. Together they leaned on him hard, trying to convince him that he should support their cause. Tyson was evasive, but Jackson, who was accustomed to having people say yes, continued to press; he wanted Tyson to visit the Marion County Jail with him and Williams. Finally Tyson said, "Okay, I'll be there." He didn't mean it, but it was the only way to get Jackson to stop pestering him. Justifying his response to Jackson, Tyson later claimed, "He wouldn't take no for an answer, and he didn't understand—he didn't respect me."

Tyson wanted to attend the Johnny Gill concert at the Hoosier Dome, so the dinner broke up early. Donna Thompson, a student at Butler University who was working for Williams as an intern, had been assigned to be Tyson's host for the evening. She was decidedly nervous, concerned that Tyson had designs on her. Jackson's bodyguards had spooked her. "Mike Tyson is a dangerous person," they said. "But don't worry, we'll look out for you." But in the back seat of Tyson's limousine en route to the Hoosier Dome she didn't see any of Jackson's bodyguards sitting between Tyson and her. Tyson noticed her fear. "Are you afraid of me?" he asked. "No, I'm afraid of the situation," she answered. Tyson laughed, told her not to worry, and had the limo driver drop her off at the Omni Severin.

The backstage of the Hoosier Dome was crowded, but Tyson was among friends. He watched B Angie B's entire forty-five-minute opening show. During the several acts between Angie's and Gill's, Tyson wandered aimlessly about, not paying much attention to the music, just enjoying the flow of the evening. He talked with Angie, signed a few autographs, met a group of Miss Black America contestants who were also backstage—the usual backstage scene, dancers coming and going, loud music making conversation difficult. An hour, maybe more, passed. Onstage, the rapper Yo Yo, gave way to yet another rap act, Digital Underground. Backstage, Tyson relaxed.

He started to make plans for after the concert. Another night with Angie was out: she had agreed to go to her aunt's house for homemade biscuits and pork chops, and although Tyson was welcome, he wasn't interested; Angie's aunt was too strict. When she saw Tyson hug Angie at the concert, she had told him, "You better get your hands off that married girl." So Tyson told Angie to have fun with her family; he would just "kick it" with Johnny. But Gill had no set plans for after the concert, either. He told Tyson to meet him in his tour bus after his act.

The concert ran late. It was after one when Gill finished his hour-and-a-half set. He met Tyson in the bus, where they talked for a few minutes, but he had another concert in Cleveland in nineteen hours and had to be on the road. Tyson would have to find his own entertainment.

Outside the Hoosier Dome, Tyson's driver was waiting for instructions. Shortly before 1:30 A.M., Tyson and Dale Edwards arrived back at the limo and told her to drive to the Canterbury. At the hotel, Edwards went inside to check for messages while Tyson waited in the car. Nothing important, Edwards reported when he returned. Tyson told Foster to drive the half block to the Omni. He still had Desiree Washington's phone number. They still had a date. At 1:36, Edwards called Desiree from the phone in the limousine. Edwards talked. Tyson talked. The conversation ended. Edwards dialed Desiree's number again. Both men talked to her a few minutes more. Finally, close to 1:50, Desiree walked around the corner of the hotel and got into the back seat of the limousine.

Sitting in the front seat, Edwards told the driver to head back to the Canterbury.

# CHAPTER 2

————

# LADIES' MAN

Monday, July 22, 1991, was a typical summer day in Indianapolis, hot and humid, as Tommy Kuzmik, sex crimes investigator for the Indianapolis Police Department, read the morning paper. Over the weekend, Florida had announced that the William Kennedy Smith rape trial would be televised. That was good news for a nation of Kennedy watchers. Police Chief Daryl F. Gates had announced his plans to retire from the Los Angeles police force in the wake of the beating of Rodney King in March. Many Americans thought that news bode well for Los Angeles's racial tensions. African-American organizations debated whether Clarence Thomas was the right choice to replace Thurgood Marshall on the Supreme Court. In sports, the Colts were in training and Greg LaMond still had hopes of winning the Tour de France.

But Kuzmik had his own problems. It was his job to try to sort out exactly what Mike Tyson had done during his brief but busy stay in Indianapolis. Tyson, it appeared, fancied himself a ladies' man, but not all the ladies agreed with his assessment.

The most serious allegation came from a young woman named Desiree Washington, who claimed that Tyson had raped her. The report came in by way of Methodist Hospital, which had passed it along to the Indianapolis Police Department.

Cindy Jenkins of the IPD's sex crimes division immediately interviewed the woman, who wasn't sure she wanted to press charges. The alleged victim was scheduled to meet with investigators that day.

So far there were no further developments. Desiree Washington had not called, and Kuzmik wasn't surprised. Most rape cases are never reported, and of those that are, the majority never go to trial. Moreover, in a date rape case the chances of successful prosecution drop significantly. If she did press charges, Kuzmik thought, the poor woman would wind up being forced to defend her own actions, while Tyson's involvement would turn the whole thing into a media circus. When Kuzmik didn't hear from Desiree on Sunday or Monday morning, he concluded that she had decided to cut her losses and leave town. No victim, no crime.

But other allegations against Tyson had moved onto Kuzmik's heavy caseload. A local woman had charged Tyson with sexually assaulting her at the Johnny Gill concert. She claimed that she and two friends were backstage at the concert, dancing to the music, when she noticed the boxer staring at her. She ignored him and kept dancing. Then, she remembered, "Mike Tyson just came up to me and proceeded to stick his tongue in my mouth." After this suave opening, Tyson told her he wanted to spend some time with her, and his bodyguard gave her his hotel name and room number. "Meet Mike there in a half an hour," he said, "and you can bring your friends." She told Edwards that she was married and wouldn't consider doing such a thing. Later her husband insisted that she file formal charges.

Kuzmik checked her story. It was a loser. The desk clerk at the Canterbury Hotel remembered two women, one who called herself by the same name as the woman filing charges, trolling the Canterbury after the Gill concert looking for Tyson. One even left her picture. The woman claimed that it was her two friends, not she, who had gone to the Canterbury, but Kuzmik's investigation placed the "victim" at the Canterbury. In any case, the most Tyson could be charged with was a misdemeanor: "And no state is going to extradite the guy on a misdemeanor. This was one lip lock that was going nowhere."

Kuzmik was sitting at his desk at the Family Abuse Office when his supervisor called, saying that Desiree Washington was at the police station with her parents and that she wanted to make a statement. "I want you to handle the case," his boss told Kuzmik. "Fine. Send her over," Kuzmik replied.

The police escorted Desiree to the Child Advocacy Center. Kuzmik introduced himself and talked briefly with Desiree's parents, who had come to town to watch their daughter in the finals of the Miss Black America pageant.

Desiree was very nervous, Kuzmik later recalled. She had trouble focusing: "She would start a sentence and trail off without ending." Before taking her statement, he listened to her story, looking for holes and inconsistencies. He knew from experience that rape victims could seldom order events fully. Surprised by the attack and overwhelmed by their subsequent reaction in feelings of guilt and shame, they would lose track of time, telescoping some details and forgetting others. Told often enough, their stories were bound to contain inconsistencies— ammunition the defense would use to shoot holes in their version of events. Kuzmik therefore took only cursory notes as Desiree recalled the early morning hours of the previous Friday, listening not just to what she said but to how she said it; listening for truth and for lies. He kept asking himself two questions: Has she been raped? Would she be a good witness?

No matter how he rolled those two dice they came up seven—first time, every time. Kuzmik believed her story. Cops hear lies every day, and learning to distinguish between a lie and the truth is a fundamental part of their training. Kuzmik had no doubt that he'd been conned a few times during his career, but not many. As he put it, "I might have been born at night, but I wasn't born *last* night." Desiree didn't overdramatize or dress herself in a heroine's robes. She told a simple story of a kid who had made a stupid but understandable mistake, a mistake that she was likely to have to live with for years to come. Her story made sense.

Perhaps even more important, she told the truth well. The more she talked, the stronger she became. She spoke quietly, but with resolve and directness and conviction. It was the voice of an honors student *cum* beauty contestant, one used to answering questions in an exact, poised manner. Only Kuzmik wasn't Bert Parks. He didn't ask, "If you were to be chosen Miss America, how would you end world hunger?" He asked about the night of July 18 and the early morning of July 19, 1991. What had Tyson done? What had he said? What was Desiree's response? What happened next? Slowly, bluntly Desiree told her story.

At one o'clock Kuzmik put aside his pen and paper and turned on the tape recorder. The dress rehearsal was over. Desiree now had to give an official statement. Kuzmik carefully followed set procedures, noting the time and the place where the statement was being taken. He asked Desiree her name, her age, her educational background, her reason for coming to Indianapolis. Then he asked her about Mike Tyson. "Okay," Kuzmik said. "Tell me what happened."

Desiree remembered the rehearsal for the Miss Black America contest as a confusing, exciting time. She and the other contestants were rehearsing the opening number. Celebrities were moving in and out of the rehearsal hall of the Omni Severin Hotel. Then Mike Tyson came in with Johnny Gill.

The arrival of the former champion jacked up the excitement level. Desiree, along with most of the other contestants, watched his every move. He walked about, watching the girls watch him, talking with Gill and Charlie Neal, a sports commentator for Black Entertainment Television who served as emcee for the pageant. Desiree saw Tyson point toward her and whisper a question to Neal. "I later found out that Charlie Neal told him that I was a nice girl and things of that sort," she told Kuzmik. Tyson walked over to where Desiree and a group of girls were standing. "I like you," he said. "You're a Christian girl. Aren't you?" He was direct, but not impressive. "Yes, I am," she answered.

A short time later, Tyson agreed to do a rap promo for the beauty contest. It was short and simple. While the contestants danced and twirled, Tyson, like a shopper in a grocery store, walked down the line, eyeing the merchandise. "I'm in a dream, day after day, beautiful women in such an array," he rapped. In the middle of the first take he stopped and hugged Desiree. "Would you like to go out on a date with me tonight?" he asked. "Sure," Desiree answered. She had planned to go to the Johnny Gill concert that night, and a date with Tyson, one of the most famous black men in America, would be a singular experience. "He seemed to have a lot of respect for me," Desiree told Kuzmik. "He kept repeating over and over again how I was a Christian girl."

After the promo, the girls started posing for pictures with Tyson and Johnny Gill. Tyson continued to charm Desiree, smiling at her and whispering, "I like you. I really like you." But Desiree saw him whispering to several other girls as well.

Late that afternoon Desiree saw Tyson again, this time at the opening of Black Expo. Tyson was wearing a button proclaiming TOGETHER IN CHRIST. When he saw her he walked over and said, "There's the Christian girl. There's the girl that I really like. We're gonna go out tonight. Right?" "Sure," she replied. They continued to talk. Desiree introduced one of her hotel roommates, Pasha Oliver, to Tyson, and he commented that the two looked like twins. Pasha laughed. "Oh, like in the picture." Desiree explained that several people had said the same thing, that she and Pasha looked like twins, and pulling out a picture, she said, "Look at this. It looks like a trick of the camera." In the picture Desiree and Pasha, wearing swimsuits and standing in the same pose, looked almost identical, except that Desiree's hair was brushed one way and Pasha's the other. "Wow," Tyson said.

As she told the story to Kuzmik, Desiree began to second-guess her actions. "I feel like maybe he took that as a come-on. But I'm not sure."

Kuzmik listened. It was always the same: the rape victim blaming herself, examining her actions under a microscope, believing that if she had done or said something different she would not have been raped. But Kuzmik's job was to take a statement; the psychological conflicts victims experienced in the aftermath of rape he left to therapists and counselors.

Tyson never showed up for the date, Desiree continued. She hadn't been surprised; she understood that a date so casually made could be just as casually forgotten. That evening Desiree and Pasha attended the Johnny Gill concert together, where they saw Tyson backstage. He waved hello and smiled, but quickly returned to signing autographs. Desiree met several other celebrities backstage as well, but she and Pasha soon returned to the audience to watch the concert. Later, she told Kuzmik, "we left the concert kind of early because it was cold."

Shortly after one-thirty the next morning the telephone rang
in Desiree's hotel room. Kycia Johnson, Desiree's other roommate, answered and handed the phone to Desiree. It was Tyson
calling from his limousine, parked outside the Omni Severin.
He was ready for their date. "Do you have Johnny Gill with
you?" Desiree asked, hoping that Pasha and she could make it a
double date. "No," Tyson answered, "but we can just talk and
get to know each other." Desiree hesitated. It was late, she told
him, and she had a full day ahead of her. It was their last
chance, he said, because he was leaving Indianapolis early the
next morning. Kycia told Desiree that she had heard about a
number of planned after-concert celebrity parties, and that a
date with Tyson—even a late-night date—was an opportunity
not to be missed. Desiree reluctantly agreed. She slipped out of
her pajamas and got dressed.

The limo was parked around the corner from the hotel's
main entrance. As soon as Desiree was inside, Tyson grabbed
her shoulders and pulled her closer for a kiss. "I kind of backed
off and he said, 'Oh, okay, okay. You're not like these city girls
here. I'm glad I met you. You're a Christian girl.' " She took his
comment as a compliment once again and thought they had an
understanding that their date would be different from Tyson's
other dates.

It was a short drive: only about fifty yards of South Illinois
Street separates the Omni Severin and the Canterbury hotels.
The limo parked outside the Canterbury and Tyson mumbled
something about stopping by. "I thought he meant stop in,
pick something up maybe. I figured his bodyguard, because he
had mentioned something about his bodyguard."

Inside the hotel a grade school–age kid recognized Tyson
and waved. "That was great," Desiree said later, "because he's
a role model and we need black role models." As the elevator
moved toward Tyson's suite on the sixth floor, Desiree said that
all the attention must be difficult to handle at times. "It's bullshit," he replied. The fame, the autographs, the fake smiles—
all bullshit.

To Desiree, Suite 606 seemed huge. "You're very lucky," she
told him. "There's three of us in a room half this size at the
Omni." He smiled and told her that the TV was in the bedroom. Desiree objected: she thought Tyson only needed to pick
something or someone up. "Well, we can talk," he answered.

"At this point," she said, "I didn't think anything bad of it. He seemed very interested in me and getting to know me as a person, and I thought that was nice."

Desiree talked about her accomplishments—her work in the Big Sister program, her responsibilities as vice president of her church's board of ushers, the different organizations she belonged to. Tyson listened, occasionally mentioning something about himself. He told her about his pigeons and about his own work in Big Brothers. He asked about her family and how they would like him. "Do you like me?" he asked. "You seem okay," she answered. "He just seemed like a very, very nice person at that point."

Then he changed—suddenly, unexpectedly, she told Kuzmik. Like the fighter he was, abruptly shifting tactics to surprise his opponent, Tyson looked hard at Desiree and said, "Oh, you're turning me on." Desiree stiffened: "I got a little freaked because that was odd for him to just come up with that, out of the blue." Still, she didn't sense danger, just discomfort. Maybe he was just impressed with her, she thought—impressed because she wasn't throwing herself at him. Kuzmik thought that part of Tyson's craft was reading body language, and for him Desiree was a *Dick and Jane* primer. She was sitting on the corner of his king-size bed, her arms and legs crossed. "You can relax a little bit," he said. She told him that it was difficult for her to relax and then made it clear that she was "not the type of girl that goes for one-night stands."

Tyson kept her off balance, ridiculing her one moment and being gentle the next. "You're just a baby," he chided. "You must be spoiled. You must be a Daddy's girl." Then he talked about his investments and real estate ventures in Newport, Rhode Island. Still, Desiree didn't think she was in any danger. The two even discussed seeing each other again when Tyson came to Rhode Island.

Desiree had to use the bathroom. When she returned, Tyson had stripped to his underpants. "I guess it's time for me to go," she said, embarrassed. But as she reached for her pocketbook Tyson reached for her, and he was faster.

Desiree then described to Kuzmik how he stripped off her outer jacket and pulled off her sequined bustier, shorts, and underpants. "Don't fight me. Don't fight me. Just relax. Don't fight me. You can't win. Don't fight me. Just relax." Then, methodically, he raped her.

As Desiree told her story, dredged up painfully before a stranger with a tape recorder, she spoke in quick bursts: "He started sticking his hands in my vagina and sucking on my breast and I was trying to squirm away and he kept saying, 'Don't fight me. Just relax.' And he kept saying that, saying that, that was like the main thing at that point, 'Don't fight me. Don't fight me. Just relax.' And I was very nervous and I said I don't do one-night stands and you don't have a condom on and leave me alone, I have a future ahead of me. I, you know, you're going to get me pregnant if you don't get away from me. I was just panicking, saying anything that I thought would trigger him to stop doing what he was doing. And he was like, 'Well, I don't have anything and I know you don't have anything.' And I said I don't need a child, please get off me and I was really trying to get away and the more I fought the more he became aggressive and violent. He said, 'I don't need a condom,' he says. 'We'll just have a baby.' That was one of the statements that he made. And I was just like, 'Please, I have a future ahead of me'—you know, 'I'm going to go to college! I don't care who you are, I don't care if you're a celebrity, I just don't do this,' and I made that very, very clear to him, but it just seemed to go in one ear and out the other and he just, his words over and over again were, 'Don't fight me. Don't fight me.' And I was trying to squirm away and at that point he put his penis into my vagina and he started. . . . I started crying and he said, 'Oh, you're crying, you're crying,' and he grabbed my legs and that's when he licked my vagina."

With a growing sense of anger, Kuzmik listened to Desiree describe how Tyson had held her legs "really tight" and "licked her vagina" for lubrication. Not wanting to break the momentum of her story, he interrupted only to ask for more detail on a particular point. Desiree continued: "I was hitting him, but he didn't seem to feel it and I was saying, 'No, please, why are you doing this to me? You said that I was a Christian girl, you said that you respected me, please, would you stop?' And he just didn't. He was saying, 'Don't fight me. Why are you trying to fight me? Don't fight me.' And then he proceeded to put his penis in me."

Kuzmik asked if he said anything else during the intercourse. Desiree answered, "He was calling me Mommy. He was saying, 'Oh, Mommy, Mommy, come on, Mommy, come on.' That really scared me, out of the whole experience. He was going, 'Don't fight me Mommy, come on, Mommy, Mommy, Mommy.' " When Desiree complained that he was hurting her, Tyson responded, "Do you want on top?" Desiree said yes, thinking that she could then get away from him. But Tyson held her tightly by the hips, and when he realized that she only wanted to escape, he flipped her to the bottom again.

Desiree continued to protest: "I said, 'Please stop, you're hurting me, please stop.' And he said, 'That's because I'm so big,' and I said, 'No, you're hurting me, please stop.' " Finally, it ended with Tyson pulling out and ejaculating on the sheet. "I told you I wouldn't come inside you," he said.

"You're welcome to stay the night if you want," Tyson offered when he was through. "Why, so you can do this again?" Desiree responded. She was crying, and her only thought was to get out of the room. She quickly pulled on her clothes. While she was dressing, Tyson arranged for the limo to take her back to her hotel.

Desiree described herself as being in a daze, but she retained a clear memory of the rest of the night. She recalled the sympathetic look Virginia Foster, the limo driver, gave her. "Oh, my goodness," Foster told her, "he's had so many girls up there all week. He tried to do something to me. He tried to rip my clothes off. What happened to you? I wouldn't be surprised if he had a disease. I knew you weren't like the rest of the girls. When you got into the car, I wanted to say something to you, but I couldn't." Desiree thought, *Why couldn't she have told me this before?*

Back in her room she tried to hold back the tears but failed. She felt "dirty and disgusting." She told Kycia that Tyson had tried to rape her, unable yet to admit that he had in fact raped her. She took a long shower, no longer trying to contain the tears and thinking that the next day "everything will be all right."

Desiree finished her statement, describing her activities on Friday, Saturday, and Sunday—what she did, whom she talked to, when she told her parents, her trip to Methodist Hospital.

Kuzmik asked more questions, and Desiree's answers became shorter, more to the point, less emotional:

Q. Did he ever strike you?
A. No. He just held me down.
Q. Did he ever threaten to strike you?
A. No.
Q. Was there any weapon involved?
A. No.
Q. Desiree, has what you've told me here today been the truth?
A. Yes. I gave it because of the fact that he could be doing this to other girls. And it is hard for me to do this because of who he is, but when I think about it, he could be doing it to younger girls than me. And it upsets me because he is a black man who basically came from nothing and who has rose up and . . . I am one who advocates black people helping each other and not pulling each other down. But if he's doing this to me, he could be doing this to other girls . . . black girls or white girls, it doesn't matter. No one deserves this.

As Desiree gave her statement, Kuzmik noted small details, sometimes an aside, sometimes a fragment of a memory, that indicated psychological trauma. Talking about her examination at Methodist Hospital, she shifted topics in midsentence: "I don't want to put my swimsuit on and I am very proud of my body and myself and I've just been feeling so terrible lately and I don't want to see anyone else have to go through something like this."

Twenty-eight minutes after it had begun, the interview was over—roughly the same length of time that Desiree Washington had spent in Suite 606 at the Canterbury Hotel.

By the time Kuzmik finished taking Desiree's statement, Jeff Modisett had arrived at the Child Advocacy Center. After the Marion County prosecutor learned the substance of the allegations, he had a short talk with Desiree's parents. Both

were upset, but Desiree's father felt somehow personally betrayed. He had admired Tyson. For him, the boxer was an example of a black man "making it" in America. He wondered
why someone who could have thousands of women would have
raped his daughter. It didn't make sense. Shaking his head, he
said, "You never know, do you? You just never know."

Modisett agreed that what had happened was bewildering,
but privately he thought that it wasn't surprising. His mind
drifted to the opening ceremony for Black Expo, when he had
been on stage with Tyson, Jesse Jackson, and other celebrities
and community officials. He had watched Tyson, fascinated by
the aura that surrounded him. And what he saw made him angry: "I had an opportunity to meet Tyson, and something told
me not to. I was already offended by his behavior. I saw that he
didn't give a damn about anything going on at the ceremonies
except for those beauty contestants. People I respected, including Jesse Jackson, would come up to him and you could see
that he basically wanted to blow them off. All he wanted to do
was talk to the beauty contestants."

After assuring Desiree's parents that he would take their
daughter's statement seriously, Modisett tracked down
Kuzmik. The detective had been awake since three o'clock in
the morning and was drinking a cup of coffee, probably his
tenth of the day. "What do you think?" Modisett asked.

"He did it," Kuzmik answered.

Modisett stared blankly past Kuzmik for a few moments. "Is
there a case?"

Aside from greeting him at a formal awards ceremony,
Kuzmik had never met Modisett, and he found it difficult to
read the prosecutor. Modisett's stiff posture and eerie gaze
threw Kuzmik off balance. Once he got to know Modisett, he
learned to interpret the penetrating eyes: "When Jeff asks you
a question or you ask him a question, his mind is going fifty
different directions all at the same time and he's keeping track
of every single direction. So you get a stare for a second or two
while he's formulating his next question or weighing his
options."

Not wanting to be thought flippant, Kuzmik reviewed the
strengths and weaknesses of the case. Physical evidence would
be a problem. Since the night of the rape, the staff at the Canterbury would have cleaned the room and changed the sheets

several times. The chances of finding body fluids or pubic hairs were slim. But Kuzmik believed that the case would come down to one of credibility: of who was telling the truth.

"I think she's going to make an excellent witness," Kuzmik said. "She's intelligent, she's articulate, she's attractive—easy to look at, easy to understand, easy to believe."

Kuzmik had handled too many victims who had seventh- or eighth-grade educations and who "talked street." They made horrible impressions on juries and were easily torn apart by defense lawyers who confused, embarrassed, and angered them. Kuzmik knew Desiree was different.

"Given her background in public speaking," he told Modisett, "you're not going to fluster this girl. She's going to sit up there and she's going to tell her story. She's going to stick to it. It's believable, it's factual."

Modisett looked directly at Kuzmik. "Can we win?" he asked. The police investigator understood the source of Modisett's concern: the case would be hot politically, to put it mildly. Modisett held an elective office. If he were to lose a high-profile case, a national case, he would look bad. In the next compaign, he would be both the man who tried to get Mike Tyson and the man who blew the case. Kuzmik knew the issues, so he answered the question as honestly as he could. In a flat voice he said, "It's as good as any case I've ever taken to court."

# CHAPTER 3

# CIRCUMSTANTIAL EVIDENCE

**D**ate rape was on the nation's mind in the summer of 1991. Less than four months before, a twenty-nine-year-old woman in Palm Beach, Florida, had accused William Kennedy Smith, the nephew of Senator Edward M. Kennedy, of raping her on the beach near the Kennedy clan's vacation estate. According to the woman's report, the two had met at a fashionable Palm Beach nightclub, Au Bar, and had talked, danced, and drunk together. When they left the club the woman drove Smith back to the Kennedy's house, where they talked some more, kissed, and took a stroll on the beach. She said Smith invited her for a swim and undressed. She declined and began to leave. She claimed he then attacked her, pulled off her clothes, and raped her.

The Kennedy name transformed a prosaic date rape case into a media sensation. On April 5, 1991, when the police identified Smith as the subject of a rape investigation, Palm Beach became the scene of the largest press corps gathering since the Persian Gulf War. Disregarding the tradition of protecting the identity of rape victims, NBC News, the *New York Times*, the *San Francisco Chronicle*, the *Detroit Free Press*, the *Des Moines Register*, and several other influential papers named Patricia Bowman, the stepdaughter of former General Tire and Rubber

Company chairman Michael G. O'Neil, as the woman Smith was alleged to have attacked. Defending his decision, NBC News president Michael G. Gartner sanctimoniously claimed that he wanted to "remove the stigma of rape" by treating the case like any other crime. Not to be outdone by NBC in the pursuit of objectivity, the *New York Times* not only identified Bowman as the alleged victim but also ran an unflattering profile of her life. Rumors of Bowman's three abortions and sexual abuse by her father filled tabloids and serious papers alike.

Through the spring and summer, the Smith case remained in the headlines. Smith called the charges an "outrageous lie" that "represent an attack on me, on my family and on the truth." Bowman and the prosecutor's office responded by announcing that she had passed two lie detector tests. Palm Beach police even released the entire 1,300-page report on the alleged rape, complete with detectives' reports, police interviews, depositions, and speculations about the role that Senator Kennedy was said to have played in the sordid affair. Part soap opera, part political football—the Conservative Campaign Fund used the case as the basis of a complaint it filed against Senator Kennedy before the Senate Ethics Committee—the story received more attention than dozens of more important national and international developments. It was listed as number one in newspapers' "what's hot" columns.

On the same day that Desiree told her tale of date rape into Detective Kuzmik's tape recorder, the temperature in the Florida case was turned up a few degrees. The prosecutor's office filed documents asserting that Smith had raped a woman in Washington, D.C., in 1988 and that he had sexually assaulted another woman in New York City in 1983 and still another in Washington in 1988. Although none of the women filed charges, the Florida prosecutors clearly believed the assertions showed a pattern of conduct that supported Bowman's claims. Once again the media devoured the story, reporting the facts—which were only unsubstantiated allegations—and speculating on the cosmic meaning. Was there an overactive mutant sexual gene in Kennedy men? pundits wondered. Had the defect been passed from Jack, Bobby, and Ted—the nation was on first-name terms with the Kennedys—to Willie and his cousins? Such idle conjectures filled miles of newspaper inches and hours of television "journalism."

In Indianapolis on the afternoon of July 22, William Kennedy Smith was very much on Jeff Modisett's mind. Two things were obvious. Conducting an investigation illuminated by media klieg lights was impossible, and trying a case in the media was a poor decision. In Florida the prosecutor's office was attempting to make use of press attention. The chief prosecutor claimed that Florida's "sunshine law" forced his office to release public records on request, but it was clear that he was trying to put the state's best case forward, attempting to influence the very citizens who would form the jury pool.

Modisett knew that the Tyson case would be just as explosive as the Smith case, perhaps more so. William Kennedy Smith, a celebrity only by virtue of his name, was a conduit, hot-wired to America's most famous family. No link to someone more important than himself, Mike Tyson was Mike Tyson—a figure seemingly blasted out of granite, one whose total disregard for his public persona and his reputation as the baddest man on the block was a tabloid editor's dream. For several years experts both within and outside the world of boxing had been predicting that Tyson would self-destruct, that his excesses and emotional binges would lead to a complete meltdown. Some said he would end up in prison. Others asserted that someone would shoot him or that he would wrap himself and some expensive automobile around a tree. Everyone agreed, however, that his pedal-to-the-metal lifestyle was out of control.

As Modisett talked with Kuzmik and his advisers he began to fathom the full implications of Desiree's charges. He tried to treat the matter as just another case, but he knew there was nothing routine about it. When reporters heard the news, they would besiege Indianapolis like an army. With their cameras, notebooks, and fax machines, they would track down and attempt to interrogate anyone even remotely connected to the case. And in the process, they would frustrate the official investigation by frightening jumpy witnesses and sensationalizing each morsel of information.

Modisett needed a plan of action, and he needed it right away. Earlier in the afternoon he had called David Dreyer, his chief counsel in the prosecutor's office. "I think we are going to have to charge Mike Tyson with rape," Modisett said, his voice somber. *Here we go again,* Dreyer thought. In the six months since he had followed Modisett into office, it had been one crisis after another: the ordeal of an election recount was followed by several well-publicized cases involving messy police action shootings. "Well, tell me what happened," said Dreyer. Modisett answered, "I'm not sure yet, but come on over to the Family Abuse Office and let's talk about it."

Jeff Modisett was the first Democrat to hold the office of Marion County prosecutor in twelve years, and he had been elected by a shoestring margin. An Indiana farm boy, sure enough, he had finished his undergraduate education at UCLA, then had gone to Oxford on a Marshall scholarship. From there he had traveled throughout Europe, Africa, Asia, and the Middle East, getting about as far away from corn and hogs as a Hoosier can get. He came back to the States for law school at Yale, clerked in San Francisco, worked in the U.S. Attorney's office in Los Angeles, and then, in 1988, found himself back home in Indiana again. But the work ethic of his native Midwest and the reserved demeanor of its inhabitants had never left him.

But not everybody saw it that way. Modisett, who came from a family of Goldwater Republicans, seemed awfully cosmopolitan to the people of Indiana. He had switched political alliances, campaigned for the election of George McGovern in 1972, and worked one summer in Washington as an intern for Senator Birch Bayh, the Indiana Democrat. He met and became friends with Birch Bayh's son Evan. When Evan Bayh made his move for the governor's mansion in 1988, he appointed Modisett as his campaign issues director. Once elected, he named Modisett his executive assistant for public safety and drug abuse prevention.

In 1990 Modisett ran for the office of Marion County prosecutor. It was a bitter campaign. Richard "Drew" Young, Modisett's Republican opponent, accused him of being a carpetbagger, raising the specter of a quiche-eating, Chablis-drinking Californian in the City-County Building in Indianapolis. Out of 180,000 votes cast, he won by a walloping margin of 285. Even less reassuring, and a complicating factor given the racial tinderbox he had inherited, his victory was based on having carried only one of Marion County's nine townships, the predominantly black inner-city region. Young demanded a recount, which Modisett successfully fended off, but not before the expenditure of $100,000 in legal costs and much moral capital. In short, Marion County's head lawyer was not feeling terribly secure as he faced the prospect of charging black superstar and multimillionaire Mike Tyson with rape.

At three-thirty that afternoon Modisett, Dreyer, Kuzmik, and several other police investigators and members of the prosecution staff started to formulate a war plan. "We just wanted to make sure everything was done by the book," Dreyer recalled. But no book covered charging the former heavyweight champion of the world with rape. It was one thing to announce that you would follow set procedures; it was another to actually do it.

After reverently paying lip service to "the book," Modisett and Dreyer decided to rewrite a few sections. Their first decision contrary to established procedure was to keep the allegations away from media attention for as long as possible. Typically, when a crime is committed and a preliminary investigation is conducted, the police issue a detective hard copy, or DHC, a simple document detailing the nature of the crime and listing the name of the victim and, if known, that of the suspect. A DHC is a public document. Once one is issued it is part of the public record, available to anyone who wants to see it.

One of the first questions Modisett asked the police was if a DHC had been drawn up. So far, he was told, only a brief interdepartmental report had been filed by Officer Cindy Jenkins after she talked to Desiree at Methodist Hospital. "Does it have anybody's name on it?" Modisett asked. It didn't. "Is that something that is a public document?" It wasn't. "Do we have to create a DHC?" Modisett knew he was moving onto slippery legal ground, that contestable area between the prosecutor's right to withhold information during an investigation and the public's right to full disclosure. As Modisett remembered, the ranking police officer at the meeting told him, "A DHC does have to be created at some point. But it doesn't have to be created right now."

"Let's hold off for a while," Modisett decided. "Let's get as much done as we can without it being public."

Modisett's decision would prove to be a controversial one. But Dreyer remembers clearly that a police officer said that the

Indianapolis Police Department had delayed issuing DHCs before, particularly in high-profile cases. "We've held them back and then made them public," the officer said. "In fact, there's an opinion from our counsel saying we can, in sex cases, delay issuing a DHC." Modisett and Dreyer agreed there was enough gray area to justify their action.

"Nobody talks," Dreyer instructed the others at the meeting—not to friends, not to associates, not to family members. "We weren't going to cover anything up," he later recalled, "but we needed space, time to investigate without being interfered with." Dreyer had no doubt that reporters would inconvenience the investigation, but beyond that he feared the power and influence of Tyson and his manager, Don King: "I knew that they would have unlimited resources. They could affect our investigation. I didn't want them talking to people before we talked to them. And if the press was in the way as well, that would have been horrible, impossible."

Kuzmik agreed. "Look, the guy's worth twenty-five million bucks a fight. Who can make that much money? Sure there was a possibility of tampering somewhere along the line. Witnesses are gotten to, things happen to people. Boxing is not the most upright of sports. Don King has done time for killing a guy, so we're not dealing with elite society."

Kuzmik was as concerned about the Miss Black America contestants as he was about Tyson and King. "Who is going to make up something so that she can get her name in the paper or her face on television? I looked at the pageant applications. Over half the girls wanted to be singers or actresses. Publicity is important to them. Who might 'forget' something because she is promised a recording contract or a part in a movie?"

Speed and secrecy were essential, but the logistics of the case worked against both. Many of the most important witnesses were contestants, and when the pageant had ended on Sunday they had scattered in all directions. Desiree's two roommates, Pasha Oliver and Kycia Johnson, had returned to their homes in Montgomery, Alabama, and McAlester, Oklahoma. Other contestants were strung across the country, from New York to California and Illinois to Texas. Kuzmik and his investigative team had to contact and take statements from each of them.

In addition, several other important potential witnesses lived outside Indiana: Johnny Gill in Los Angeles, Charlie Neal in

Arlington, Virginia, J. Morris Anderson in Philadelphia, Frank Valentine in Atlanta, Dale Edwards in Cleveland. Most of these men were also friends of Mike Tyson's.

Although other police officers outranked him, Kuzmik was put in charge of coordinating the investigation. Given the interstate nature of the probe, the FBI agreed to help locate and conduct brief interviews with potential witnesses. This aid was part of a program the FBI had worked out with local law enforcement agencies. "There was no way that we could have done it on our own," Kuzmik said. "We didn't have the time, manpower, or budget to travel around the country to contact all of these people individually. Just impossible. A nightmare." Jim Rice, Kuzmik's FBI contact, supervised the out-of-state search for witnesses, significantly aiding the prosecution's case.

Dreyer and Kuzmik decided to divide the Indianapolis phase of the investigation among three police investigators. Sergeant Jeff Duhamell was assigned to interview employees at the Canterbury and the Omni Severin hotels. Kuzmik took the staff at Methodist Hospital. Charlie Briley, a grand jury investigator, and Kuzmik worked together to find and interview the woman who drove Tyson's limousine and the various persons connected with Black Expo and the Miss Black America pageant. The testimony of desk clerks, maids, bellboys, drivers, doctors, nurses, chaplains, preachers, and businessmen would either buttress or undercut the charges made by Desiree Washington. None, of course, could prove that Tyson had raped her, but each could provide a story that would become part of the circumstantial evidence pointing toward guilt or innocence.

Time worked against them. The allegations would leak; Modisett, Dreyer, and Kuzmik only hoped that they could keep their collective finger in the dike long enough to build a case. The rape had occurred early Friday morning; Desiree had gone to the hospital early Saturday morning; she had given her statement to Kuzmik late Monday morning. Not only had the maids at the Canterbury changed and cleaned the sheets in Suite 606, but they had vacuumed, dumped the wastebaskets, and most likely destroyed all evidence that Mike Tyson had ever slept there.

Crime lab investigators made a detailed search of the suite and discovered only two objects that might link Desiree or Tyson to the rooms. The first was a tiny white sequin, discovered in the carpet along a floorboard in the area between the sitting room and the bedroom. It was from the bustier Desiree had worn that night, but by the time the sequin was discovered the garment had already been sent back to Providence. A loose sequin might indicate that it had been torn while Desiree was in the suite. Perhaps other sequins came off during the struggle but were vacuumed up afterward. Then again, maybe the sequin wasn't from Desiree's clothing at all. Either way, Kuzmik needed the garment.

The other object was as big as the sequin was small. Although the sheets and blankets on the king-size bed in Suite 606 had been changed, the bedspread had not.

The standard forensic test for sheets, blankets, and bedspreads involves looking at the bedding under ultraviolet light, which, given the chemical composition of certain body fluids— sweat, urine, semen—makes them fluoresce. Technically, they emit electromagnetic radiation resulting from the absorption of incidental radiation caused by ultraviolet light.

The bedspread in Tyson's suite glowed like a lightning bug on a dark night. It had stains large and small and every size in between. Perhaps there was a stain that could be linked to Tyson, but it would have taken a year to find it; there were just too many others on the bedspread. Kuzmik recalled his thought when he saw the bedspread under an ultraviolet light: "Look, this is a four- to five-hundred-dollar-a-night suite, a five-star hotel. And one stain was huge, just huge. Pretty easy to guess that one. It taught me a lesson—I'll never sleep under another bedspread."

The staff at the Canterbury were more informative than the bedding. The hotel aimed for an atmosphere of Old World gentility, with bellmen who held open doors for guests, desk clerks who remembered their names. The Canterbury wasn't interested in convention trade. With only ninety-nine rooms, it was the smallest, most exclusive hotel in downtown Indianapolis, a member of the Preferred Hotel and Resorts Worldwide network. Guests at the Canterbury paid to be noticed and pampered, and the hotel's staff catered to those expectations.

When Jeff Duhamell interviewed the staff on duty the night of July 18–19, he discovered that they had been alertly attending to their business. Most had sharp memories of Tyson, and together those memories supported Desiree's story.

Denisa Stevenson, the hotel's PBX switchboard operator, had no trouble recalling Tyson's mood on July 18: he was on the make, definitely looking to get laid. She had seen Tyson and Johnny Gill at the front desk in the early afternoon, and since she was a fan of Gill's, she walked over from her post to shake hands. Tyson quickly let her know that he was interested in something more physical than a handshake. He told Denisa that he "liked short and well-stacked women. They can handle it." If she had any doubt what "it" was, Tyson clarified his intentions by simulating cunnilingus with his tongue. "How would you like to handle that for an hour?" he asked. Denisa answered that he should have more respect for women, and that such behavior would lead to "various diseases." Tyson laughed and replied that he used condoms, then again asked if Denisa "could handle it." If Denisa would follow him to his room, Tyson added, he would give something to her. Once more, she took the comment as a unmistakable sexual reference.

Denisa told Duhamell that the conversation ended when Tyson became aware of another man standing behind him at the front desk. The man reminded Tyson of a preacher. "I know God," Tyson told Denisa, suddenly becoming serious and polite. Not wanting to be confused with a preacher, the man informed Tyson that he was a politician. Denisa used the interruption to return to her desk.

Denisa had no knowledge of Tyson's behavior with Desiree, but her story did suggest a state of mind and a pattern of behavior. His shift from vulgar suggestiveness to upright religiosity was the mirror reverse of his behavior with Desiree. More important, it suggested a man who was accustomed to getting what he wanted. In Mike Tyson's myopic world, women were objects to be used for his pleasure.

Stationed at the front desk from 11:00 P.M. to 7:00 A.M. on the night of July 18–19, McCoy Wagers also remembered Tyson's stay at the Canterbury. Tyson wasn't the only person on the make that night, he recalled. Two women were searching for Tyson, prowling the lobby and the sidewalk outside the hotel. Several times they asked Wagers whether Tyson had returned to the hotel, and one even gave the desk clerk a picture of herself for him to pass on to the boxer. Their perambulations and nervous behavior fitted the stereotype of the groupie.

By the time Tyson returned to the Canterbury, the two women had given up. Wagers saw Tyson enter the hotel with a black woman and walk toward the elevator. He didn't see Tyson again until the boxer unexpectedly left the hotel a few hours later. But he did see Dale Edwards, Tyson's bodyguard, several times that night. About two-fifteen or two-thirty, Edwards returned to the lobby, made several phone calls, and ordered room service while he waited for a return call. Wagers didn't see Edwards or Tyson again until the two left the hotel around four. "Did they stop to check out?" Duhamell asked. "No," Wagers answered. "Went straight out. Didn't talk to a single person."

Christopher Low, the Canterbury's night bellman, confirmed Wagers's account and added several important details. He too saw Tyson return to the hotel with a woman, but whereas Wagers remembered only that she was black, Low recalled that "she was fairly conservative [looking]. She wasn't dressed trashy." Not at all like the other women who had accompanied Tyson, Low told Duhamell: the others "were dressed sort of trashy, sort of like hookers."

Low also remembered delivering a room service order to 604—Edwards's room—at about two-thirty. As he was standing at the door delivering scallop chowder and a cheeseburger, he saw Edwards look past him at something down the hall. Low turned around and saw a girl emerge from Suite 606. The girl took a step or two toward Room 604 and the elevator farther down the hall, then turned around and walked the other way, down a dead-end hallway. Low looked back at Edwards and saw a "smirky smile" cross his face as he watched the girl.

Shortly after Low returned to the lobby, he walked outside and had a short conversation with Tyson's limo driver. Tyson and Edwards were poor tippers, they agreed. Low mentioned seeing the girl come out of Tyson's room after only a short stay, and the driver responded, "Well, she wasn't going to be playing any of Mike Tyson's games." She then told Low that Tyson had tried to play his game with her, but that she had put him straight. Tyson used women, she believed—but then, they all seemed to want something from him, too.

The last Low saw of Tyson and Edwards was when the two left the Canterbury. Low was at his bell stand, five feet from the lobby door. Tyson and Edwards breezed past him at a brisk pace.

Ivy Rodgers, a housekeeper at the Canterbury, agreed with Low and Wagers that Tyson left the hotel "real fast." When she cleaned his room the next day, she discovered clear indications of Tyson's quick departure: he had left behind an expensive shirt and some cash as well as his toothbrush and toothpaste. Deaf in one ear and hard of hearing, Ivy had difficulty understanding several of Duhamell's questions, but her memory was unimpaired. The shirt was black and white, she remembered, and the two dollar bills were on the nightstand by the phone. One more thing she remembered was the sheets; when Ivy stripped the bed she noticed that they were spotted with fresh blood.

Although Kuzmik and Dreyer didn't realize it at the time, Wagers's and Low's accounts were vitally important. In an early attempt to prove his innocence, Tyson would assert—and Edwards would confirm—that his bodyguard was in Suite 606 during the time Desiree was with him. Tyson said that he hadn't raped Desiree, and Edwards backed up his employer's story, but the evidence showed that Edwards wasn't in Tyson's suite. Eyewitnesses and phone records placed him in the Canterbury's parlor and lobby as well as his own room. Tyson's hastily manufactured alibi would form an important part of the prosecution's case as the question of Edwards's whereabouts hovered over the trial.

While Duhamell interviewed the staff at the Canterbury, Kuzmik began his search for Tyson's limousine driver. She had talked about Tyson with Desiree and Chris Low. She had been propositioned by Tyson and had observed his behavior during his stay in Indianapolis. Kuzmik was certain her story would be important, but he had no idea who she was. All he knew was that the limousine was gold.

Most police work doesn't take great imagination; patience is usually the most important requirement. "Charlie Briley and I did some classic detective work," Kuzmik said. "Got on the phone, got a list of limo companies, and started calling. We tracked the limo down. It belonged to a company named Solid Gold Limousine Service. Figures.'' Kuzmik called Solid Gold and got an answering service that in turn gave him the phone number of the company's owner. Having assumed that the company's owner, Virginia Foster, wasn't the same woman who had driven Tyson around Indianapolis, he then served Indiana Bell with a subpoena to obtain subscriber information—name and address—for the number. Kuzmik and Briley were surprised to find out that they were wrong; Foster had been Tyson's driver during his stay the week before.

Though Foster might have talked freely with Desiree and Chris Low and any number of other people about Tyson's behavior, she wasn't anxious to discuss the matter with two white policemen. Her background and her poise, though, impressed both officers. While working full-time as a keypunch operator for the State of Indiana, she had begun college, earning her bachelor's degree in education in 1977. She then taught in the Indianapolis public school system while working toward a master's degree in counseling, which she received in 1983. She took a job as a career counselor, and then in 1986, after still more schooling, she became a guidance counselor. Two years later she and her husband started the limousine service. She served as both president and chief driver.

Charlie Williams, the head of Black Expo, had hired Virginia Foster as Tyson's chauffeur during the boxer's stay in Indianapolis. Foster picked up Tyson and Dale Edwards—who Foster thought was named Daryl—at the USAir gate at 4:45 P.M. Tyson had had her take him from one night spot to the next that first evening. Tyson's date was the rap singer B Angie B, and the two were accompanied by Edwards—and a male associate of B Angie B's. After spending some time at the Holiday Inn on East Twenty-first Street, the rolling party made stops at the Seville and the Mirage nightclubs. At about 2:30 A.M., almost ten hours after picking up her client, Foster dropped Tyson and friends off at the Canterbury Hotel.

But she wasn't through for the night. Shortly after Tyson and Edwards registered at the Canterbury, Edwards returned to the limousine to get their bags. Foster helped, following Edwards's instructions to take Tyson's bag to Room 604. Tyson told her to have a seat, but something about the situation made her uncomfortable. ''You act like you're afraid of me,'' Tyson said. "Don't be afraid of me." She lied and said she wasn't. Tyson seemed to feed on the fear he sensed. He grabbed her, pulling her closer to him for a hug. Pushing him away, Foster stiffened. She was his chauffeur, and she wasn't interested in anything other than a professional relationship. She cautioned Tyson to "keep it clean and respectful," then left the room. "I was kind of getting scared at that point," she told Kuzmik. But by the time of Kuzmik's questioning, bravado had replaced the fear. "If he had tried anything more with me, I'd have knocked that sucker out."

"Lady, if you could do that," Kuzmik replied, "I want to be your manager."

"She was so strong," he later recalled. "I thought, 'If we can keep her this strong, if we can keep her this confident, she's going to kill him.' " Her words, if not her fists, could deliver a knockout blow.

Kuzmik began to steer the conversation away from Foster's frightening confrontation with Tyson in the early hours of Thursday morning toward the events of Thursday afternoon and evening and Friday morning. Thursday, she said, had been a confusing day. It was difficult to keep track. She waited for Tyson outside the Canterbury only to find out that at around noon he had walked the block over to the Omni to watch the rehearsal for the Miss Black America pageant. Next she waited for him outside the Omni, then discovered that he had again decided to walk, this time to the Hoosier Dome for the opening ceremony. For most of the afternoon she waited by her gold Cadillac limousine, hoping that Tyson would be able to find her when he wanted her. Advance warning and keeping to a schedule, she soon realized, were not his strong suit.

The evening was more predictable. Tyson, Edwards, and Charlie Williams met Jesse Jackson at the Black Orchid for dinner. Then Tyson and Edwards went to the Johnny Gill concert at the Hoosier Dome. The concert ran late, and it was almost 1:30 A.M. when the two returned to the limo. That's when Tyson, after checking his messages at the Canterbury, had Foster drive him and Edwards to the Omni.

Urban redevelopment had given the area between the Canterbury and the Omni Severin a bombed-out look. Behind the Canterbury and St. Elmo's restaurant and a few other historical buildings was a large hole, twenty feet deep and several blocks across, an area of seemingly permanent construction. Foster parked near the construction site while Edwards, sitting as usual in the front seat, dialed a number at the Omni. Subpoenaed telephone records later listed the time of the call as 1:36 A.M. Edwards talked for a few minutes and then passed the phone back to Tyson. Foster heard Tyson trying to convince someone to go out with him. He was pleading, she said, begging in the beseeching voice that men use when they want something from a woman. "Please, please. I only want to talk to you," he said. Then, after a pause, "It will only take you a few minutes to put something on." Another pause, more "pleases," then, "No. It has to be tonight. We'll be gone tomorrow."

He hung up at 1:42. Six minutes later Edwards made another call, but this one, Foster noted, seemed to irritate Tyson. A few minutes after that call had ended, a woman walked toward the limousine. She looked to be in her twenties, Foster remembered, and her hair was "fixed pretty." Foster helped her into the passenger side of the limousine and noticed that she looked like a "real nice girl . . . real pretty . . . very friendly." Foster then drove back to the Canterbury.

Foster was exhausted, but Edwards told her to wait in the limousine because he and Tyson planned to catch an early flight. Since Tyson was supposed to stay in Indianapolis until Saturday, at shortly before two she called the Reverend Williams, the man who had hired her, to inform him of the change of plans. She dozed for a short time. "I don't remember too much of the conversation because I was tired," she told Kuzmik. But she did remember the look of the young woman who rushed out of the Canterbury.

"That poor child, that poor, poor child," she told Kuzmik. "She looked so scared." Foster immediately hit the button to unlock the doors, but before she could get to the passenger's side to help her, the woman had scampered into the back seat. Foster sensed something bad had happened. The girl looked as though she was in a state of shock. Her hair and clothes were mussed up. Her eyes were frantic, dazed and disoriented.

Foster had seen that look before. She had done her practicum for her master's in counseling at the Midtown Indianapolis Mental Health Crisis Intervention Center, where she had attended women who had been raped or beaten. In her earlier work as a school counselor, she had comforted junior high girls who were victims of rape, child abuse, and incest, girls who had attempted suicide or suffered complete breakdowns. Something had happened, all right. This wasn't the same girl who had gone into the Canterbury with Tyson less than an hour before.

During the four-minute drive back to the Omni the girl kept repeating, "I don't believe him. I don't believe him. Who does he think he is?"

Foster suspected that Tyson had "put her out because he didn't get from her what he wanted." She knew from experience that Tyson was quick to make demands. Perhaps Tyson had laid a hard hit on the girl and she had overreacted. When they arrived at the Omni, Foster helped the girl out of the limousine, shook her hand, and watched her enter the hotel. She then drove back to the Canterbury.

The girl wasn't the only person in a rush to leave the Canterbury; soon afterward Edwards told Foster that he and Tyson would be departing. At around four-thirty boxer and bodyguard made their quick retreat. Foster drove them to the home of B Angie B's aunt on Indianapolis's north side. She beat on the door and Edwards banged on the horn, but the house was empty. They located B Angie B at the Holiday Inn on the east side and told her to meet them at the airport. Then it was off to catch the five-thirty flight to Cleveland. In the back seat, Tyson was quiet. He spoke only to complain that Foster wasn't driving fast enough. He wanted Edwards to drive. Foster refused, saying she was driving at the speed limit and that she would get them to the airport in time for the flight. Once a sheriff's car pulled ahead of them. Foster suggested that they ask him for a police escort. "No," Tyson and Edwards answered. There was no need to rush; they would get there on time. Foster thought it was strange that suddenly time was no longer important.

They arrived at the airport at about five-fifteen, cutting it close but still arriving in time to catch the flight. Tyson and Edwards departed on a Continental flight. Foster found this strange too; they had arrived on USAir. Wouldn't it be cheaper to use the same carrier? It wasn't important, she guessed, but still, it was odd.

Virginia Foster's story was critical to the case. She was the first person whom Desiree talked to after leaving Tyson's room, and she had been trained to observe signs of emotional stress. *A great witness,* Kuzmik thought, *but reluctant.* Kuzmik talked to her several times between Tuesday, July 23, and Friday, July 26, aware each time of her discomfort at her central position in the case. Kuzmik recalled her gradual change: " 'That poor child,' she kept saying over and over and over. When we went back a couple of days later to get a taped statement from her she'd started to become, well, she just backed up a little bit, less forceful. She was like everyone else—'I don't want to get involved in this.' "

Fortunately for the case, however, Sergeant Darryl Pierce, a black Indianapolis police officer, knew Foster, and she trusted him. He acted as police liaison with her, helping to keep her spirits up even after the case turned into the circus everyone knew it would become.

The Reverend Charlie Williams also cooperated with the investigation. "He was cautious and he was guarded," Kuzmik said, "and I'm sure he knew more than he let on. Most people do. But he didn't try to cover anything up." Kuzmik appreciated Williams's position. He had toiled to build Black Expo, and the organization worked to instill pride in Indianapolis's black community and to build bridges with the white establishment. It was supported by the Lilly Foundation and other largely white-controlled foundations. Could Black Expo survive a major scandal, one whose sordid details would be reported worldwide in graphic detail in newspapers and magazines and on television? Would the board of the Lilly Foundation want to see its name reported in connection with charges of rape?

Sure, Williams told Kuzmik, Mike liked the beauty contestants. It was mutual. Everybody wanted to get a picture with the champ. Yes, he had heard rumors—unsubstantiated rumors—that something had happened between Mike and one of the contestants. But he didn't know what, and besides, he wasn't in charge of the Miss Black America pageant. It was a completely separate entity, organized and run by J. Morris Anderson of Philadelphia.

J. Morris Anderson, Kuzmik believed, like Williams, knew far more than he was willing to say. When Kuzmik spoke to him a few days after the episode in Tyson's suite at the Canterbury, he struck the detective as a man who made it his business to learn secrets. Anderson smiled easily, but somehow his eyes remained fixed and sharp, revealing no trace of mirth—at least, not around a white cop. As Kuzmik characterized it, "I think he lied through his teeth the whole time. But I can't prove it."

Illusion—something short of an outright lie—was the basis of Anderson's livelihood. He ran the Miss Black America pageant, a throwback to the time when the Miss America pageant was a lily-white affair. But that particular phase of Jim Crow had ended. During the 1970s and 1980s, black women entered the pageant, and in 1983, Vanessa Williams became the first black woman to win. The Miss Black America pageant in the 1990s was similar to the Negro Leagues in baseball after Jackie Robinson joined the Brooklyn Dodgers: the best talent went into whatever integrated organization offered the best prizes and the most publicity. Although Negro League team owners tried to keep their franchises alive after Robinson erased the color line, the organizations languished and eventually died. Anderson faced the same problem—and that wasn't all. Some critics of Anderson's organization said the Miss Black America pageant was an anachronism. Others said that *all* beauty pageants were anachronisms. But with smoke and mirrors, Anderson kept the illusion alive, the illusion that America had not changed since 1965.

Through the J. Morris Anderson Production Company, Anderson had been running the pageant for twenty-four years. Since 1989, the Miss Black America pageant had been held in conjunction with Black Expo, a union that had not escaped disparaging comment. "Beauty contests are meat markets," said one black Indianapolis resident. "They don't showcase the accomplishments of women—white or black. They treat women as ornaments, as jewelry." Another remark was more pointed: "Black beauty pageants are even worse than integrated ones. For too many centuries, black women and men have had to stand on auction blocks. I don't care if the audience is all black or all white. The whole process is too similar to slavery. It's degrading."

As Kuzmik continued his investigation, he began to side with the critics. To begin with, the pageant was more an exhibition than a contest. Although some of the contestants had won state or regional competitions, others had simply paid an application fee to enter. Of the twenty-three contestants, several represented the same state. "The first thing the Andersons [J. Morris and daughter Aleta] wanted when the girls got into town," Kuzmik said, "was a check for more money. These girls paid their own way. They paid their own entry fees unless they had someone backing them. One of the girls I talked to actually had to call home and say, 'Look, they are not going to let me in this thing until I come up with more money.' And the family members all got together, gathered up what they could, and wired it to her so she could stay in the pageant. You got the money, you're in. This is horrible. This is embarrassing."

The level of supervision appalled Kuzmik. At the Miss America pageant, each contestant has at least two chaperones with her at all times. The contestants are unapproachable by anyone not officially cleared through pageant administrators. In public areas they are shielded from both men looking for dates and reporters seeking interviews. No such precautions were taken at the Miss Black America pageant. Although Anderson claimed that the contestants in his pageant were also chaperoned, he wasn't exactly sure who the chaperones were. His pageant was staffed by a senior coordinator, a choreographer, an assistant choreographer, and several volunteer representatives. In addition to their other duties, Anderson suggested, these persons served as chaperones. Moreover, the contestants had tight schedules that kept them busy most of the time and were provided with instructions outlining rules of behavior. "They're told to adhere strictly to the schedule," Anderson told Kuzmik. "They are told that they are accountable for their actions. They are told that in order to appear bright and sharp on television they need to get their rest. And they're all given tips in terms of how to answer questions. . . . We have an oath of positivity which we give the girls which has all the points that control being successful in given endeavors."

None of the "general rules of positivity," however, addressed being trapped in the suite of a former heavyweight champion. Kuzmik recalled his first interview with Anderson: "I asked, 'What kind of curfew did you have?' 'Well, they know they have to start at six in the morning.' I'd say, 'Didn't you have a bed check?' 'No.' If these girls had the energy when they were through with the day's rehearsals, they could pretty much do what they wanted."

But Kuzmik was less interested in how the pageant was run than in what material evidence Anderson might have and what he had heard about the rape. Anderson disappointed the investigator in both areas.

Anderson remembered Tyson's behavior on the afternoon of July 18 in the Omni Severin's Allison Ballroom. The boxer was completely at ease. He was "elated to be with the girls and the girls were elated to be with Mike Tyson." Everyone was relaxed and friendly. Tyson even agreed to do a promotional piece for Black Expo, strolling to a rap beat along a line of the contestants, admiring their beauty, touching a waist here and a shoulder there. Kuzmik had heard rumors that Tyson was touching more than shoulders and waists. He asked Anderson what he had seen or heard. Anderson answered that he didn't see anything, although he too had heard rumors. "What rumors?" Kuzmik urged. "Just general conversation that Mike Tyson was making overtures to the contestants and that the contestants were making overtures to Mike Tyson." Anderson didn't recall anything more specific.

Nor did he remember much about the rumor that Desiree Washington had been raped. Toward the end of the pageant, Desiree's father told Anderson that his daughter had been raped by Tyson, and that he and his wife had persuaded Desiree to press charges. Anderson relayed the news to the Reverend Williams. Anderson told Kuzmik that his primary concern was for the Miss Black America pageant: rape charges would have a "negative effect." Williams shared Anderson's concern—he had Black Expo to worry about—and told the pageant director that he would talk to Don King and try to solve the problem. Anderson stressed that all he knew was hearsay and that he didn't want to be involved in the case.

Kuzmik realized that Anderson wasn't going to tell him anything he didn't already know. But on one point he wanted to press Anderson: the raw videotape footage taken at the pageant. J. Morris Anderson Production Company's most valuable product was the edited tape of the Miss Black America pageant. It was that tape, not the live pageant, that generated the most revenue. Anderson rented the tape to television stations to broadcast whenever they could fit it into their schedules. During the course of the pageant, Anderson's photographers filmed anything and everything that might make the final edited tape an attractive show, including the rehearsals, shots of the contestants in Indianapolis, celebrities at the pageant, and the contest's finals. Kuzmik had no interest in the final tape, but he did want to see all the raw footage in which Tyson appeared.

Desiree had told Kuzmik that Anderson's cameraman was shooting a promotional commercial when Tyson first approached her. "Do you want to go out?" he had asked. "Sure," she answered. Simple innocent conversation—but one that helped to corroborate her tale. "It's all on the videotape," Desiree repeated. "They were taping when it happened."

Before Kuzmik spoke with Anderson, he had received a tip that the entrepreneur was using Video Management Systems in Indianapolis to edit the videotape of the contest. The information was strong enough to obtain a search warrant. But when he went to serve the warrant, the doors to the business were locked. Kuzmik and several other detectives then went to the Omni Severin, where Anderson was staying. The only description Kuzmik had of Anderson was that he was a "tall black guy." In the middle of Black Expo, Kuzmik began his search for a tall black man. After saying "Excuse me, Mr. Anderson?" to several dozen tall black men in the Omni and getting only blank looks, one at last answered "Yes?"

Anderson allowed Kuzmik to search his rooms for the tapes and arranged for him to get the others at Video Management Systems. Kuzmik recovered enough tapes to start his own film library. The owner of Video Management Systems even located the edited tape that contained the Tyson segment. It was just as Desiree had described it: the dance number, Tyson walking down the line and repeating his rap lines, Tyson flubbing up a line, laughing, and reaching out and pulling Desiree to him. Then, abruptly, the tape cut to another scene. The footage where Tyson had asked Desiree out was missing from the edited version. "Where's the rest of this tape?" Kuzmik asked. The manager waved his hand at the stack of raw tapes: "Somewhere in there."

Kuzmik looked through all the unedited tapes. Nothing. It wasn't there. The only videotape containing Tyson was the edited version. Of all the tapes, why was the one with Tyson the only one missing? Five days after the search, Kuzmik questioned Anderson on the whereabouts of the missing tape:

> **Q.** To your knowledge, you have produced all the videotapes involved with the Miss Black America pageant?
>
> **A.** Yes.
>
> **Q.** Who has ultimate control over these tapes? Someone obviously has to be responsible for maintaining the tapes that you need and to put in your archives later on. Whose job is that?
>
> **A.** We don't have any. . . . There's nobody. . . . The only thing we're concerned about is what's going to be on the television show.

Kuzmik was certain that someone either knew where the tape was or had destroyed the tape. In addition, he was fairly sure who that someone was. He also had a feeling that he had a better chance of finding Jimmy Hoffa than of locating the raw videotape of Mike Tyson.

Aleta J. Anderson, J. Morris's daughter and the pageant's producer, echoed her father's observations. Tyson had been aggressive, yes, but the contestants were flattered by his attentions. "No one registered any complaints," she said—and Desiree was no different. When Tyson grabbed her, Desiree appeared to enjoy the attention. She wasn't upset by his actions. Nor, like her father, did Aleta Anderson hear Tyson ask Desiree for a date or know anything about the missing tape.

After taking the statements of Charlie Williams and J. Morris and Aleta Anderson, Kuzmik knew that he wasn't going to learn much from the organizers of Black Expo or the Miss Black America pageant. He understood their reluctance to get involved, but as the case wore on it began to eat at him. Too often he had heard his department criticized for ignoring black-on-black crime. Now he was investigating a major black-on-black crime, and "all of a sudden it's the white prosecutor and it's the white police department that are after Mike Tyson because he's a successful black man. What a crock! I didn't commit the crime. Jeff Modisett didn't commit the crime. We didn't make the accusations. But we caught the heat. I've got an eighteen-year-old black victim who leading black spokesmen are trashing. I saw some professor from some small southern school on television explaining that what Mike Tyson did to Desiree was part of some black dating ritual. It's normal, he said, for black men to treat black women this way. That's just the way it is. What a crock!"

The staff at Methodist Hospital were more forthcoming. Dr. Thomas Richardson was on duty in the emergency department of Methodist Hospital in the early hours of July 20. In over seven years in the emergency department, Richardson had confronted every sort of injury and condition. For two years he had taken care of trauma patients on Lifeline helicopter flights. By 1991 he was coordinating the Lifeline flights, monitoring the status of patients with the helicopter crew and organizing a team to take care of patients once they reached the hospital. But 95 percent of Richardson's patients walked— or were carried—through the hospital door. Each year over seventy-five thousand patients were treated in Methodist's emergency department.

Like other emergency physicians in inner-city hospitals, Richardson routinely performed gynecological examinations, especially on women too poor to afford either medical insurance or doctor's bills. On a typical day he would give two or three pelvic exams; during his years at Methodist he had done between two and three thousand. Occasionally he would perform pelvics on women who had been raped.

Richardson attended Desiree Washington when she walked into the emergency department at about 3:30 A.M. and reported that she had been raped. Desiree, Richardson told Kuzmik, was composed, but she was clearly struggling to keep her emotions under tight control. Though she answered questions with precision, her voice betrayed a slight quiver. She told Richardson that Mike Tyson had raped her—that he had lured her into his room and sexually assaulted her. Like other rape victims with whom Richardson had talked, Desiree quickly described the attack, refusing to linger on the painful details.

Richardson proceeded to give her a physical. There were no bruises or abrasions on her arms or legs, no signs that she had been hit or squeezed. There was no trauma to her labia majora or labia minora. But there were two small abrasions, an eighth of an inch wide and three-eighths of an inch long, on her introitus, the opening to the vagina. When Richardson attempted to insert a speculum into her vagina to look for internal injuries, Desiree winced and pulled away.

Richardson told Kuzmik that Desiree's injuries and reactions were consistent with rape. Between 10 and 20 percent of all rape victims suffer injuries to the introitus. Such injuries are virtually unknown in consensual sex. In the thousands of pelvics he had given, Richardson had seen them only twice. In fact, Desiree found the exam so uncomfortable that Richardson decided not to do a full pelvic and rape examination. Desiree told him that she had been raped over twenty-four hours before. To subject her to the standard rape tests, which involved fingernail scrapings, combings for pubic hair, and vaginal washings, seemed pointless. It would entail more pain and probably produce no evidence.

Instead, Richardson counseled her. He talked to her about her greatest fears: pregnancy and disease. Given that she had just begun her period, Richardson said it was highly unlikely that she was pregnant. Disease was another matter. He gave her an antibiotic injection to prevent the development of gonorrhea and informed her about the need to have an HIV test.

In questioning Richardson, Kuzmik found the doctor to be likable, helpful, and thoroughly professional. Richardson wouldn't say whether or not he thought Desiree had been raped; it was a question he could not answer with certainty. But he did suggest that her injuries and behavior were consistent with rape. Other members of Methodist's staff who had helped Desiree agreed with Richardson. Both the nurse and the chaplain confirmed that Desiree had been brave but badly frightened. There was no doubt that something bad had happened to her.

Virginia Foster, Chris Low, McCoy Wagers, and now Thomas Richardson—all confirmed parts of Desiree's story. Kuzmik had always believed Desiree, and now he saw a case against Tyson beginning to form. As date rapes go, it was even a good case. But one that would lead to a conviction? That was another matter entirely. What would happen when the press got hold of the story? The police investigator could already see Virginia Foster beginning to waver. What would happen when reporters started to fight for leads and began grilling witnesses important to the case? He had seen cases stronger than this one go south. By Thursday, July 25, one week since the day Desiree Washington first met Mike Tyson, Kuzmik suspected that the press would soon have the story.

# CHAPTER 4

# "Get the Fuck Out of My Office"

Jack Rinehart was accustomed to cryptic messages, but the one he received at a quarter of eight on the morning of July 24 was even more vague than usual. He was driving to work when he answered a call on his portable radio. A police officer at the City-County Building wanted to talk to him. The caller left no name and no details, but he insisted that it was urgent.

Urgent messages with details left vague were the substance of Rinehart's professional life. As the leading news reporter for WRTV–Channel 6, the ABC affiliate in Indianapolis, he covered the City-County Building. He had been a reporter for the station for sixteen years and had won a reputation for uncommon professionalism. Everyone at City-County liked Jack: prosecutors and police because he was an honest news reporter who faithfully reported the facts and didn't slant stories or engage in irrelevant sensationalism, defense attorneys because he wasn't a stooge for the prosecution, secretaries and janitors because he remembered their names and was always courteous and friendly. And almost everyone at City-County talked to him—in private, off the record. "He has more sources than a narc," admitted one detective. A deputy prosecutor said, "If City-County has a father confessor, it's Jack. Christ, Jack knows every secret in the building."

Fishing was Rinehart's only diversion. It was more than a hobby; it was his passion. Night after night, after work and dinner and tucking in his kids, Rinehart would leave the comforts of his home to throw his line for an hour or so into the nearest body of water. He was a "catch and release" man. Dead fish can never play the game again. Live fish put gently back in the water may be smarter next time—and thus more of a challenge.

Like fish, good stories normally don't jump into your boat, but they're out there, swimming around, waiting for the reporter with enough skill and patience to catch them. City-County was Rinehart's stream. He knew every rock, every eddy, he knew where to cast his line, and he could sense when something big was getting ready to bite. The only difference was that at City-County he never let go of anything he caught.

Before Rinehart could reach his office, the police officer who had left the message met him at the top of the escalator. He touched Rinehart's arm and said, "We've got to talk. Let's go get some coffee." Rinehart had known the man for years. A seasoned cop, he was not easily unnerved, and mystery stories were not his style. Rinehart felt a sharp, familiar tug on his line.

There was no small talk, no polite inquiries about wives and children. Before they were out of the building, the officer told Rinehart that a rape had occurred during Black Expo and that the rapist was either Mike Tyson or Evander Holyfield. That uncertainty was the strange part. Even within police circles, information was scarce. Normally police talk among themselves about their cases, exchanging gossip and war stories, but nobody at headquarters was saying much about this particular case. The normal DHC had not been filed. The usual paperwork was conspicuously absent. The officer didn't know if the prosecutor's office or the police department was trying to cover up the crime, but the whole affair seemed suspicious.

Rinehart learned months later that the police leaked the story to him because the department was "pissed off" at the *Indianapolis Star* for its coverage of several other stories involving the police. At the time, however, Rinehart's only thought was, *Holy shit, this is a huge, huge story.*

Still, all Rinehart had was a very vague rumor. He trusted his source, but the officer himself was only one step beyond complete ignorance. It was now up to Rinehart to fill in the missing information.

For the moment Rinehart was the only reporter on the story, but he knew it would not stay his for long. He called his managing editor, Ray Bredemann, and told him the sketchy details. Rinehart said he needed a photographer for the day, adding that Bredemann could tell Bill Skroko, the acting news director, what he was working on, but no one else. The last thing he wanted was some film editor or reporter at the station calling his or her spouse with the hottest news in town.

By late morning, with the help of photographer Mike Grimes, Rinehart had begun the search for confirmation. He didn't have to prove that a rape had taken place, just that the police were investigating the allegations. From the first, he suspected that the charges—if indeed there were any charges— involved Tyson, not Holyfield. Although both boxers had attended Black Expo, Tyson's and Holyfield's public images contrasted sharply. Holyfield seemed as clean as the young Steve Garvey—a Christian role model for America's youth who seldom did or said anything controversial—whereas Tyson was a black Sean Penn; trouble and discord followed him across continents.

Rinehart's search began at a computer terminal. Normally the police dumped every report of a crime, or DHC, into the computer, gave it a computer aided dispatch (CAD) number, and sent it out to reporters over the telefax. But there had been no telefaxed DHC in the Tyson rape case. There was, however, something in the computer, if one had the CAD number to access it. Earlier that morning, Rinehart had obtained the number. He typed 899837 F-H into the computer terminal at police headquarters. A few pieces of information flicked onto the screen, enough to confirm that something had taken place. He learned that the crime was reported to have occurred at the Canterbury Hotel and that a white sequin and a bedspread had been turned in to the property room at police headquarters. But that was all the information the computer would give him. To get the rest of the DHC—names and specifics of the crime—Rinehart needed another access number, and none of his informants had it.

Rinehart's next stop was the headquarters of Black Expo and the Reverend Charles Williams on Indianapolis's near north side. Without telling Williams what he was looking for, Rinehart conducted a brief taped interview. He asked a few general questions about Black Expo and the schedules of Tyson and Holyfield. Then he started to focus his questions on Tyson's behavior. How had he acted? What did he do at night? Who was he with? Williams said that Tyson had had "a good time with the ladies," telling Rinehart that the boxer exchanged phone numbers with several contestants and that there was a significant amount of touching going on.

The interview with Williams certainly didn't verify any rape allegations, but it did add background depth and color to the story Rinehart was building. The narrowing focus of Rinehart's questions made Williams suspicious. The two men had known each other for years, since the days when Williams had worked in the mayor's office. When the interview ended, it was Williams's turn to ask questions. "What's going on? Did something happen that I don't know about?" Rinehart said he wasn't sure. He refused to say any more, but Williams's earlier conversations with the police had already tipped him off.

If a story is a fish, this one was moving closer to the boat, but it still had lots of line and plenty of fight left. There was one person who could confirm absolutely if Tyson was under any kind of investigation for rape or anything else: Marion County Prosecutor Jeffrey Modisett. Good fortune plays a part in chasing down every successful story, and Rinehart seemed to be rolling sevens—he already had an interview scheduled with Modisett for one-thirty that afternoon, an interview set up the day before that had nothing to do with Tyson.

"No reporter can survive in the City-County Building by screwing people," Rinehart said later. "You just don't say 'Let's talk about this' before the camera goes on and then talk about something different once it's rolling. It's not professional. And no one story is big enough to burn Modisett." But this was a big story, and Rinehart was not about to pass up the opportunity. Toward the end of the interview, after he had asked a series of questions about another matter, Rinehart inquired if Michael Gerard Tyson was under investigation for rape. Modisett's face seldom registered much emotion; "malleable" is the last word one would use to describe it. But with the question still in the air, Rinehart could see the blood drain from Modisett's face. "No comment," Modisett answered. Rinehart approached the subject from a different direction. The blood returned to Modisett's face, along with the stony gaze. The prosecutor had nothing, absolutely nothing, to say about Mike Tyson or any subject pertaining to Mike Tyson.

Modisett would later claim that he expected Rinehart's question, noting that he had heard that "Jack had been asking around." Before they went into the prosecutor's library for the interview, Modisett said, he asked Rinehart to tell him the subject of the interview. "Jack said no, that he would just rather turn on the camera. Well, that's not like Jack, so I knew what it was." Rinehart, however, contests this claim, and the tape of the interview supports him. If Modisett expected the question, then Al Pacino could not have done a better job of feigning total shock.

Had Modisett gone off the record and told Rinehart, "Yes, there is an investigation, but it is at a very sensitive stage and I would rather keep it quiet for a time," Rinehart would have sat on the story. But Modisett's only comment was "no comment"—which, of course, spoke eloquently to the newsman. If Tyson were not under investigation, Modisett would have said so; he wouldn't have left the subject open to speculation. But though "no comment" is in fact an important comment to a reporter, it isn't a confirmation. And Rinehart needed an absolute confirmation.

After failing to get substantiation of the story from Modisett, Rinehart left the Office of the Prosecutor on the fifth floor of the City-County Building and walked to police headquarters in the east wing of the building, where his own office and those of his most friendly sources were located. One of his friends was "at the highest levels" of the police department. Like Modisett, he would be in a position to know with complete certainty if Tyson were under investigation.

Rinehart entered the policeman's office, sat down, asked how his day was going, and then inquired if Mike Tyson had raped anyone while he had been in Indianapolis. Rinehart later recalled the scene this way: "So, I'm sitting in this person's office and I ask him and I can see him just, you know, shit. He says, 'Get out of here. I don't need this. I promised I wouldn't say anything.' " Rinehart could see, however, that the officer wanted to say something and that, unlike Modisett's, his "no comment" was equivocal, capable of sliding into a confirmation. Rinehart reasoned. He pleaded. He begged. He tried to cash in IOUs and mentioned the public's right to know the truth. No confirmation; the officer had promised not to say anything, and he wouldn't.

Rinehart tried another tack: perhaps he could get a confirmation that wasn't an official confirmation. "Look," he told the officer, "if you can confirm the rape allegations, just tell me to get the fuck out of your office." The officer stared at him and without missing a beat said, "I don't want to talk about this anymore. Get the fuck out of my office." Rinehart left, satisfied.

By Wednesday afternoon, Rinehart had his story and was ready to go public. As television reports go, it was compelling. On tape, Williams confirmed that Tyson had acted improperly during his brief stay at Black Expo. Off tape, several high-placed officials in the police department confirmed that there was an investigation. Rinehart had footage of the Canterbury Hotel and videotape of Tyson in the ring. The story, he told the managing editor and news director, was "definitely doable."

At WRTV, Bredemann and Skroko disagreed. Worried about lawsuits by Tyson and King, they wanted what Rinehart could not provide: either Modisett or the Indianapolis chief of police on camera verifying the investigation. Rinehart was livid. He remembered being in a phone booth on the south side of town, screaming at his managers, telling them that the story was going to break and that Channel 6 had the opportunity to break it.

Rinehart had entered a region that reporters refer to as the "paranoid zone." Actually it's a state of mind, based on an unshakable belief that you have discovered the truth about a story but your superiors won't run it. Since the truth is irrefutable, only a conspiracy can account for the actions of those above you. Perhaps they are part of an elaborate cover-up. Perhaps some outside element is calling the shots. Whatever the reason, your story, your truth, is being buried.

That night Rinehart called Don Thrasher, a former reporter for the *Indianapolis Star* who had become a Washington-based producer for ABC's "20/20." Rinehart had known Thrasher for some time and had even given him a major lead in an investigation of a scandal at the Pentagon. He told Thrasher his story, complaining about the cautiousness of his superiors. If Channel 6 refused to run his report, he wanted Thrasher to break the story nationally. "Don't fuck me on this," Rinehart said. Thrasher promised Rinehart that he wouldn't tell anyone. Rinehart believes that Thrasher promptly telephoned R. Joseph Gelarden of the *Indianapolis Star* and told him Rinehart's story, then made reservations to fly to Indianapolis. (Gelarden, for his part, claims that Thrasher first heard of the story from a contact he had in the Indianapolis police department.)

That night Rinehart didn't need to sleep to have nightmares. All he could think about was reading the story in the next morning's *Star*. He thought about his sources, men who had never lied to him, and the unwillingness of his managers to accept their accounts. He turned the story over and over in his mind, examining it from every angle. It was flawless. No doubt about it, there was an ongoing investigation.

By Thursday morning both Rinehart and the team of Thrasher and Gelarden were working independently on the story. Rinehart had most of the story; all he needed were a few more details and, if possible, an on-tape confirmation. He set out to fill in the gaps. He interviewed another police officer who spoke openly about the investigation, although not in front of the camera. He also spoke to J. Morris Anderson, the promoter of the Miss Black America pageant, who at first denied everything, insisting that Tyson had done nothing wrong. But finally he did confess that there had been an "incident." During the last two days of the pageant Desiree Washington had supposedly initiated some talk of the rape, but Anderson doubted that any rape had occurred.

Unknown to Rinehart, Thrasher and Gelarden were attacking along a different front. Joe Gelarden was a forceful reporter who was every bit as competitive as Rinehart. He was passionate about a number of subjects—fly-fishing and good writing among them—but on no subject was he more adamant than the public's right to know what its elected officials were doing. By Thursday morning he and Don Thrasher were hounding Modisett for a confirmation. They accused the county prosecutor of protecting Tyson and engineering a cover-up. When they discovered that no DHC had been filed in the case, Gelarden went ballistic, arguing that the open records statutes of Indiana required that every DHC be made public within twenty-four hours of a crime's being reported. By Friday, Edward O. Delaney, the *Star*'s attorney, was explaining Indiana law to Modisett and Dave Dreyer, Indianapolis's two leading law enforcement officials. During the three-way conference call, Dreyer explained to Delaney that there was considerable gray area in the law, especially in rape cases, where privacy statutes allowed police to withhold the names of both the victim and the accused. Finally, Modisett interrupted the legal disquisition. He and Delaney were friends; Delaney had handled the legal work on Modisett's fight over the election recount. Off the record, Modisett asked for Delaney's gut reaction. "Look, Jeff," the lawyer answered, "the cat's out of the bag. I know we could probably argue this thing through the courts, but the bottom line is that everyone knows about [the investigation], and what do you have to gain by secrecy at this point?"

Modisett agreed. He told the police department to release the DHC and make a brief statement that Mike Tyson was under investigation for rape. At four-thirty that afternoon, police spokesman Lieutenant Timothy Horty made it official. As Modisett had requested, the statement was brief and details were sketchy. Horty handed out an edited DHC, said Tyson was under investigation, and then read a one-sentence report: "The victim stated she was at 123 S. Illinois with the suspect on the above time and date [1:30 A.M. on July 19] when she was forced to submit to vaginal intercourse." Unlike in most other rape cases in Indiana, he gave the victim's name.

For Rinehart, the timing was ideal. While the other reporters scrambled for interviews to support their lead, Rinehart opened Channel 6's "News at Five" with the full story, replete with interviews and videotape of Tyson. By the time the *Star* reported the story the next morning, most of America had learned of the charges.

The next hour was the longest and most complex in Rinehart's life. At five o'clock he broke the biggest story of his career live at the City-County Building. Then he headed back to the station to put together a longer and more complete segment for the "News at Six." Around five-thirty, his wife called, in tears. Her regular ob/gyn checkup that morning had prompted an ultrasound examination that detected a large mass in her ovaries. Ovarian cancer had killed her mother. In her mid-twenties, she herself had had breast cancer. And on the following Monday she was scheduled to have her cancerous thyroid gland removed. Now the doctors were telling her she would need a complete hysterectomy that Monday as well.

Suddenly the Tyson story didn't seem so important to Rinehart. The adrenaline that had sustained him during the previous two days drained from his body. His first instinct was to go home to his wife and two young sons. But he didn't, at least not immediately. He asked his wife if she could wait until after his six o'clock report. She said she could. With an eerie emptiness, he returned to work. His five o'clock report had already resulted in his phone being lit up like a Christmas tree. A security guard claimed that he had seen Tyson "manhandle some gal." A woman insisted that Tyson had sexually assaulted her at the Johnny Gill concert, and that she had filed a complaint but the prosecutor's office had ignored her. Rinehart listened to these stories, but in his mind he was already home with his wife. After doing his report at six o'clock, he turned everything over to the night crew and left the Tyson case.

Jeffrey Modisett soon had reason to wish he could leave the case as well. He had withheld a great story from hungry news reporters, and they were angry. Within a few days they turned on Modisett, accusing him of allowing leads to grow cold and shirking his duties as an elected public official. Editorials in Indianapolis's two leading newspapers, the *Star* and the *News,* both Republican, condemned his behavior. The *News* was particularly hostile: "Rape—like murder and many other violent crimes—is not merely a crime against an individual. It is a crime against the public—against the citizenry's sense of security." That, the editorialist argued, was why the government, supported by taxpayers' dollars, hunted down and prosecuted the criminal. "Citizens . . . recognize that it is not in any decent person's interest to have rapists, murderers or thieves walking around unrestrained." The tenor of the editorial suggested that Jack the Ripper was loose on the streets of Indianapolis and that Jeffrey Modisett had chosen to keep the fact secret.

Modisett knew that he had tried to keep the charges secret to conduct a more, not less, thorough investigation. As a federal attorney he would conduct secret investigations for months before handing down indictments. In some cases that were especially sensitive, secrecy was essential to protect important witnesses. The last thing he wanted was for the press to get the story and interview witnesses before his office reached them. Only later, after several other confrontations with the press during the Tyson trial, would he grasp an essential political axiom: If the press thinks you're screwing it, it'll screw you.

Quick to advance the public's right to know everything, the press was equally swift to begin trying the case. Running just beneath the surface of the early reports was the assumption that Tyson was probably innocent, a reflection in part of who spoke most to reporters. Modisett and the police department refused to answer all but the most basic questions. Desiree Washington answered no questions at all. Tyson's camp, however, treated the investigation as one of the hazards of new fortune. "We hear the same kind of thing about once a month," said Charles Lomax, a Chicago lawyer who represented Don King and Mike Tyson. "Mike is a target for just about anyone who wants to take a shot at him."

Many contestants in the Miss Black America pageant supported Tyson's claim of innocence. Tonya Traylor, the thirty-year-old first runner-up in the pageant, claimed that she and several of the contestants were with Tyson in the Hoosier Dome at the Johnny Gill concert when the rape was supposed to have occurred. "That's probably about right," agreed Aleta Anderson, the pageant's producer. Tyson, added Traylor, was "real nice. You assume people are going to make a pass or whatever, but he didn't."

Other contestants believed that Iron Mike wasn't real nice. Rosie Jones, Miss Black America of 1990, told a television reporter about a photo session with Tyson: "When we turned to take the pictures, he put his arm around me, and he grabbed my rear end. And then I took his hand and knocked it off my behind, and I said to him how I didn't appreciate that. He just kind of chuckled, and then he goes, 'What's wrong? You don't want to help a black man out?'"

Modisett quickly discovered that his instincts had been right. Once the allegations became public the story began to spin out of control, with the press publishing reams of he said–she said stories. The media demanded to know what he was going to do about the case. Was he going to charge Mike Tyson with rape or not? Modisett had two options. First, he could charge Tyson with rape and issue a warrant for his arrest. He had Desiree's story, statements from Virginia Foster and the Canterbury's staff, physical and medical evidence—more than enough probable cause material to charge Tyson. Modisett's second option was to convene a grand jury. The regular grand jury's caseload was too full to hear the Tyson case. But Modisett could call a special grand jury to hear this one case.

The grand jury option had an attractive feature: politically, it was safe. It removed the burden of decision from Modisett's shoulders and gave it to six members—black as well as white—of the Indianapolis community. They, not Modisett, would have to decide whether or not to indict the famous black celebrity. The grand jury option also made sense strategically. It allowed Modisett to present the state's case without trying it. He could give all the evidence to the grand jury and in essence say *Here, you decide. Is there enough probable cause to indict or not?* The grand jury's reaction would provide an indication of how a real jury would respond. Moreover, the grand jury's subpoena power made it easier to compel witnesses outside Modisett's jurisdiction to testify. The grand jury, in effect, could help to strengthen the state's case. Finally, there were financial considerations. The Tyson case would be expensive to investigate and try, and Indianapolis taxpayers would have to pick up the bill. A grand jury would be composed of and would represent Indianapolis taxpayers. If the grand jury indicted Tyson, no one could later accuse Modisett of trifling away taxpayers' dollars on a frivolous issue.

The fear that he would be accused of advancing the case to spotlight himself gnawed at Modisett. Rape victims, and particularly victims of date rape, are different from victims of other forms of assault. As sex crime prosecutors cautioned Modisett, rape victims often blame themselves for the crime. Desiree, for example, had been raped, but she had gone to Tyson's room voluntarily. Psychologically, she might hold herself at least partially responsible, and that feeling of guilt, however baseless, might reduce her level of commitment to the case. And this was not a typical rape case. Added to the emotional trauma that any rape victim has to confront, Desiree would have to deal with the intense glare of publicity that would inevitably result from her charges—the photographers in her face, the crush of reporters at the trial, the sleazy stories that would circulate as facts in newspaper, magazine, and television reports. Modisett did not want to try Tyson without Desiree's complete support.

"The grand jury process," Modisett argued, "would allow her to spend more time thinking about the level of her cooperation, and it would give her a sense of what it's going to be like if she pursues the case."

One final consideration pushed Modisett toward convening the special grand jury: he was a product of the federal court system, where every important case goes to a grand jury. He was comfortable with the system; he knew how to use a grand jury as an investigative tool, and he knew that a grand jury indictment aided the state's case once it went to court. Over the weekend, as the Tyson story exploded nationally, Modisett discussed his options with Dreyer. On Monday, July 28, he called a press conference and announced that he had decided to impanel a special grand jury to look into the allegations.

# CHAPTER 5

# "THIS AIN'T MAYBERRY"

Though they were both cops, Tommy Kuzmik didn't like Dale Edwards much. It wasn't because Edwards pocketed extra money moonlighting as Mike Tyson's bodyguard/gofer, nor was it anything the Cleveland policeman had said to the Indianapolis sex crimes investigator. It was just a cop's sixth sense, a vague feeling that Edwards had cut too many corners in his career, that he was on the lookout for the easy score. "There are some cops that no matter how much they bathe, they stink," Kuzmik said. "When you look at them you see dirt."

To be sure, Edwards had faced official problems during his career. He had been tried on a charge of possessing cocaine—and found not guilty. Looking at the record in the case, Kuzmik believed that Edwards had been set up. A Cleveland grand jury returned a no bill on a rape charge. Kuzmik knew that cops had enemies, and that those enemies liked to throw around unsubstantiated accusations. But Kuzmik believed that even if Edwards had not been guilty of those specific charges, his strong suit wasn't innocence.

On August 30 Edwards was called to Indianapolis to testify before the specially convened grand jury investigating the rape charges against Mike Tyson. At the conclusion of his testimony, Kuzmik invited Edwards into his office for a cup of coffee, mostly to keep the bodyguard away from his boss, who was testifying the same day. On Kuzmik's office wall Edwards noticed a year-old headline from the *National Enquirer* announcing that Mike Tyson was going to retire from boxing to marry a beauty pageant contestant. The sick irony of the story had appealed to Kuzmik, who had tacked it up and then forgotten about it. Edwards looked at the headline, smiled, and then began to pump Kuzmik for information.

"You get a lot of rape charges against celebrities in this town?" Edwards asked.

"No. If we did, they'd go to trial."

"How's the investigation against Mike going? You know he's innocent. I was in the other room the entire time. I heard them laughing and having a good time in the bedroom."

There was a question there somewhere, but Kuzmik ignored it. Edwards kept asking questions and looking at the scattered papers on Kuzmik's desk concerning the Tyson case. Kuzmik let him look. He knew from experience that Edwards was a snoop, and he expected him to look. Just that morning he had manufactured several memos and bogus cryptic phone messages intended to interest Edwards. Now he even occasionally turned around on one or another pretext to give Edwards more time to look. As Edwards talked and not so furtively peeked around, Kuzmik thought, *Do I have "stupid" written across my forehead?*

Recalling the episode, Kuzmik said, "I'm no hayseed. I grew up in his turf. Now he was on my turf, pulling this shit like he was in some hick village. Check the population figures; Indianapolis has over two hundred thousand more people than Cleveland. I wanted to say to him, 'This ain't Mayberry, pal. And my bullet ain't in my pocket. It's in the chamber.' But I didn't say anything. Maybe it was better if Edwards, Tyson, and the whole bunch thought they were dealing with Andy and Barney and Opie. Let them take us for granted."

If Tyson and King ever took Indianapolis authorities for granted, they were not blasé about the charges. While Charles Lomax, Tyson's lawyer who handled his ordinary legal problems, was publicly saying that rape charges were common for wealthy celebrities like Tyson, the boxer and his manager moved to retain extraordinary legal counsel. Within twenty-four hours after the charges had been made public, Tyson hired Vincent Fuller, senior partner of the Washington firm of Williams & Connolly, and James Voyles, one of Indianapolis's leading defense lawyers, to represent him. Fuller was one of the premier defense attorneys in the nation; he had defended clients ranging from John Hinckley, the man who shot President Ronald Reagan, to Don King, when the boxing promoter faced serious income tax problems. Although Voyles's practice was confined mostly to Indiana, he had experience in rape trials.

Tyson's uneasiness increased the next week. On Monday Modisett announced that he would convene a special grand jury to investigate Desiree Washington's charges. On Tuesday Rosie Jones, Miss Black America 1990, told reporters that Tyson had propositioned her at the opening ceremony of Black Expo. Then on Saturday, August 3, Tyson noticed unusual activity around King's Ohio training camp. Most Saturdays King opened the camp free to the public to allow people to see a few of his fighters train. On this Saturday, however, more than a few curious fans showed up. Tyson, who often used off-duty Cleveland policemen as bodyguards and was thus familiar with many members of the force, spied several plainclothes cops looking around the camp. Quick to reach the logical conclusion, he called King and said that the police had come for him.

He was only partially right. Dave Dreyer, the chief counsel under Jeff Modisett who was in charge of the grand jury investigation, didn't want Tyson arrested, only located. Police lab technicians needed blood and saliva samples from Tyson, and the Cleveland police agreed to locate the former champion, which they did. Tyson's hasty retreat, however, set off a round of confused telephone calls. Tyson called King; King called Voyles; Voyles called Modisett; Modisett called Dreyer. Dreyer, who was worried about how he was going to get Tyson to give him blood and saliva samples, called Voyles and said that the police were not going to arrest Tyson, but only wanted the samples. Tyson was so relieved that he agreed. The samples only proved that he had engaged in sexual intercourse with Desiree, an act he never denied.

The mix-up, however, demonstrated to Dreyer that he wasn't dealing with just another Class B felony. Team Tyson had access—to Modisett, to him. Its lawyers could get answers on a

Saturday afternoon, and get them fast; Tyson didn't have to take a number and wait in line. As much as the prosecutors and investigators working on the case tried to deny it, the case had an implicit priority code.

As he began communicating with Williams & Connolly, Dreyer also realized that he was not facing just another law firm representing just another client. When Fuller wanted something, he wanted it immediately, and expense wasn't a problem. In the prosecutor's office, budget constraints made workers debate whether or not to send important letters via overnight mail. Fuller functioned in a different economic zip code. At one point during the grand jury investigation, Fuller called Dreyer one morning to complain that he hadn't received some trivial document. "It's in my office. You need to pick it up," Dreyer explained. "Fine, I'll send someone over," Fuller politely answered. By noon, that person, who Dreyer assumed worked for Voyles, arrived in his office. Though Dreyer didn't recognize him, he asked him a question about the Indianapolis lawyer. Another mix-up: the man didn't work for Voyles, but for Williams & Connolly. Instead of relying on Voyles's office, Fuller had instructed a member of his own Washington staff to fly to Indianapolis, pick up the document, and get it back to him by early afternoon. No problem—all it cost was a few thousand dollars.

The Tyson case was Dreyer's baptism in office. After earning his law degree at Notre Dame, he had gone to work for the Legal Services Corporation, providing legal aid and advice to the poor. For six years he was in court steadily, fighting the government to obtain housing, Social Security allowances, Medicaid, food stamps, welfare, and other benefits for his clients. He also handled civil disputes over child custody, landlord-tenant disagreements, and consumer problems. He tried cases in courts ranging from small claims court to the Seventh Circuit Court of Appeals, which is only a step away from the Supreme Court. The Legal Services Corporation was a place where a young idealistic lawyer could help people tangibly, and in the process gain experience. He left the Legal Services Corporation in 1986 and joined a midsize private firm, where he worked until late 1990, when he accepted Modisett's offer to become chief counsel in the Marion County prosecutor's office. It was part of his job to oversee all cases taken to the grand jury. From the time Dreyer took office there had been one crisis after another, but nothing that rivaled the Tyson case.

The week of August 12, the week the members of the special grand jury were selected, was one of the worst of Dreyer's life. On Monday the standing grand jury reported on two controversial police action shootings; on Tuesday he and sex crimes prosecutor Linda Lovin participated in the selection of the Tyson grand jury; on Wednesday he interviewed a local sports star on a fraud and racketeering investigation; on Thursday he took a convoluted murder case to the grand jury; and on Friday the Tyson grand jury began deliberation. The week was a blur. Every case was at least potentially explosive. But only the Tyson case attracted national and international attention.

If it was a bad week for Dreyer, it was a worse one for Tyson. In 95 percent of the cases that prosecutors present to them, grand juries return a "true bill," or as it is more commonly known, an indictment. This is not because grand juries are rigged or filled with right-wing, law-and-order-type citizens, but rather because all the prosecutor has to present is probable cause. The question before the Indianapolis grand jury was simple: Was there enough evidence against Tyson to indicate that he might have raped Desiree Washington? If the answer was yes, the grand jury was expected to return an indictment, which in theory was an indication not of guilt, but merely that there was enough evidence to justify a trial. In most cases, the grand jury never hears from the accused, and certainly not from his lawyer.

Unlike in a trial, Tyson had no right to face or cross-examine his accuser or tell his full story before the grand jury. If invited to testify, he could choose to appear and answer the prosecutor's questions. But in most cases the accused does not testify before a grand jury because the chance that it would lead to a no bill, or *ignoramus,* is outweighed by the liability of giving the prosecution a sworn statement.

But the nature of the grand jury was only one of Tyson's problems. His behavior in Indianapolis had led to other civil suits. Attorneys for Rosie Jones filed a $100 million suit in New York against Tyson for grabbing her buttocks. Determined to exceed Jones in language if not damages, J. Morris Anderson, director of the Miss Black America contest, filed a $21 million (later to escalate to $607 million) suit in Philadelphia against Tyson and Black Expo. According to Anderson, Tyson and Charles Williams had conspired "to ravage, rape and despoil the Miss Black America Pageant in general and to specifically ravage, abuse and assault Miss Black America Contestants . . . by grabbing, rubbing and fondling their buttocks and by specifically fondling the breasts of another contestant in addition to specifically assaulting and raping a specific contestant in the pageant. . . . " In a rambling legal document, Anderson accused Tyson of being a "serial buttocks fondler" and of striking "a ferocious blow against the face of the Miss Black America Pageant in general and a lick against the face of Black Women in general." Williams, he added, "had hid behind the cloth of the ministry and brought Mike Tyson into the rehearsal hall to feast on the flesh of the Miss Black America Pageant Queens." In an Associated Press release, Anderson asserted that Tyson had sexually assaulted or harassed eleven of the twenty-three contestants.

It was in this atmosphere of suits, charges, and rumors, all featured prominently in newspapers, magazines, and tabloid television, that the Tyson grand jury began deliberation. Three men and three women, one of whom was black, randomly selected from a list of registered voters, the jurors agreed to meet once or twice a week for three or four weeks until they heard the evidence in the case. Their sessions, like all grand jury sessions, were conducted away from the glare of publicity. During most sessions only ten people were in the grand jury room— the six jurors, a reporter, two prosecutors, and a witness.

From the start, Dreyer and Modisett gave Tyson every chance to clear himself. They agreed to present to the jurors any evidence or witnesses Tyson's attorneys requested. They did not try to push the jurors toward an indictment. "If they didn't want to indict, fine," Dreyer said. "If they did, that was fine too. We played it down the middle, did our job, and left the rest up to the jurors. As a matter of fact, when the jury began its deliberations, I wasn't sure in my own mind if there had been a rape or not."

On Friday, August 16, Desiree told her story. Dreyer was struck by her poise. Answering questions for hours, she never broke down or cried, even when she was discussing the details of the rape. Her answers were forthright, credible, and detailed. If there was any problem with her testimony, Dreyer thought, it was her *lack* of emotion. She seemed too much the beauty queen—detached, maybe even a bit cold. But to Dreyer she didn't appear to be a person who would make such serious allegations to gain publicity or out of some neurotic compulsion.

For the next four weeks the process continued. The grand jury met every Friday and occasionally on Wednesdays. One after another, those who had witnessed the activities and behavior of Tyson and Desiree came forward, told their tales, and answered questions. Virginia Foster, Dr. Thomas Richardson, Chris Low, McCoy Wagers, Pasha Oliver, Charles Williams— twenty-seven witnesses in all testified for over fifty hours. Unlike in a trial, during the hearing there was no judge present. The jurors controlled the proceedings. They asked questions, considered hearsay evidence, ordered detectives to investigate important points, and subpoenaed witnesses. Although Dreyer exerted some control, ultimately he too did what the jurors requested. There was always a small but real possibility that the grand jury would move in an unexpected direction and make an unexpected decision.


No one doubted that the grand jury had enough probable cause against Tyson to return a true bill. If Tyson had not been a celebrity, the case would have never gone to a grand jury; Modisett would have felt confident that he had enough probable cause to charge, arrest, and try him without further ado. But Tyson *was* a celebrity; and never had such a famous athlete been charged with such a serious crime. In 1921 Roscoe "Fatty" Arbuckle, one of America's most famous comic actors, was charged with the rape and second-degree murder of Virginia Rappe. In 1942 Errol Flynn, the country's favorite swashbuckling actor, was charged with the statutory rape of two teenage girls aboard his yacht. Both men went through sensational trials, and neither was convicted. Celebrities, jurors seemed to say, *were* different. Their morals, their behavior, their activities were exempt from normal sanctions.

Tyson had an additional advantage. He was touted as a black role model, an example of a black man who had made it in America. In a national survey of black heroes conducted by the

*Miami Herald* in 1990, Tyson ranked seventh. Yes, he had a troubled past: he had been arrested for purse-snatching at twelve; was sent to the Tryon School for Boys in Johnstown, New York; later he was expelled from Catskill High School; he had had persistent problems with women. He had been accused of beating his wife, assaulting a parking lot attendant, propositioning a clerk, and pawing women from New York to Los Angeles. But he always had an explanation, and he told his side with disarming charm in a sweet, childlike voice that insinuated, *You know, these charges are wildly exaggerated. Those women, they're just after my money. And besides, it wasn't really my fault.* Through the turmoil, he remained in demand for commercials and personal appearances.

In an editorial in the *Washington Post,* Arthur Ashe explained the basis of Tyson's popularity: "Many establishment blacks . . . winked at Tyson's escapades, legal skirmishes and marital woes, envious of his millions of dollars in earnings despite his limited education. They were condescendingly amused as the tabloid press derided his excesses; they were earnestly convinced that ex-wife Robin Givens was probably just a gold digger." Tyson was their Teflon hero. When scandal hit him, it slid off harmlessly.

Tyson's one chance to evade indictment was to exploit that quality of blamelessness: to go before the jurors, sit down just a few feet away from them, talk to them, use his intelligence and charm, tell them that he was completely innocent. It was a calculated gamble. If he lost, he gave the prosecution his whole story, which could later be used against him at his trial. But if he won, he walked—no indictment, no trial, and a $15 million payday for a championship fight with Evander Holyfield before the end of the year. After consulting with Don King and Vincent Fuller, Tyson decided to take the gamble.

On Friday, August 30, Tyson returned to Indianapolis to testify, accompanied, it sometimes seemed, by half the world's journalists and photographers. When he arrived at the grand jury building at 129 East Market Street, journalists crushed against him, shouting questions and snapping pictures. Beside him King hollered, "This man is innocent. Mike Tyson says he's innocent." Mixing legal theory with hype, he continued, "He's testifying because I think that's what we're supposed to do. I'm going to let due process take its course. I'm not an attorney,

I'm just a promoter of the greatest fighter in the world, and he's going to win the championship in the fall." As King talked, Tyson muscled his way forward, eyes focused on the elevator door, saying only, "Please let me through." Although he was dressed in a conservative dark blue double-breasted suit, he looked as if he was moving toward the ring to regain his championship. The crowd of reporters and protesters was out of control, pushing, shoving, yelling, especially in the narrow foyer between the front door and the elevator. But the fighter seemed above it all. It was all part of being Mike Tyson.

Fuller, however, was not accustomed to fighting crowds. "Fuller was very shaken physically," Dreyer said. "He was nervous, you could tell he was nervous; the reporters had jostled him, and it took him awhile to collect himself." In fact, he had not fully recovered when Dreyer began to explain to Tyson that by testifying before the grand jury he was waiving his Fifth Amendment rights. Since the law required that Tyson sign a document to show he understood Dreyer's warnings, Dreyer assumed that Fuller and Voyles would want to read, discuss, and even negotiate the ground rules. Instead Fuller said, "Fine, fine. Whatever." No discussion or negotiation.

Defending a man accused of rape was not Fuller's métier. There was something of the Victorian about him; he didn't seem to have noticed the sexual revolution of the sixties and seventies. "Fuller's defense was, 'Well, she wanted it . . . she had to know . . . look how she dressed,' " Dreyer recalled. On one occasion he showed Dreyer and Modisett a picture of Desiree in a bathing suit, the same picture she had shown Tyson at the opening ceremony of Black Expo. For Fuller, the picture demonstrated that Desiree wanted to have sex with Tyson. "See," he said, extending the picture to Dreyer, "look at this." Dreyer thought, "Does he want me to say 'Gosh, you're right, she did want it'? It was just a picture, taken during the bathing suit phase of the pageant."

Dreyer's primary concern outside the eighth-floor grand jury office was keeping Tyson away from Edwards, who had testified for three hours before the boxer was to give his evidence; he didn't want Tyson to have a chance to talk to his former bodyguard. So while Edwards was holding forth on the case in Tommy Kuzmik's office, Dreyer ushered Tyson into the grand jury room.

Tyson also testified for three hours. In a quiet, polite voice, he recounted his brief, pleasant trip to Indianapolis. He admitted that he had engaged in sexual intercourse with Desiree Washington but insisted that it was consensual. Dale Edwards, Tyson claimed, was in the parlor of the suite while he was in the bedroom with Miss Washington. Edwards had told the same story, in much the same words, earlier in the day. Dreyer asked if the door was closed; Tyson said yes. If the door was closed, how did Tyson know that Edwards was in the parlor? Well, Tyson suggested, that was where he was supposed to be.

The jurors, of course, had already heard three witnesses testify that they saw Edwards outside the room, and they didn't buy Tyson's story. "He just looked and acted and spoke like he was guilty," Dreyer said. "He was evasive; his attention wandered like a person who does not want to talk about something. I'm sure the jurors picked up on it."

When he was finished testifying, Tyson again pushed through the journalists, protesters, and interested bystanders. Fans cheered him. One woman gripped him in a hug. Several men shouted encouragement: "Keep your chin up, champ"— "You've got friends here"—"We're behind you all the way." Tyson signed an autograph, slapped a few palms, mumbled his thanks, and got into a rented Ford Taurus while King repeated, "My man's innocent. Mike Tyson's innocent."

"**W**hat do you think?" Modisett asked Dreyer later that evening. Until Tyson and Edwards had testified, Dreyer hadn't been sure. Now he was. "He's guilty," said Dreyer. "He lied. Edwards lied. He said Edwards was outside his room; Edwards wasn't. He said Desiree had left messages for him at the Canterbury; she hadn't. If he's not guilty, why is he lying?" Modisett had hoped to complete the grand jury investigation by Labor Day, but after talking with Dreyer he told reporters that the jury needed to hear a few more witnesses. He didn't add that those witnesses would confirm Dreyer's belief that Tyson had lied.

After hearing several more witnesses, the six jurors began their deliberations on Monday, September 9. The rules were simple: the jurors were to make their decision on their own in the grand jury room, without prosecutors, judges, or investigators present. To return a true bill, five jurors had to vote to indict. If only four voted to indict, there would be no trial. When they had finished talking and voted, Dreyer asked the foreman, "Are there at least five jurors who have voted for an indictment?" "Yes," the foreman answered, and although he was not supposed to spell it out, he added, "The vote was five to one." Tyson's gamble had fallen short of success.

At the press conference announcing the indictment, Modisett said that "it was not [Desiree Washington's] intention to have sex when she met up with [Tyson] after the concert. Evidence will show that it was by force." He was under no illusions, however, that the trial would be pro forma. "I think it will be difficult because of who the defendant is. Rape cases are often difficult, and a rape between two people who know each other . . . is additionally difficult."

Two days later, Tyson flew to Indianapolis from Las Vegas for his arraignment. The State of Indiana had charged him with one count of rape, two counts of criminal deviate conduct, and one count of confinement. Bond was set at $30,000. Tyson pleaded not guilty to the charges. Judge Patricia Gifford asked him a few standard questions, then scheduled the trial to begin January 27. The arraignment lasted only four minutes, after which the boxer was escorted to a basement room where he was booked, fingerprinted, and photographed. He then paid his bond in cash and left.

The press conference afterward, a show arranged by and starring Don King, wore on for close to an hour and a half. While Tyson sat and listened, King rattled off a list of celebrities who had run into trouble—Judy Garland, Elvis Presley, James Dean, Marilyn Monroe. All had died young, but Tyson, an "urchin from the ghetto," "a target and a martyr," had handled his celebrity status better than the others. It was Tyson, King claimed, who was the victim, Tyson who had suffered most. But he would emerge from the experience "bigger [and] better."

Tyson said little, which was not uncommon for anyone around King. "I know what happened. I know I'm innocent," he said. "I didn't hurt anyone. I didn't do anything. I love women—I mean, my mother's a woman. I respect them as well."

As the press conference ended, King talked to a few stragglers while most of the journalists packed up to go home. Tyson turned to a friend and said, "I should have killed the bitch."

# PART TWO

# CHAPTER 6

# Friday the Thirteenth

From July to November the Tyson case was the county prosecutor's problem, not mine. When I first heard of the allegations I was in a car driving to my father's cabin at West Bearskin Lake, Minnesota. News heard first on a car radio stays with you, probably because you have time to do little else but think about it, miles and miles to turn it over in your mind and consider the ramifications.

Like others who have spent years as prosecutors, I suffer from near terminal cynicism, a condition that manifests itself most readily in disbelief of the spoken word. Prosecutors live with lies: "I didn't do it"—"It wasn't me"—"I wasn't even there"—"I never met the guy"—"Believe me, you got the wrong man." In law school, professors tell you to suspend belief or withhold belief, to maintain some such unattainably abstract state. Listen to the evidence, trust the autopsy reports, have faith in forensic science. But the streets teach you to disbelieve, to distrust everything you hear. Anyone who is deeply involved in a crime should disbelieve everything that is said unless there is a compelling reason to do otherwise.

The news reporter announced that a woman had accused Mike Tyson of rape. The details were sketchy, but evidently the rape had occurred in Tyson's hotel room at about two o'clock.

*Oh, please,* I thought. *Right! Two in the morning in his room! Come on!* It was a knee-jerk reaction, but one millions of other people who heard the story also had. Mike Tyson was one of the most widely recognized men in the world. Nearly every informed person knew three things about him: First, he was the meanest, toughest man on the block. Second, he had money to burn, which was perhaps the only way he hadn't tried to rid himself of it. Third, he was attracted to women who believed that their reason for being was to dispose of his fortune. Controversy stalked him like a leading contender. Accusations abounded: "Mike Tyson fondled my buttocks"; "Mike Tyson fathered my child"; "Mike Tyson abused me." The memory of Robin Givens being interviewed by Barbara Walters in September 1988 rose in my mind. Before some sixty million Americans watching "20/20," and with Tyson sitting docilely at her side, Givens told about her life with the fighter: "It's been torture. It's been pure hell. It's been worse than anything I could possibly imagine. He's got a side to him that's scary. . . . He gets out of control, throwing, screaming, he shakes, he pushes, he swings. And just recently I've become afraid, very, very much afraid."

Accusations about and even evidence of Tyson's behavior were so widely known that he had become an easy mark. But of all the many times a woman accused him of some sexual impropriety, I had no recollection of any of the charges reaching a courtroom. Moral, even criminal, issues had been transformed into financial concerns and were settled out of court. The report on the radio sounded like just such an accusation—hardly anything that would make it to a police blotter.

This story, however, had a curious aspect to it. Prosecutor Jeff Modisett, the report noted, had decided to convene a special grand jury to consider the accusation. A mistake, I thought; a grand jury hearing would drag the case out for weeks. If I were in Jeff's place, I would get to the nub, and fast—no grand jury, no wasted taxpayers' dollars. I would have hooked the woman up to a polygraph machine and gotten Mike Beaver—to my mind, the best polygraph man in the world—to ask the questions and interpret the results. If she was clean, if she was telling the truth, I'd gather my evidence and go to court. It was that simple. I wouldn't give Tyson's lawyers the state's case as presented to the grand jury.

But I wasn't a politician who had recently knifed into office by a razor-thin margin. The case was a political live wire, and Modisett understandably wasn't anxious to grab hold of it. How would the black community regard the case? The black vote had put Modisett in office. Would blacks view charging Mike Tyson with the rape of a black woman as doing something about black-on-black crime, or as persecution of a black hero? And how would whites regard the charges? Besides, Jeff had cut his teeth in the federal system, and he was comfortable with grand juries. It was the cautious route, but in the end maybe it was the best one.

Beyond these thoughts on first hearing of the case—musings to while away the time on a long drive—I had little reaction to the story. As a prizefighter, Tyson had never interested me. When I was a kid I had followed the career of Floyd Patterson, a fighter who didn't brag, seldom spoke, and just flat knocked each and every opponent on his ass. I loved his looks and style: he was a smallish man who held his hands high in that famous peek-a-boo stance, his eyes looking through the gap between his gloves, his mouth tight and expressionless, his head swaying to some internal music that must have been like that of a snake charmer. His concentration seemed utterly pure. Then—*pow*—his whole body would uncoil as he sent a perfectly timed left hook to his adversary's jaw. Afterward, emotion drained from his face, he would speak quietly and perfunctorily to the reporters: "It was a good fight. My opponent is a good fighter. I was fortunate to win." In the late 1950s and early 1960s, watching Patterson fight seemed as good as Christmas.

Then, of course, Sonny Liston killed Santa Claus. After that came Muhammad Ali and the age of athletes doing the play-by-play for their own careers. I knew Ali was the greatest, but I hated to hear him say it. I hated the Brian Bosworth and Neon Deon–style athletes with four-letter words carved in their hair and big endorsement contracts.

I remembered that famous picture of Ray Nitschke. He was on the sidelines, resting as football players used to do, on one knee with his hand on his helmet. Sweat, mud, and blood streaked his face like warpaint. The caption read simply MR. NITSCHKE. If today's kids wanted different idols, fine. I'd keep the Nitschkes and Pattersons, the Giffords and Robinsons.

Tyson didn't interest me because I was never sure who he was. There were too many Mike Tysons. For a while Madison Avenue tried to market him as a nostalgic return to the past, to a time of Dempsey white-wall haircuts and Louis bum-of-the-month-club opponents. Tyson seemed completely programmed. His robeless, sockless entrance into the ring was theatrically contrived. The "Cus and the Kid" story belonged to Disney Studios. Then Tyson started to get into trouble outside the ring and to say things meant to humiliate his opponents. He told one, "I'll make you my girlfriend. I'll make you kiss me with those big lips." It was worse than pro wrestling.

Though I was in and out of the Marion County prosecutor's office on various legal matters, I was aware of only the broad outlines of his problems in Indianapolis. I knew he had testified before the grand jury. I knew he had been indicted. I had a general sense of his story and the woman's story. I followed the Tyson case about as much as I followed the William Kennedy Smith case. The media wouldn't allow you to ignore the charges, but I had no passion to learn more than I picked up on nightly news reports. For me, the Clarence Thomas confirmation hearings were more important because his confirmation would change the direction of the Supreme Court's rulings and thus affect my work as a lawyer. But that was before Friday, September 13, 1991.

That afternoon I had a meeting scheduled with Dave Dreyer, Modisett's chief counsel in the prosecutor's office. We met in his cramped corner office on the fifth floor of the City-County Building in Indianapolis. Now, Dreyer is a bright man, and more than one woman has commented about his good looks, but his office was an unholy mess. Too many cases and too much paper had to pass through.

I had been handling RICO cases for the prosecutor's office for several years, and the topic of this meeting was a settlement. I did forfeiture work in these cases, for which I was paid a percentage of everything confiscated from the offenders according to a sliding scale. The work was sometimes lucrative—too lucrative, ultimately, for the prosecutor's office to let it go outside. When Modisett took office in early 1991, he notified me that he planned to handle the forfeiture cases in-house. He agreed, however, to phase in the new program, and he extended my contract to the end of 1991.

Dreyer met me as I entered the door, and as we shook hands he grinned and asked, "So, are you going to come back and try Tyson for us?" I looked at him for a second. He had an impish half grin on his face, as if to suggest that the question amounted to no more than a Friday the Thirteenth joke. I laughed and replied, "Right. When donkeys fly." Then we quickly zeroed in on the subject of the meeting, and Tyson wasn't mentioned again.

I learned later that when I left his office, Dreyer walked next door and told Modisett that I wasn't interested in the Tyson case. "I just mentioned trying Tyson," Dreyer told the chief prosecutor, "and Greg blew me off." Dreyer had wanted to catch me off guard just to get a gut reaction. Modisett was, to use his own word, pissed. "You son of a bitch," he said; "*I* wanted to ask Greg." Modisett's style wouldn't have been to blind-side me. He would have made a serious proposal, careful to lay out the case in detail to try to convince me that it would be the right thing to do. But it probably wouldn't have made any difference; if Modisett had asked me first, my reaction would have been the same. I would have mirrored his seriousness and said, "Not a chance."

Unaware of the conversation that had taken place after I left the City-County Building, I gave little thought to Dreyer's strange greeting. That night, though, David Young, a crazy, creative artist and advertising executive as well as an old friend, came for dinner at my house. As an artist, Dave paints with passion and boldness, characteristics that mark his conversation as well. After too much wine and a couple of beers, I mentioned that Dreyer had kidded me about trying Tyson. Dave lunged forward, eyes bulging. "You got to be shitting me," he exclaimed. "You're going to take the case, aren't you?"

"It was a joke. Gallows humor. Friday the Thirteenth."

"Bullshit. He meant it. They want you to try Tyson. And there's no way that you can turn them down. Simply no way. This case was made for you."

"Watch me. There's no way I would touch it." I had tried my last capital murder case in March 1988 in an old high-ceilinged, brass-railed courtroom in Richmond, Indiana. When it was over, a judge sentenced a man to die in the electric chair for killing a deputy sheriff, and I promised myself that I would never take another high-profile case.

And I meant it. My life in the prosecutor's office had been a constant two-minute offense with the juice turned all the way up. I was forced to live in a state of perpetual advocacy. Unlike in civil law, where cases are only rarely tried, and where the closest to court a lawyer ever gets is filing the occasional motion regarding discovery or a summary judgment, as a prosecutor I was in court constantly, facing juries and arguing the standard of proof beyond a reasonable doubt. The burden of proof never shifts: the defendant doesn't have to prove his innocence. We were always on offense—always. If we ever went on defense, we were dead meat.

Working as a prosecutor also made life unnatural. I had grown accustomed to seeing sights that should make a normal person retch—autopsies, sandwich-size plastic bags full of fingers, blood-splattered walls, punctured, mutilated bodies. Most of my time was spent in the company of cops—men and women whose jobs routinely included being lied to, shot at, beaten up, and left for dead. Fraternal to the point of being conspiratorial, they dealt constantly with the worst of our society, and they hardened young. Every day they were expected to confront the results of drug abuse, gross parental negligence and abandonment, shoddy education, and poverty, not to speak of just plain thoughtlessness or, on the other side, calculated inhumanity. Living and working with cops, prosecutors soon adopt their attitudes. The fallout had contributed to the breakup of my first marriage and left me cold, cynical, and distrustful. I had seen too little of my kids and too much pain and death.

I wonder now if I believed my promise to steer clear of the prosecutor's role—or if, like a drunk after a particularly long binge, I was saying "Never again" with deep, heartfelt conviction but little real intent. I wonder now about my conversation with Dreyer. Had I felt the surge of excitement a new case always brought? After my three years of abstention, was I dried out but still craving the taste? All I know is that when Dave Young left that night, I began to think about the Tyson case. And I began considering the costs.


I hadn't planned much in my life, but there was a consistency in the choices I made. I was always drawn to challenges, especially when something important hung in the balance.

I come from a family with a pretty strong sense of right and wrong. My maternal grandmother had a big heart, a short fuse, and would argue about almost anything. She was a frontier woman—came to Indiana in a covered wagon, cooked everything from scratch, and could scrub the floor without a mop, standing up: she just jack-knifed in the middle and went to it. She had a birthmark on her face that changed color when she was mad, and waist-length hair that she rolled up on both sides. She was a working fool and had no uncertain views about people who played cards, smoked cigarettes, or drank alcohol. And she hated vacations; never took them herself, and worried when any members of her family went on one. I suspect she was afraid they wouldn't return. She's been dead twenty years, and I still miss her every day.

What I most admired about her were the things she held as absolutes: integrity, the merits of hard work, truth, and the risen Christ. She had unshakable values; and you could take her word to the bank. If you asked her opinion about anything, she would give it instantly, whether she knew what she was talking about or not. I believe I have inherited many of her strengths as well as weaknesses. Like her, I am too judgmental and too quick to voice my opinions. It has probably cost me a marriage and more than a few friends. I also have her industriousness and self-discipline. If manure needs to be cleaned out of the stable or a murderer needs to be taken off the streets, I don't mind doing the job.

My grandmother's values were shared by many of the people I grew up with in rural Indiana. Although as a young woman my mother was a New Deal Democrat, by the time Eisenhower took office she had repented and joined the rest of my family in the Republican fold. Everyone in the family discussed politics, but nobody had much faith in politicians. "If you can't lie, cheat, and steal all at the same time, you can't make it in politics" was a maxim my family believed. My grandmother and several other members of the family were, however, attracted for a time to a right-wing radio commentator named Tom Anderson. I listened to his show as a kid. He had a thick, syrupy southern accent that made him sound as though he was from Hellbound, Mississippi, and his message was a cross between those of Father Coughlin and the John Birch Society. But sometimes he said things that made sense. One time, I remember, he claimed that the hottest places in hell were reserved for those who remained neutral in times of crisis.

All this is to say that I am a product of rural Indiana, a land of conservative Republicans and hard-working, decent people who tend their own fields, respect the law, and help their friends when needed. Family, faith, and the price of corn and soybeans matter most in life. It's a land of tradition and stability, where change is treated like an unwanted guest. My divorce, for example, created a family crisis. For several years, everyone looked at me as though I had the clap. Only one other family member, an uncle, had ever divorced, and he received the same treatment, as though he had upset the sacred balance of rural Indiana.

Make no mistake, Tyson picked the wrong place to commit his crime. Indianapolis is different from Palm Beach or Washington, D.C., or Los Angeles. In the prosecutor's office, Jeff Modisett and Barb Trathen grew up on farms in Tipton County in central Indiana. My own father was a country doctor. Only Dave Dreyer and George Horn were exceptions: Dave was raised in Indianapolis itself and George across the state line, in rural Michigan. At times we debated tactics, but never goals. And when it came time for the trial, we understood the people who sat in the jury box.

I am more certain of the shared values of that Indiana courtroom where Tyson was tried than I am of how I ever ended up there. As a boy, I had harbored no great interest in the law. I lived for the weekends—for my piano lesson at eight-thirty on Saturday morning, and then hours alone out in the hedgerows and ravines of central Indiana, hunting for rabbits or squirrels or crows. I'd roam around in the woods and ditches and fields until dark.

After graduating from high school I entered Indiana University, starting out as a music major and taking my degree in social studies education. By then I was married and commissioned in the army. But it was 1970, two years after the Tet Offensive, and the army didn't need officers. After four years of ROTC, basic training, civilian pilot training, and cadet school, my military career came to an abrupt and permanent end.

It was about the time I was being set adrift by the army that I started to think about becoming a lawyer. I was back in Indianapolis, where my wife had gotten a job teaching music in the public school system. A friend suggested that I apply to law school. After looking at my undergraduate transcript and casting a few critical glances in my direction, the dean of admissions at the Indiana University Law School in Indianapolis advised me to try the night school—part-time. Angry and insulted, I argued with him until giving in was easier than listening to me any longer.

There was something pure and logical about law that attracted me from my first day in class. More than any other person, Professor William F. Harvey inspired me in law school. He taught a civil procedures course that made the subject breathe. He also taught the course on evidence. I remember sitting in the classroom, listening to him discuss some point of evidence, and thinking that the courtroom was going to be my world. I didn't want to practice tax law or corporate law or international law. Criminal law intrigued me. I wanted to be a trial lawyer.

My internship in the Marion County prosecutor's office reinforced this inclination. The work was more fun than robbing banks. Most of the lawyers who were supposed to supervise the interns disappeared to the golf course as soon as the last frost was off the pumpkins, and they didn't show up again until August or September. It wasn't unusual to go a week or longer without seeing a deputy prosecutor in the room. Working the complaint desk served as a crash course on crime and its consequences. Battered, swollen figures would file in to make complaints; winos would drift in to pick fights. We would take each complaint, fill out an affidavit, and obtain an arrest warrant. At the probable cause desk we interviewed police officers every morning and took the new charges. But the best stint was in Municipal Court, where interns could try traffic offenses, misdemeanors, petty thefts, and small-time marijuana charges.

Drunken driving cases were the most challenging. To avoid losing his license, a wealthy drunken driver would hire the best lawyer in town to argue his case. I tried my first case against Jim Voyles, the Indianapolis lawyer who later represented Tyson, in Municipal Court. I won the case because Voyles's client had indeed been drunk, and the police had followed the proper procedures in his arrest. Working in Municipal Court was an education in itself.

After graduating from law school, I took a job in the prosecutor's office. Then as now, prosecutors spoke a different language from that used by most other lawyers. The difference surfaced first in their hiring practices. The best private firms spoke the language of commerce—salary, vacations, benefits, revenue sharing, pension plans. They trafficked in financial security and economic advancement. The prosecutor's office was the only place where the word "justice" was mentioned. A prosecutor is the state's "sworn minister of justice"; he or she is the legal conscience of the state. Though the prosecutor's office doesn't promise wealth—why start off with a lie?—it does allow the pursuit of justice. In my years as a prosecutor, I never—*never*—prosecuted a person whose guilt I doubted. In every case I handled, I believed that I was on the side of truth, and any prosecutor who could not make the same claim was guilty of an obscenity.

I became a deputy prosecutor in 1973. I handled hundreds of cases, plea-bargaining them when I could and trying them when I couldn't. Drugs, battery, theft, prostitution, rape—I covered the full range. If you took a case to court, you were expected to win, but occasionally something would go wrong and a person you knew was guilty would walk. At those times a painful sense of having failed the public—the citizens who had entrusted my colleagues and me with the task of securing justice—accompanied the wounded ego.

It's difficult to forget the failures. I remember my first murder case. Patrick Joseph Kelly, a man who drank too much and had a lethal taste in women, was the victim. He had been shot dead by his girlfriend in front of a handful of witnesses at the Silver Fox tavern, an Indianapolis dive. She was real charming—five feet six inches, three hundred pounds, about four teeth in her mouth, mostly bald, and as mean a person as I had ever seen. She shoved a twelve-gauge shotgun in Patrick Joseph's belly and pulled the trigger, emptying the polyethylene sleeve and a load of buckshot into his gut. During the autopsy, a physician dug the power piston out of his intestines. Both

Kelly and his girlfriend had been drunk; Kelly's blood alcohol level tested at .32.

She requested and received a change in venue, and her trial was moved from Indianapolis in Marion County to Greenfield in Hancock County. Jim Brand, the premier defense attorney in Hancock County and perhaps the best I have ever faced, represented the defendant. He was subtle and quick-witted, and if he couldn't get a piece of information in one way he would try another. His success was the result of the sheer joy he derived from the contest. You could see it in his eyes, animated like a child's on Christmas morning. He simply liked to play the game.

Jim concocted a story out of whole cloth about the sear malfunctioning on the automatic shotgun. If you aren't familiar with guns, a sear is the internal mechanism in a gun that holds the firing pin spring in a compressed position once the weapon is cocked. When you pull the trigger, the sear releases the firing pin. But if the sear were broken, the gun would go off as soon as it was cocked. And an old gun might—just might— have a worn sear, which might—just might—slip if the gun were jolted in some way. Jim Brand manufactured a case out of the collective "mights." Yes, he admitted, his client had jammed a loaded, cocked shotgun into Patrick Joseph Kelly's stomach. Yes, she was angry and drunk and mean. But she didn't pull the trigger. The sear slipped and she accidentally killed her boyfriend. It was an accident—a tragic accident— but not murder. As defense counsel, he didn't have to prove that the automatic shotgun malfunctioned; all he had to do was create a reasonable scenario in which it might have. If he could inject a reasonable doubt of his client's guilt into the minds of the jurors, they were obligated to find her not guilty.

Jim worked magic with those "mights"; confusion was written all over the faces of the jurors. It took them seven or eight hours to reach a verdict. My local counsel, John L. "Red Dog" Davis, and I got drunk and sobered up twice with Jim before the jury returned. Unfortunately, we were in a sober phase when we heard the verdict: not guilty.

The defendant was guilty; about that I had not the slightest doubt. But instead of going away for life, she walked. She had shot a man at zero range and gotten away with it. Although it was twenty years ago and the last jury trial I lost, I still clench my teeth when I think about it. Justice was not fulfilled in that courtroom. But I learned. I was young and innocent, and Jim Brand was just better than I was. He taught me some important, painful lessons: primarily, that facts alone do not win cases. If they did, there'd be no need for courthouses, juries, and lawyers. Prosecutors set out to win the cases they try, and so do defense lawyers. There's no second place.

For months I turned the case over in my mind, examining what Jim had done and thinking about what I should have done but didn't. At the same time, there was something about the experience of prosecuting a murder case that attracted me. It was so intense. Most of it was unpleasant and sad. There were the relatives of the victim, all believing that the accused should be hanged in the town square at sundown, regardless of the circumstances. Telling these good, grieving people that justice would not be swift and might never be complete was difficult. Reading autopsy reports and examining photographs of the dead body was also no holiday. But the trial itself, where life and death were literally on the line, was like a drug, and I was hooked.

No sooner had I lost my first murder case than I was assigned to another one. The Sacks Eagle Loan Company was a pawnshop on Indiana Avenue in Indianapolis. Four black militants had decided to rob the shop for the good of their cause. As they later admitted, they wanted to obtain rifles and shotguns to "harass the pigs." They planned to hit at 11:00 A.M. on Indianapolis 500 race day, when every cop in Christendom was out on Sixteenth Street directing traffic or working inside the track. It wasn't a bad plan, but they should have checked the weather report. It rained, hard, and the race was postponed, but they went through with the robbery, during the course of which one of the men pulled out a .41 Magnum and shot a clerk named Archie Landy just beneath his right eye. The bullet must have had a metal jacket because it left a perfect cross where it exited through the back of Archie's head.

Four of the robbers, including the shooter, pleaded out for a flat ten. The driver, a young man named Jerry Roseberry, wouldn't take the plea, so we tried him for murder. When the trial was over, the shooter got ten years and Jerry got life. After the trial, Jerry wrote me from the penitentiary asking if the ten-year option was still available. It wasn't.

The two murder trials, however, were unusual. Most of my time during those early years was spent bargaining with defense lawyers. I pleaded hundreds of cases. Sometimes I had twenty cases on my calendar for one afternoon. It was like being at a flea market; you soon got a sense of how much everything was worth. A trial was the result of failed negotiations, of lawyers not being able to decide on a fair price.

The flea market ended in 1974, when the Republican prosecutor for Marion County was voted out of office and I went back to private practice. In the next four years, the Democratic prosecutor made such a mess of the office that he didn't even bother to run for reelection. In 1978 the Republican Stephen Goldsmith won the prosecutor's race, and I returned to the City-County Building.

I soon became homicide supervisor. Death occupied most of my days—investigating crimes, working with homicide detectives, dealing with the families of victims, taking death penalty cases to trial. If you work close to death long enough you become hardened by the accumulation; murders become merely cases; dead bodies, instructional mannequins with the life sucked out of them. Your interest focuses on the forensics of a case. You have to discover what brought any one corpse to the examining table. The cause of death is usually obvious: a bullet hole in the head, a body part that got blown away is difficult to overlook. Beyond that, dead bodies are full of information. There can be signs of struggle or indications of which way the person was standing when he or she was first hurt. You look at the soles of a person's feet and the toenails to see whether the victim spun around in an effort to withdraw or lunged forward to fight. You use long probes to trace the line of a bullet through the body to discover the angle of entry and the direction of fire—small details that can become vital during the trial.

As a homicide prosecutor, I dealt mostly, though not always, with the photographs taken at the crime scene and in the autopsy room. But even photographs exact their emotional price. Occasionally I would enter a detective's office and see two plastic bags holding human fingers, five in each bag—meaning that the police had found some unidentified, decomposing body. They would photograph the teeth and snip off the fingers for identification before disposing of the corpse. The calluses grew. Eventually my interest was aroused only when I saw the photographs or looked at a corpse on an autopsy table with a Y-shaped incision from its thorax to its abdomen. The corpse had become an "it," and the qualities of the person who had inhabited it important only as they related to the case.

The essence of a trial is convincing the jury that you are right. The jury has to believe you and believe *in* you—believe your facts, your witnesses, your interpretations, your arguments. From opening statement to final argument, the jury has to look to you for answers. If someone in the courtroom raises a hand to ask to go to the bathroom, twelve sets of eyes should look at you to see if permission will be granted. Jurors need to have as much faith in you as they do in the judge. The defendant in my first murder trial was freed not because she was innocent, but because the jury didn't believe me.

When I returned to the prosecutor's office in January 1979, some of the murder cases I began to try on a regular basis were no-brainers. I worked with Steve Goldsmith on a case against Wayne Hooks, who was charged with shooting his estranged wife on January 17, 1978. It wasn't difficult to convince the jury of Hooks's guilt. Nellie Hooks had worked as a waitress and go-go dancer at the Slow-Poke Tavern in Indianapolis. One night Wayne walked into the tavern and pointed a gun at his wife. When the bartender-owner tried to defend her, Wayne shot him in the back. He then shot his wife three times as she cowered under a pinball machine. It didn't take Clarence Darrow to persuade the jury that Hooks's gun had not misfired four times.

Domestic murder cases are usually the easiest. Rarely is the murderer a professional. There are often witnesses, the murder weapon is generally easy to trace, and there is always a motive. About the only place in the United States where a man kills his wife or a woman kills her husband and gets away with it is in the movies. But other murder cases are more difficult. Sometimes there are problems with the evidence or with witnesses. When your key witness is testifying to get a reduced sentence on another charge, the jury is bound to be suspicious. Other cases arouse community emotions. Crimes in which race is a factor are particularly volatile. Pressures come from outside the courtroom. Rumors and death threats materialize in the poisonous air. In that miasmic atmosphere, jurors can begin to doubt themselves and second-guess what they know to be true.

Between 1979 and 1985 I tried a series of difficult, high-pressure racial cases. These cases both prepared me for the Tyson trial and dictated my strategy and tactics in the courtroom. I am certain that what happened in Criminal Court IV in late January and early February 1992 was a converging of biographies—Desiree's, Tyson's, Vincent Fuller's, and my own. Each played a role in the case of *State of Indiana* v. *Michael G. Tyson.*

# CHAPTER 7

---

# PRELIMINARIES

**O**n Monday, September 16, I hadn't stopped thinking about Mike Tyson. I was intrigued by Dreyer's offhand remark. Was he serious? Dave Young had thought so, and the more I considered it, the more I believed so too. Tyson had retained Vincent Fuller as his counsel—Fuller of Williams & Connolly, the man who had aided one of his firm's founding partners, Edward Bennett Williams, in several important cases; the man who had defended John Hinckley and Michael Milken. Would I ever have another chance to work opposite a lawyer of Fuller's stature? Not likely. Would I ever have another chance to try a case that would attract the attention of the world's media? Out of the question. If that's not enough challenge to stir your ego, you don't have one. And of all the things I have been accused of, not having an ego wasn't on the list.

On Monday I went to Cleveland to take a deposition. During a break I called Dave Dreyer about a RICO case. Toward the end of the conversation I asked, "Dave, how much were you kidding about the Tyson case, and how much were you serious?" "Oh, about fifty-fifty," he said, laughing. There was no way he was going to give me a straight answer—and I wasn't about to sound eager. "Well," I said, "if you want to talk about one of those fifties let me know." I left it at that. We were playing footsies. Maybe we had a date, maybe not.

In the event I got a call, I discussed the case with my partners, Mike Kiefer and my brother Chris. My brother said I should accept it. "It'll get the firm's name out on the street," he argued. "You'll get to kick butt in front of a national—hell, an international—audience. The money's not as important as the publicity." He also volunteered to pick up some of my caseload to allow me to devote more time to the trial.

Mike Kiefer disagreed. "If Modisett calls," Mike said, "leave the office. Run, pass go, and don't look back. Look," he continued, "Modisett will call if he thinks his office is going to lose the case. If it's a dog, he'll call. If he's in trouble, he'll call. If the community pressure gets too intense, he'll call. If it's a strong case, one that will make his office and himself look good, he won't call. So if he calls, why would you want the case?"

Mike tends to see conspiracies, and the notion that Modisett would farm out the Tyson case made his eyes narrow with suspicion. "This isn't Hick County, Indiana," he reasoned. "Marion County is the most populous county in the state, and Modisett has an experienced, professional staff. There's no good reason for him—a Democrat—to hire an independent Republican prosecutor unless he wants to distance himself from the case."

As usual, we argued back and forth. Mike contended that the Tyson case was wrong for our firm. Touching his fingers, he listed his objections. "One: It will completely consume your time. You'll have to devote months to the case and won't be paid enough for the hours you put in. Two: The case will overload other members of the firm. Maybe a large firm could afford the luxury of taking the case, but Garrison and Kiefer can't. We don't have the pool of associates, interns, and research assistants to handle the paperwork. Three: The case will divert the entire firm away from the work that pays our salaries. Secretaries, receptionists, everyone will get sucked into this thing. Four: What if you hang up a big L? If the case is a dog but you accept it and lose, whose picture will be plastered across the front page? Count on it, you lose the case and the first time you drop your head some photographer is going to take your picture."

Mike didn't press the final point, but he didn't have to. In any highly publicized case the risk of failure is always part of the equation. You try not to dwell on it, and you almost never talk about it with anyone, but it's always there, clutching at your stomach. Follow trial lawyers while a jury is deliberating a case. Where do they go while they wait for the verdict? What do they do? Some go directly to a bar and drink; others dress up drinking by doing it in a restaurant. But even in a restaurant, if you look at their tables after they leave, you'll notice plates piled high with food, but every glass will be empty. You eat after the verdict. You drink before it. The empty glasses testify to the fear of failure.

The other side of the equation is that the risk of failure gives meaning to success. The higher the risk, the more satisfying the reward.

Mike knew the risk equation as well as I did. We didn't discuss it. But I couldn't ignore his contention that the case would have a significant negative effect on the firm. Over a two-week period, I went hot and cold on the case. One minute I would focus on the challenge, the opportunity to try a case against one of the leading trial lawyers in the country in a national media spotlight. The next minute I would think about the downside, the financial effect the trial would have on the firm. But that the case remained on my mind for two weeks was important. I knew that if Modisett called and offered me the case, I would accept. And I knew that once I accepted, Mike would support me fully.


The call came on Tuesday, October 1. I was out of the office at the time, but my secretary scheduled a meeting with Modisett for the following day at the City-County Building. October 2, the day Modisett would offer and I would take the Tyson case, was Mike's birthday. The timing could have been better, but at least Mike would have something tangible to wish for before he blew out the candles.

Jeff Modisett, Dave Dreyer, and I met in Jeff's office. Unlike Dreyer's small corner office that looked like a trailer park after a hurricane and had all the personal charm of the Office of Traffic Safety, Modisett's office was fastidiously neat. It was a power office, straight out of some Furnishings for Success manual. Nothing was out of place.

Modisett's style was more serious than Dreyer's: no jokes, no oblique questions with shades of meaning. He started off the meeting by apologizing for the casual manner in which Dreyer had first mentioned the case. He then detailed why he had asked for the meeting. It was a classic description of how to build an elephant, starting with the big toe. It all boiled down to the fact that Jeff had talked to a number of people and they had given him two crucial pieces of information. First, and contrary to Modisett's own suspicions, they told him that I was a team player. Coming from the federal system, where teamwork was the not-so-secret password, he concluded that I had made his first hurdle. Second, almost as important as being a team player was that I had enough of a "fuck you" attitude not to be pushed around or intimidated by high-priced D.C. lawyers in Armani suits.

Eventually getting around to what had been obvious from the moment I walked in the door, Modisett offered me the position of lead counsel in the Tyson trial, with full control and complete cooperation from his office. We had a short discussion about my fee. I had been paid $20,000 for an earlier case, and I told Modisett that I would prosecute Tyson for the same amount. I thought $20,000 was fair—for me as well as Marion County. I had worked for the prosecutor's office long enough to know that there wasn't much fat in the budget. Under the administrations of Democratic governor Evan Bayh and Republican mayors William Hudnut and Stephen Goldsmith, even that small amount of fat had been trimmed substantially. Billed at $100 an hour, $20,000 only buys two hundred hours. I would pass the two-hundred-hour mark in early December. For the next two months, when I devoted the most time to the case, I essentially worked for free. Later, when Mike Kiefer remarked that he had heard Tyson was paying Vincent Fuller $500 an hour, I confessed to my lack of business skill, but few if any important cases are about money.

Dave Dreyer walked me through the facts of the case. He did a good job of describing what Desiree Washington said had occurred and what were likely to be the problem areas. I sensed Dreyer believed Desiree's story but wasn't confident it would meet reasonable-doubt criteria.

Back in my office, Mike and I discussed the case as we glanced over the file. As I expected, Mike voiced no reservations. As we read the contents of the file, in fact, he became as enthusiastic about the coming trial as I was. "There's nothing wrong with the case," he said. This seemed to trouble his absolute belief in conspiracies. There had to be something wrong, some reason why Modisett wanted to unload it. But the more he read, the more he became convinced that it was without serious flaws. No credible witnesses had corroborated Tyson's story, and the circumstantial evidence supported Desiree. Mike wasn't certain we could win the case, but he believed we had a chance.

We brainstormed about what tactics Fuller and his associates at Williams & Connolly would likely employ on Tyson's behalf. Mike knew more about Fuller and the firm than I did. He was a lifelong student of the history of the law—the great cases, the famous lawyers, the landmark decisions. He knew details of Edward Bennett Williams's important cases, and of Vincent Fuller's, and he gave me background on Fuller's representation of Michael Milken, Don King, and John Hinckley.

Mike anticipated two things of Tyson's defense lawyers. First, Fuller would be meticulously prepared for the trial. He mastered the minutiae of his cases, the statistical and financial data of complex white-collar crimes, for example. Although he had a commanding presence and a deep, rich voice, he did not depend on his courtroom performance to win an acquittal. "You're going to have to be as prepared as him," Mike reasoned, "and he'll have more help getting prepared. Williams and Connolly has deep pockets, almost unlimited resources. And you can bet that Tyson will be billed for more than two hundred hours.

"Second," Mike went on, "expect to be papered to death. Williams and Connolly will file scores of arcane motions and conduct endless depositions in an attempt to force you to spend your time responding to their paper lions. You have to insulate yourself from the paper and the media." I agreed. To win the trial I needed to spend as much time as possible with my witnesses and on preparing my case. I couldn't go on the defensive. I could not allow Williams & Connolly to dictate the pretrial phase any more than I could permit Fuller to dominate the courtroom once the trial started. If I personally spent time responding to Fuller's motions and King's wild charges, I would lose.

**M**onday, October 7, was a steel gray midwestern day, the kind of day that makes you think of winter. I had a two-day break in my calendar; two days to work on nothing but *State* v. *Tyson*. At 8:30 A.M. I met Dave Dreyer in the grand jury room to review the basic evidence. I had read Tyson's grand jury testimony over the weekend. His story bothered me. It was logical and consistent, but too pat, almost as if his "date" with Desiree had been scripted by a hack Hollywood screenwriter. What Tyson presented the grand jury with was a perfect house of cards. Remove one or two cards and the house would crumble. I knew from my homicide and forensic science background that physical evidence does not shade the truth.

Early in any case, I hole up in a grand jury room or police evidence room with the written record and the artifacts and try to reconstruct what happened. In a murder case the artifacts include weapons, blood-stained clothing, cartridge casings, bullet fragments, and photographs of the crime scene and from the autopsy. I move back and forth between words and artifacts, reading a witness's statement or a police report and then examining a bullet hole in a shirt or an automatic weapon. Back and forth, from words to objects—reading one and touching the other—I listen for echoes.

I wanted to follow the same procedure in the Tyson case. Although I believed Desiree's version of her encounter with Tyson, I was particularly troubled by the lack of physical injury. Oftentimes in a rape there are bruises on the thighs or on the insides of the knees, but Thomas Richardson, the emergency room physician who had examined Desiree, reported no evidence of bruising. The absence of bruises did not in itself contradict her account, but it did present problems in terms of carrying the burden of proof. In all cases of date rape, it is important to show the jury some physical evidence that is demonstrably inconsistent with consensual sex.

On a table in front of me in the grand jury room in a series of plastic bags were the clothes Desiree had worn on her outing with Tyson—the jacket, the bustier, the pants, and the panties. There were photographs of Desiree dressed in the outfit, and more photographs of the other contestants. A videotape cassette contained the footage of Tyson's promo for the Miss Black America pageant.

I watched the videotape, and for the first time I saw Mike Tyson in an arena where he was surrounded by impressionable young women, many of whom were very attractive. As I watched him move and smile and laugh it became obvious to me that here was a man on the prowl—flirtatious, physical. It made my blood run cold when he walked up to Desiree and said something to her, and she giggled in that childish way of hers while he put one of his huge arms around her and pulled her close.

Next I arranged the garments on the table as if someone was wearing them. I looked at the outfit and then at a photograph of Desiree in the clothes. It seemed like a risqué costume when you just looked at it lying on the table. The pants were baggy and not form-fitting, but the upper part of the outfit, the bustier, would have stopped traffic on the right woman. It was nothing more than a strapless, decorative brassiere. On Barbara Ucchi, the friend who had lent it to Desiree, the bustier would have had a sultry effect. It was wrong for Desiree, however. The photograph showed that it did nothing for her slight, girlish figure. If anything, it looked as though it might slide off her slender body.

I looked at the little tear on the wide sequined waistband— the tear that would take on weighty importance in the trial. It seemed to me that the tear was consistent with Desiree's grand jury testimony and inconsistent with any sort of contrived setup. The tear was significant but not immediately noticeable, and it looked too small to have been fabricated for the purpose of trumping up a charge of violent attack.

Looking at the bustier and the pants—really just long shorts with an elastic waistband that kids call "jams"—it was clear to me that a man of Tyson's strength and quickness could have grabbed the front of the bustier and pulled it down, catching the elastic waistband of the pants and pulling them off along with the bustier in a single swipe. In one fast, powerful snap of his wrist, Tyson could have gone from Desiree's shoulders to her knees and gotten all the clothes that were in the way as he went. Desiree told both Kuzmik and the grand jury that Tyson had stripped off her clothes in seconds.

The last garment I examined were the panties. Made of white cotton, they were printed with polka dots—hardly some garment from Frederick's of Hollywood, or even the kind of silky panties one might expect an eighteen-year-old girl to wear. They were the bottoms to her pajamas, which she had simply left on when she dressed to go out on her fateful late-night limousine ride. It was curious. My thirteen-year-old daughter, Kate, or two-year-old, Ashley, might be seen sporting about in a pair of pink polka-dot underpants. The panties were certainly not consistent with the image of a young gold digger heading out to get into the pants and pocketbook of the former heavyweight champion of the world.

The panties were scarred from where the forensics people at the crime lab had cut out snippets in their attempt to identify body fluids and blood types. Wherever there was a hole, traces of blood or some other fluid surrounded it. I opened the panties and looked down at them as if I were going to put them on. In the crotch there were two larger holes and stains, one at twelve o'clock and the other at nine o'clock. Both were discrete bright red blood stains, the color of blood from a cut or abrasion and not the darker color of a menstrual discharge. I then looked at Dr. Richardson's report on Desiree's injuries. On a diagram of a vagina he noted two abrasions, one at twelve o'clock and the other at three o'clock. I must have spent an hour looking at those panties and reading the medical report, looking at the panties, reading the report, looking at the panties, and trying to figure out if the stains correlated to the injuries. Then I realized that when a physician examines a woman's vaginal opening, he charts the injuries as they appear to him: twelve o'clock is the top of the opening near the pubic bone, three o'clock the left side, six o'clock the bottom, and nine o'clock the right side. Looking down into the underwear, however, three o'clock and nine o'clock are reversed. The holes in the panties corresponded to Desiree's injuries.

I visualized Desiree dressing after her encounter with Tyson. She had been angry, humiliated, but most of all scared. She wanted to get out of that room as quickly as possible. In her haste she jerked on her panties, hiking them too tight into her crotch and blotting them at the points of the introital injuries. She then put on her jams and bustier and jacket and left the room, not even taking the time to sit down and put on her shoes. I saw her walk into the hall, take a step toward Dale Edwards and the elevator farther down the corridor, notice the smirk on his face, and then turn and walk toward a dead end. It all fitted. At that moment, I knew that Desiree was telling the truth. Mike Tyson had raped her.

I quickly began rifling through police statements and grand jury testimony, looking for a discussion of the relationship between Desiree's panties and her injuries. Nothing. A small alarm went off in my head. *Wait a second,* I thought, *this is a smoking gun.* Here was direct and painful corroboration of Desiree's story. She had said, "I didn't want him to do that. And it hurt when he did." If I could show that the abrasions were inconsistent with consensual sex, then half the case was won. And all it would take would be some common sense. *Hell, I said to myself, I'm forty-four years old and have had sex a few times in my life. And you don't hurt a woman that way. Not and keep it up. If it hurts, you get told to stop.*

I had also read Tyson's lurid grand jury testimony. According to Tyson, he had engaged in oral sex for ten or fifteen minutes before he and Desiree had had intercourse. Again, his description of the event veered wildly counter to everything I knew about sex. Women who are frightened do not lubricate. If Desiree wanted to have intercourse with him, and if he had engaged in oral sex with her for ten minutes, there would have been no vaginal injuries. His saliva and her vaginal secretions would have lubricated her.

Sitting alone in the grand jury room, I could see my case taking form. First, have medical experts testify that Desiree's injuries were inconsistent with consensual sex. Second, show that those injuries were bad enough that they bled. Third, impress on the jury that Tyson's description of their sexual encounter didn't make sense. And what would the defense argue? That tiny Desiree was some kind of sexual athlete who made love with such abandon that she didn't care that she was suffering painful vaginal injuries? Bullshit. That wasn't going to fly. Tyson should never have testified before the grand jury.

Back in my office, I reviewed the evidence with Mike. I was so hopped up on adrenaline that I was jumping around the office like a kid, talking about panties and twelve o'clock and three o'clock and what the doctors and investigators had and hadn't done. At this stage I certainly needed a less biased opinion.

Mike's judicial balance lasted about five minutes, at which point his excitement about the evidence matched my own.

We talked at length about Tyson's motivation. Much gassy psychologizing, Freudian mumbo jumbo, was batted about. We talked so much about power and inadequacy and compensation that we seemed to be primed for "Oprah." After trying out several exotic, and no doubt previously unimagined, theories, I admitted I had no idea why Tyson would have chosen to rape Desiree when he could have had any one of a score of women. But I also knew that if I was going to cross-examine Tyson, I had better learn more about him. Mike agreed to do the background research. During the next few months he read every book and article he could find on the former champion. At the time I little realized how important Mike's research would be to the final verdict.

I left the office late, ate nothing for dinner, and had trouble getting to sleep that night. I started to visualize the courtroom—the face of each witness, what I would ask, what each would answer. I envisioned myself putting into evidence items that would clearly attest to the violent act. I began planning how I would ask this question, how I would present that document, how I would introduce articles of clothing or lab results. I knew that before I ever stepped into the courtroom I would live the drama a thousand times in my mind.

Such thoughts, I knew from experience, could distract me from the hard work of preparing for the trial. The thoughts buzzing around in my head could prevent me from focusing on the next step in the case. Occasionally over the next several months I had to battle my own imagination. If you envision a scene too often, it starts to seem real. When you ask a question about a garment or a crime lab report or a medical detail, you expect to get the same answer you heard in your mind. I therefore waged a constant struggle to keep to the reality of the case.

On the afternoon of October 8 I was sitting in the control room of Channel 8 News in Indianapolis. Lee Giles, the station manager and an old friend, had contacted Modisett, informing him that Channel 8 had a piece of tape that might be important to the Tyson case. The tape was from Tyson's post-arraignment press conference at the Hyatt Regency Hotel in Indianapolis on September 11. Most of it was routine. For the record, Tyson asserted his innocence: "The situation that occurred was totally ridiculous. . . . I love women—I mean, my mother's a woman. I respect them as well." Also for the record, Don King charged that Mike Tyson was the victim of an unprovoked personal crusade by forces who sought to discredit and ruin all successful black men. Tyson, King charged, had become "a target and a martyr" because "he wants to be with the people, one of the masses." He called for Desiree to come forward and answer the question "What were you doing in that man's bedroom at 2:00 A.M.?" The press conference went as King planned: he adroitly painted Tyson as a defenseless victim of racism and Desiree as a ruthless, aggressive, gold-digging opportunist.

It was the unplanned part of the rambling eighty-minute conference carefully orchestrated by King that Giles believed would interest the prosecution. I learned a cameraman's trick that day: the little red light that comes on when the camera is running can be turned off manually, so that it looks as though the camera has been shut off. But it actually continues to record both the video and the audio hooked up to the microphone. Unknown to Tyson, when the press conference ended and the red camera light shut off, the camera kept filming and the audio hookup continued recording. The result was that I could eavesdrop on Tyson's private musings.

Perhaps even Tyson had become bored with King's rantings, for when the conference ended he tuned out King—who continued on his verbal roll, criticizing Tyson's current manager—and turned to an aide, John Horne. "I should have killed the bitch," he said. It was a statement of fact, nothing personal. If he had just killed the bitch he would have been spared all this.

During the previous three years, Horne had become an important part of Team Tyson. He had met Tyson when he was living in Albany and Tyson was a fifteen-year-old amateur boxer training twenty minutes away in Catskill, New York. For a few years they lost touch. Tyson turned professional, and Horne moved to Los Angeles to pursue a career as a comedian and actor. Horne got bit parts in *Harlem Nights* and *Coming to America,* two Eddie Murphy movies, and he made several commercials, but he failed to turn the corner in his acting career.

He did, however, revive his friendship with Tyson, and whenever the boxer was in Los Angeles the two got together. In 1989, when Tyson was going through a difficult time, emotionally, Horne shelved his acting career and became Tyson's camp coordinator.

Horne always knew where the action was and where to find women, and his primary function in Tyson's entourage was to keep the boxer happy. When Tyson had wanted to meet Robin Givens in March 1987, it was Horne who dug up her phone number. During Tyson's divorce from Givens he moved to King's estate in rural Ohio. King, according to Tyson biographer Montieth Illingworth, gave Horne the phone numbers and addresses of Cleveland prostitutes who stood ready to service Tyson. Over the years, Horne had become Tyson's "main man"—his friend, his procurer, his confidant.

It was clear from the tape that Horne knew exactly who Tyson was talking about killing because he immediately launched into a fine bit of street philosophizing. In a high-pitched voice he asserted that no, Tyson shouldn't have "killed the bitch" because that would have caused even more problems, and besides, there were other ways to solve his difficulty. People wanted to see Tyson fail, Horne explained; they wanted to see the great man in prison and his career ruined. But Tyson would win another victory. Horne then gave a discourse on power and money—how Tyson had both, and how that fine combination would keep him out of prison.

As I watched the tape and listened to the audio, I felt as if I was looking into the cold, pitiless soul of Mike Tyson. It was a strange feeling. Sitting in the catacombs of a television station, where the rooms are little cubicles and the walls are lined with exotic-looking equipment that can review, replay, slow down, and separate and enhance audio and video, I also gained a sense of how Tyson might behave on the witness stand.

The question Modisett, Dreyer, and I faced was whether this diagnostic tool would be accepted as a legal one. Would the tape be admissible in court? Modisett and Dreyer argued that we should try to place the tape into evidence. I wasn't sure. The inflammatory nature of such comments can outweigh their probative value. Although we all agreed that Tyson's statement was directed at Desiree, his lawyers might argue that it was not directed at Desiree, or that it could not be interpreted literally.

In fact, Horne later claimed in his deposition that Tyson's remarks had been directed at Tina Cosby, a black reporter for
Channel 8 who had seemed embarrassed at King's use of the
word "nigger," and that the statement amounted to no more
than Tyson's belief that she was uppity. Tyson corroborated
this version of the incident. It was all a mistake. But then, both
Horne and Tyson also maintained that the rape charges were a
mistake as well, a joke that had gone too far.

More important than the probative uncertainty of the comments, I didn't want them to muddy the real issue of the trial:
the rape of Desiree Washington. Tyson's remarks demonstrated a serious lack of sensitivity toward Desiree in particular
and women in general. Though they disqualified him for consideration as the National Organization of Women's Man of
the Year, neither revelation was startling. We would have ample
opportunity during the trial to explore Tyson's character and
attitude toward women.

# CHAPTER 8

# THE RACE CARD

**D**rive far enough southeast from Indianapolis and you'll reach Palm Beach. The Florida home of America's super rich is not on a different continent, and I knew from the beginning of the Tyson case that it would be paired in the public mind with the trial of William Kennedy Smith. Throughout 1991, *Time* and *Newsweek* ran lengthy articles on date rape, and tabloid television made it a mainstay of after-dinner viewing. Although I couldn't predict if it would make my job easier or more difficult, the surfacing of the issue in Palm Beach would definitely shape how twelve jurors in Indianapolis thought about it.

During September, well hidden from public notice, another drama had started. It began quietly with a telephone call from Washington, D.C., to Norman, Oklahoma, when Jim Brudney, a staff lawyer for Senator Howard Metzenbaum (D-Ohio), contacted Anita Hill, a professor at the University of Oklahoma Law School and a former assistant at the Department of Education and the Equal Employment Opportunity Commission. Brudney had learned from Nan Aron, the head of the liberal watchdog group Alliance for Justice, that Hill claimed to have been sexually harassed by Supreme Court justice nominee Clarence Thomas when she worked for him both in the Department of Education and at the Equal Employment Opportunity Commission.

Aron and Brudney had a common goal: both were searching for a way to block the confirmation of the conservative Thomas to the Supreme Court of the United States. Both also knew that it would take something explosive to derail the Republican campaign to put Thomas on the bench. After the confirmation defeat of Robert Bork in 1987, Republicans had settled on a less confrontational confirmation strategy for their appointments, and Edward Kennedy, the leading liberal on the Senate Judiciary Committee, had taken yet another of his periodic shots at his own foot. His behavior in Palm Beach with his nephew William Kennedy Smith destroyed his effectiveness on the Judiciary Committee and threatened even to ruin his career. Anita Hill was the liberals' last, best chance to keep Thomas off the bench.

First Professor Hill told staffers for both Metzenbaum and Kennedy that she didn't want to talk about her experience. Then, following Thomas's testimony at the hearing, she told committee aides about the sexual harassment with the provision that her name not go further than the committee members. For several weeks, telephone lines between Norman and Washington buzzed with calls to and from Hill and Judiciary Committee staffers. Finally Hill agreed to allow her name to be used in an FBI investigation and sent a personal statement to the committee.

Toward the end of September, Hill's statement was distributed to the committee members. But the all-male Judiciary Committee seemed singularly uninterested in her lurid story. Sexual harassment was hardly news on Capitol Hill. There were hundreds of skeletons rattling in closets from Alexandria to Georgetown to Chevy Chase, and none of the senators seemed anxious to unlock the first door. If Hill wished to preserve her anonymity, then fine; the members of the committee were content to let her remain an unknown law professor in Norman. Senator Joseph Biden of Delaware, the Democratic chairman of the Judiciary Committee who had weathered his own ethical storms, didn't press Hill to come forward. He and his colleagues didn't interview other Equal Employment Opportunity Commission employees to ask if Thomas had sexually harassed them; they didn't attempt to corroborate Hill's account. Instead, on September 27, they deadlocked 7–7 in the vote to recommend the confirmation of Thomas to the full Senate. In a time-honored manner, the Judiciary Committee struggled to avoid the volatile issue—"political nitroglycerine," said one friend of Biden's—and pass it as delicately as possible up the ladder.

But the allegations were too combustible. They exploded on the public scene on Sunday, October 6, when both Nina Totenberg on National Public Radio and Timothy Phelps in *Newsday* broke the story. I had just accepted the Tyson case and was mulling it over in my mind when I learned about Hill's charges. I assumed the Hill story was simply a particularly nasty bit of dirty politics. That it would in any way influence my case never crossed my mind.

It was on Monday, October 7, while I was pouring over the evidence in the grand jury room, that Anita Hill gave a news conference in Norman. That night as I watched her statement on CNN, Hill looked to me to be reasonable and honest and poised. She denied that her allegations were part of some "political ploy" and asserted that Senate staffers had approached her rather than the other way around. Nor had she carried her charges to the press; reporters had come to her. Most of her statement was predictable. She was a lawyer, and the statement resounded with legal phrasing. She claimed that "her integrity had been called into question" and called for an "official resolution" of the matter. As I watched her performance, my thoughts kept drifting back to my own case.

Then she said something that made the hair on the back of my neck rise. It was at the end of her statement, before she was ushered out of the conference room. Speaking of sexual harassment, she said, "It is an unpleasant issue. It's an ugly issue. And people don't want to deal with it generally and particularly in this case. . . . I resent the idea that people would blame the messenger for the message rather than looking at the content of the message itself and taking a careful look at it and fully investigating it."

Blaming the messenger for the message; killing the bearer of bad news. I thought of Desiree and how she was being treated by leading members of the black community. They had charged that "the champ" was a victim of a racist assault. They claimed that Tyson was the innocent target of white racist prosecutors and black money-grubbing women. Desiree Washington was being painted as the perpetrator, and both the NAACP and women's groups such as NOW stood by and watched it happen.

Like most of the rest of America, I watched a good deal of the he said–she said spectacle of October 11 and 12. The endless questions about pubic hairs on Cokes, breast size, and Long Dong Silver made me feel like a voyeur. The same Senate Caucus Room that had been the scene of the investigations into the Army-McCarthy controversy, the Watergate scandal, and the Iran-Contra affair was now the stage in an X-rated theater. Hill's ten-year-old charges and Thomas's obviously self-serving and less than forthcoming defense made me wonder which one I resented more.

The Judiciary Committee itself squirmed the lowest. Asking detailed questions with the sanctimoniousness of offended Baptist preachers, committee members sat in judgment. Like other Americans, I watched, both transfixed and amazed. Kennedy and Biden, Alan Simpson and Orrin Hatch, Howard Metzenbaum and Strom Thurmond, Dennis DeConcini and Arlen Specter, and the others—many of them had much more flagrant skeletons banging around in their own closets, yet several spoke with well-nigh fraudulent self-righteousness. Never had I seen so many lawyers, both on the committee and in the witness chairs, conform so closely to the lowest popular images of the profession.

Every litigator knows that no witness ever gives a hundred cents' worth of truth on the dollar. Truth—not metaphysical truth, but the approximation of truth—is arrived at in the crucible of cross-examination. Without cross-examination, all you have are statements by witnesses—and that's not much. The Caucus Room was not a courtroom, and the hearings were by no means a trial. The public wanted the truth, but none of the senators, regardless of their reputations, were effective litigators. Although many of them were lawyers, it had been a long time since they had practiced law; even when they *had* practiced, the majority had been transactional lawyers or involved in administrative law and not trial lawyers. They posed for the cameras, asking the same questions over and over again so they could get equal time on television. It almost seemed that they believed that if they only allowed everyone to tell his or her story, the truth would somehow emerge. Well, it doesn't work that way. As a result, most lawyers were embarrassed by the hearings; in the public's eye they were identified with the lawyers on the Judiciary Committee.

When the affair went show business, it was no longer about Thomas's fitness for the Supreme Court or even about determining the justice of the charges, since neither of the central figures could prove the truthfulness of his or her statements. Instead, the issue shifted to concerns about race and gender and power—the very subjects that preoccupied the media in the Tyson case. In the political arena, they were all wild cards. I watched the hearings and listened to the commentary to see how the cards would be played.

Thomas played his first. Emotionally distraught and outraged after Hill's testimony, he reappeared before the committee and condemned the entire process: "I think that this . . . is a travesty. I think that it is disgusting. I think that this hearing should never occur in America. . . . How would any member of this committee, any person in this room, or any person in this country like sleaze said about him or her in this fashion? . . . The Supreme Court is not worth it. No job is worth it. . . . I think something is dreadfully wrong with this country when any person, any person in this free country would be subjected to this. . . . This is not an opportunity to talk about difficult matters privately or in a closed environment. This is a circus. It's a national disgrace."

He was right. It was a circus. It was a disgrace. Who could defend him- or herself against such a personal, public attack? Then he played his wild card: race. "And from my standpoint, as a black American, it is a high-tech lynching for uppity blacks who in any way deign to think for themselves, to do for themselves, to have different ideas, and it is a message that unless you kowtow to an old order, this is what will happen to you. You will be lynched, destroyed, caricatured by a committee of the U.S. Senate rather than hung from a tree."

In an ironic twist on his own personal and legal philosophy, Thomas advanced his claim as a victim. In the past Thomas had mocked civil rights groups for playing the race card. All that civil rights organizations did, he once commented, was "bitch, bitch, bitch, moan and moan, whine and whine." Reliance on the race card and affirmative action programs, he once asserted, "was a narcotic of dependency." But now, like Adam Clayton Powell and Marion Barry before him, Thomas was throwing it down on the table.

When it came time for the Senate to vote on confirmation, the conservative Democrat Robert Byrd of West Virginia trumped him. Byrd, of course, had an abysmal record on racial issues. He himself was once a member of the Ku Klux Klan, and he had attempted to filibuster the Civil Rights Act of 1964. But as a card-carrying conservative, he had supported Thomas as President Bush's appointee to the Supreme Court. After the hearings, however, he changed his position. He believed Anita Hill, and more important, he was offended by Thomas's "stonewalling the committee." But he was even more offended by the "interjection of racism into these hearings." Toward the end of his rambling discussion of his vote not to confirm Thomas, Byrd declared, "I'm very sorry that the matter of race was injected here, not in an effort to clear one's name but in an effort to shift the ground. . . . I think it was preposterous. A black American woman is making the charge against a black American male. Where is the racism? Nonsense. Nonsense."

For Byrd it might have been nonsense, but the charge played well in the black community. Especially among black men, there was a circling of the wagons. Editorials in African-American newspapers and African-American spokesmen on television expressed the belief that Hill should have kept quiet and not attacked a successful black man. "I do not think that a black woman under any circumstances should report any kind of sexual issue to the white man, unless it's rape or something like that," commented Shahrazad Ali, author of *The Blackman's Guide to Understanding Blackwomen*. Rosemary L. Bray, writing in the *New York Times Magazine*, agreed. She charged that Hill had broken a fundamental black taboo: "Anita Hill put her private business in the street, and she downgraded a black man to a room filled with white men who might alter his fate— surely a large enough betrayal for her to be read out of the race." Harvard sociology professor Orlando Patterson added his voice to the criticism of Hill in an essay in the *New York Times*, claiming that the issues raised by the hearings could not simply be interpreted through the lens of mainstream white

America: "Judge Thomas on several misjudged occasions may have done something completely out of the cultural frame of his white, upper-middle-class work world, but immediately recognizable to Professor Hill and most women of Southern working-class backgrounds, white or black, especially the latter. . . . Professor Hill perfectly understood the psycho-cultural context in which Judge Thomas allegedly regaled her with his Rabelaisian humor . . . which is precisely why she never filed a complaint against him." In short, even if Thomas was technically guilty, he was culturally innocent.

"Many black men see black women as aggressive man-haters, and black women are sensitive to that image," noted Diana Hayes of Georgetown University. Polls confirmed that most blacks, and particularly black men, supported Thomas, even if they did think there might be some truth in Hill's allegations. The message coming out of the black press was clear: black women shouldn't attack black men.

Barbara Mikulski of Maryland, one of the two women in the Senate in 1991, touched on my concerns in one of her statements on the lack of support for Hill: "To anybody out there who wants to be a whistle-blower, the message is: Don't blow that whistle because you'll be left out there by yourself. To any victim of sexual harassment or sexual abuse or sexual violence, either in the street or even in her own home, the message is nobody's going to take you seriously, not even the United States Senate."

I thought about Desiree's fight during the upcoming months. I knew that she would face an even more difficult struggle than had Anita Hill. Behind Hill were legions of liberal and feminist organizations who were ideologically opposed to Thomas. They believed that Thomas's confirmation would turn the Supreme Court into a reactionary body and threaten the legacy of the Warren and Burger courts. For them, the fate of *Roe* v. *Wade* hung in the balance. They split with such traditional black allies as the NAACP and supported Hill, in part because she suited their agenda. But would they be as interested in an eighteen-year-old black beauty contestant who bolstered no political agenda but had nevertheless been badly wronged? Would the National Organization of Women and other liberal and feminist groups oppose the black ministers and leaders who had enlisted in the Free Mike Tyson army?

I couldn't help keeping an eye on the developments in the William Kennedy Smith case in Palm Beach. In Florida, feminist organizations were lining up behind Patricia Bowman. But both she and Kennedy were white; certainly gender and power were issues in Palm Beach, but not race. I didn't see any support for Desiree's position in the liberal or feminist camps. It was a development that made me nervous. I had yet to meet Desiree. My case would depend on her testimony, which rested on the strength of her character, and I had only the vaguest notion of how strong an individual she was. After the Thomas-Hill controversy, I knew that she would be publicly condemned in the black community. How would she stand up under the attacks? Would anyone come to her side?

Two voices from the confirmation fight kept echoing in my mind. The first was that of Senator Alan Simpson of Wyoming, Bush's closest friend on Capitol Hill, who predicted that some rough times lay ahead for Hill when she confronted the Judiciary Committee: "She will be injured and destroyed and belittled and hounded and harassed, real harassment, different from the sexual kind."

The second voice was Ted Kennedy's. Although I was not a great Kennedy supporter, he made one statement during the Senate vote with which I fully agreed: "The issue here is sexual oppression, not racial oppression. . . . I reject the notion that racism is relevant to this controversy. It involves an Afro-American man and an Afro-American woman, and it ultimately involves the character of America itself. The struggle for racial justice in its truest sense was meant to wipe out all forms of oppression. No one . . . is entitled to invoke one form of oppression to excuse another."

The American legacy of racism—of lynchings and Jim Crow laws—did not excuse a black man if he raped a black woman. To charge Mike Tyson with rape was not a form of racism or oppression.

# CHAPTER 9

---

# HOOSIERS
# IN RHODE ISLAND

**S**itting in an uncomfortable chair in the grand jury room, reading police reports, witness statements, and grand jury testimony, I wondered what the expensive team of Williams & Connolly were coming up with as they read the same materials. *State* v. *Tyson* wasn't a one-person job. I needed help preparing for the trial, and I needed it shortly before immediately. On the record, Mark Jones, Modisett's chief deputy, was my co-counsel, but we had yet to discuss the case, and during the week of October 14 he begged off entirely. He had too much else to do.

Jones was not the only prosecutor who passed on the case. Carol Orbison, head of the sex crimes division, was a natural. She had tried dozens of rape cases and understood the psychology of sex offenders better than anyone in the office. But she too already had a heavy caseload, and the emotional relationship that develops between the victim of a sex crime and the prosecutor would make it difficult to transfer those cases to someone else.

**M**odisett and I agreed that my co-counsel should be from the prosecutor's office and should be a woman. Barb Trathen was my choice. We had known each other for fifteen years but had never tried a case together. She had joined the prosecutor's office in 1977, a year or so before I signed on to help the newly elected prosecutor Stephen Goldsmith. By the late 1980s she had become homicide liaison. Around the office she was known as Miss Preparation. Outwardly friendly and cheerful, inwardly she was single-minded and had a steely tenaciousness; when she got a hold on a case, she wouldn't let go until she had won a conviction. Even before Jones dropped off the case, Barb had agreed to be part of the informal team. But I needed her complete commitment.

Barb was a farm girl from Tipton County who had attended an all-girl convent grade school and high school replete with nuns, uniforms, and strict rules and discipline. Her proper Catholic education perhaps had one slight drawback in that it left her linguistically unsuited to handle rape cases. I had noticed over the years that Barb blushed whenever she heard any vulgar word describing the male or female anatomy or sexual behavior, and of course she never used such language herself.

On October 23 we met for lunch at one of those restaurants that offer a choice of twenty different salads and thirty varieties of tea but don't serve cheeseburgers. Sensing what I was going to ask, Barb picked at her salad as though it was her last meal before going to the chair. She had just finished a difficult month. During the last week of September she had retried the death penalty sentence of a man I had convicted of murder. Several times during the trial, Barb called me to ask about one detail or another, and we developed a feel for each other's style.

Now the trial was over, the man's sentence reconfirmed. The Tyson trial was set to start at the end of January: in three months. That gave us three months to study the case, to roam all over the country taking depositions, and to prepare to go to trial. "There goes Thanksgiving, Christmas, and New Year's," she said. "Happy holidays." She was on the case.

On Saturday, November 9, Barb and I scheduled a trip to Providence, Rhode Island, to meet Desiree Washington. We spent hours during the week of November 4 going over Desiree's grand jury testimony and her police statements as well as talking with forensics technicians and Tommy Kuzmik.

I had started calling Tommy "my beef," but I was only half joking. Wherever we went, he was armed with a 9mm Beretta with sixteen shots in the box and another fifteen in a magazine he carried in his pocket. Shortly before our trip, rumors of bribes and tampering with witnesses began to mushroom. We all knew that Tyson was a valuable commodity, a source of nearly unlimited wealth that was spread unequally among a group of promoters, managers, trainers, advisers, and assorted hangers-on. And that source would run dry as soon as he was convicted. What would the men behind Mike Tyson do to ensure that he didn't go to prison? When I started getting death threats, Tommy took them seriously, and I wasn't unconcerned about them myself. "Your picture's been plastered all over—in the newspapers, *Sports Illustrated,* television, everywhere," Kuzmik said. "We have to be prepared for anything." His edginess increased in direct proportion to the distance we traveled from Indianapolis.

I tried to focus on Desiree, laboring to get an idea of what she would be like. Dave Dreyer, who had gotten to know her during the grand jury phase, said she had maintained the facade of the beauty queen during her appearance. She had come across as too tough, almost as if she seemed unfazed by what she had been through, but Dreyer's evaluation conflicted with the transcript from the grand jury. Reading through Desiree's testimony, it struck me as a simple, unstudied description of events similar to what I had heard dozens of times from other rape victims. But reading testimony is vastly different from being in the grand jury room, where you can listen and watch. I knew what she said, but I couldn't gauge her voice or her body language. Juries, I knew, listen and watch. They render decisions based as much on a person's presentation as on the story that person tells.

Barb, Kuzmik, and I flew to Providence in a State Police airplane, an uncomfortable four-hour trip. Barb and I took turns second- and third-guessing Desiree's account before the grand jury and tried to decide what would be the best way to approach her. We knew, however, that everything depended on

Desiree and how she reacted to us. When we tired of playing "what if" games, we turned to Kuzmik.

He had developed the closest bond with Desiree and her parents. "She's real clean-cut," Tommy told us. "An all-American type. She's intelligent, articulate, very worldly in some ways. But her upbringing—her family is very polite and genteel— sure hadn't prepared her for a date with Tyson." Kuzmik had liked Desiree instantly, and he assured Barb and me that she would be a strong witness. In addition, he liked her parents: "Real nice folks. Dad is a blue-collar kind of guy—honest and direct. Mom is a very prim, very proper, very attractive lady."

Edward Gerstein, Desiree's civil lawyer, met us at the airport. I had no idea at the time what an important and infuriatingly disruptive role Gerstein would play in the case. A Providence lawyer, Ed, as he insisted on being called from the start, was a short man with curly red hair, incredible passion for meddling, and a preoccupation with the media that, it seemed to me, bordered on obsession. He talked constantly about what had been written about the case in the *New York Times* or the *Washington Post,* what had been said on ESPN's "Sports Center" or some other television program. Driving from the airport, Ed talked nonstop, bringing us quickly up to date on his law practice, his likes and dislikes, his ability to handle the media, and about a hundred other subjects about which I had not the slightest interest.

Ed shared offices with Walter Stone, a lawyer who had been retained as a counsel for the International Boxing Federation and who had served as a judge for the Miss Rhode Island pageant. It was Stone who first approached the Washingtons about their obtaining legal counsel. As Desiree's father, Donald Washington, remembered, Stone spoke persuasively about the need for someone to "run interference with the media"—as if the Tyson case were a football game and the Washington family unit was carrying the ball and trying to break through for a touchdown. At the time he asked the Washingtons to come to see him in his office, no mention was made of civil lawsuits, retainers, or contingent fees. He was just an individual lawyer, himself a black man, endeavoring to aid an individual black family.

The Washingtons had met with Stone in his office, and he explained that he could not represent them because his affiliation with the International Boxing Federation might, in a few distant corners of the land and by a handful of overly legalistic citizens, be construed as creating a conflict of interest. Stone then introduced Edward Gerstein, who faced no such potential conflict, and who, he avowed, was a seasoned veteran in warding off the media. Ed, in short, was the Washingtons' man. Perhaps naively, the Washingtons believed that whoever Stone referred them to would be good.

According to what Desiree later told us, Gerstein had already managed to fragment the family with unfounded conjectures by the time I made my first trip to Providence. He seldom spoke with more than one of the Washingtons at a time, seeing Desiree in one room, her mother in another, and her father in a third. To each of them he would explain that there were certain secrets that had to be kept strictly confidential, even from the other members of the family.

Donald and Mary Bell Washington had separated. Desiree herself had just gone off to college. Soon the lines of family communication broke down completely, but I didn't realize the extent of the breakdown until the trial started.

Nor was I beyond the range of Ed's conniving. We hadn't known each other fifteen minutes before he started to work on my mind. He told me that I must rush the case to trial. Donald Washington, he warned ominously, was out of control, preparing to break ranks, hire another lawyer, and file a civil suit himself. This news was a live wire. If there were even a hint of pending litigation out of the Washington family, the case would be hurt. It would be impossible to refute the gold-digger charge. I looked at Barb, and we both shook our heads. *What the hell is going on here? Has friendly Ed just handed us a different case?* We thought we had discussed every possibility on the plane, but we hadn't anticipated this soap opera.

I learned later from Donald Washington that he had never considered filing a civil suit or hiring another lawyer. In fact, Ed himself was the only person I ever heard mention a civil suit. Eventually, when the Washingtons started to talk among themselves and compare notes, they realized that Gerstein had been saying different things to each of them. But that revelation was almost three months away. All I knew on November 9 was that I had a knot the size of a fist in my stomach and a headache that wouldn't go away.

Oddest of all, I liked Ed Gerstein. And I kind of half-assed trusted him. He was a guy with a barn full of personality, a splashy demeanor, and was a past master of the off-color story. He would have been an instant success at any lawyers' convention. I laughed at his jokes and listened to the plots he was endlessly unraveling, but I noticed that Barb wasn't amused.

Eventually I cut in to his monologue and asked him how Desiree was holding up. Bad question. Desiree, Ed informed us at great length, was having second thoughts, what with the publicity and all. Don King had shaken her badly when he used her name repeatedly at a press conference. In fact, Ed continued, more than once he had had to "sit on" Desiree to keep her from dropping all charges. His story was so vivid and detailed that I conjured an image of him physically sitting on Desiree in an effort to restrain her sudden impulse to hoist the white flag of surrender.

We finally arrived at Gerstein's office, where Ed left us with Stone while he drove on alone to pick Desiree up. I could only imagine what stories he told her about Barb and me.

Shortly before noon, Gerstein returned with our star witness. By then I had no idea which Desiree to expect—Dreyer's ice queen, Gerstein's anxious victim, or Kuzmik's nice kid. The surprise was as delightful as it was unexpected. Until that moment I had only seen pictures and pageant videotape of Desiree, so in my mind she was the beauty contestant with poufed-up hair, wearing evening clothes and heavy makeup. The image had no voice. But here before me was a young woman in an oversized sweatshirt and jeans, her hair pulled straight back from her fresh-scrubbed face. She was so thin that, lost in the sweatshirt, she looked no more than fourteen. She seemed like any other teenage girl on a Saturday morning, looking as though she had just rolled out of bed, brushed her teeth and hair, and stumbled over for a visit.

She was vaguely nervous, but she seemed to like Barb immediately. They shared a love of animals. Barb showed her a picture of her basset hound, Rosebud, and Desiree acted as if the overfed pooch had just won the grand prize at the Westminster dog show. They chatted about animals and Desiree's work in the Big Sisters program. I remembered that Desiree had talked about the same subjects with Tyson only minutes before he raped her. Watching Desiree become increasingly animated and wide-eyed as she talked about dogs and children, I thought about her statement to the police. It all fitted. I was seeing what Tyson had seen—an innocent, attractive girl, more a child than a sophisticated woman.

Gradually, Desiree started to direct a few questions to me. She was eighteen, and she seemed reassured by the fact that my two older daughters, Juli and Betsy, were nineteen and seventeen. For me, talking to Desiree was as comfortable as talking to them, and she seemed to realize this and relaxed. I told her that we had some hard things to do, some painful subjects to discuss, but that Barb and I were there to help her.

We took a short break for lunch and then returned for the more weighty discussion. Desiree never hesitated in speaking about the rape, never refused to provide me with any information I requested. It quickly became clear that she would do whatever was asked of her, whether it was difficult or not. Was this the Desiree Gerstein had described two hours before? The young woman talking to Barb and me never even hinted that she wanted to drop the case. She was fully committed and under no illusion about how upsetting it was likely to become. And more important, beneath her giggles and quick, big smile, she was tough. I wondered how Ed had reached his conclusions about Desiree. Only a fool would have so badly misjudged her. And Ed Gerstein was no fool.

Using Desiree's prior testimony as an outline, we went over her trip to Indianapolis for the Miss Black America pageant. When we reached the point when she and Tyson entered his suite, it was evident to both Barb and me that her memories of that night were still very painful, but she steadfastly continued to answer my questions. Once I had determined for myself, now that I had met her, that I did in fact believe she was telling the truth, I needed to begin to flesh out her story. Critical information was missing from her earlier statements. A police officer taking a statement is not necessarily interested in the details and nuances that would command a jury's attention.

I wanted her to show me what had happened, just as a director would demonstrate to an actor how to play a certain scene. We talked about Tyson's touch when he hugged her in the Omni Severin ballroom; about what he did with his hands;

about how he looked at her; about whether he made eye contact when he spoke. We discussed his voice when he called her from the limousine and how he behaved when she got in. Both these issues were important. Desiree said that Tyson's voice sounded insistent and pleading over the phone, but not suggestive or coarse. "He had such a little boy's voice," she said. "Quiet, soft, gentle. Not mean at all."

"What did he say when you asked whether one of your roommates might come along?" I asked. Desiree's conversation with her roommates was crucial. A teenage girl who wants a friend to come along on a date is either not planning on a sexual encounter or wildly kinky, and Desiree was not the latter. I knew the jury would be interested in the phone calls Tyson made from the limousine.

"He wasn't bothered by the idea of one or even both of my roommates coming along," Desiree answered. That response interested me. Perhaps sex wasn't even uppermost on Tyson's mind at that moment. If that was true, his grand jury testimony must be false. He had suggested that Desiree knew that he had only one object on his mind: sexual gratification. If they had reached an implicit or explicit agreement about the nature of their "date," why all the talk about who would join Desiree? If they only planned on getting it on, why complicate matters by inviting someone else? If Desiree was a gold digger, why would she be willing to share the source of the gold with two roommates whom she had known for only a few days? Talking with Desiree, I began to see holes in Tyson's testimony big enough for an eighteen-wheeler.

"What happened when you got into the limousine?" I knew from Desiree's testimony that Tyson had kissed her as soon as she got in. I had tried enough cases to know what jurors would think when they learned about the kiss. I had wondered myself. *Where's this kid's head if he did something like that? If a man grabs a girl he hardly knows and kisses her before he even says hello, why would the girl follow him up to his hotel suite?*

"It wasn't a serious kiss," Desiree answered. At my prompting, she demonstrated the kiss: taking her two hands, she lightly touched the sides of her face with her fingertips and gave a little familial peck at the air with her lips. It was a gentle gesture, not at all passionate. As she did it, I thought, *That's what we've got to get this kid to do in front of the jury.* The kiss was like a friend's greeting, without sexual overtones.

I thought about Tyson. He had been on the go that night for almost twenty hours—eating, drinking, talking, roaming from one place to another. As far as I could tell he hadn't returned to the Canterbury to change clothes or freshen up. I played a hunch. "What did he smell like when he got in your face?"

Desiree responded immediately: "Oh, his breath was awful." The sentence came out in one quick exhalation. Her answer had the timing of complete and unrehearsed honesty. *There's another response I want the jury to see*, I thought. It was exactly what an eighteen-year-old kid would say. As every juror would know from experience, nothing can put the damper on romantic inclinations faster than somebody up in your face smelling like a cocktail party.

As my probing got closer to the hotel room, Desiree's demeanor changed. Her tone of voice had been delicate and childlike, but now it became apprehensive. She sounded like someone telling a ghost story instead of just spinning a yarn. She told how Tyson suddenly changed, how his eyes went cold and dead and he became aggressive and mean. She kept using the same descriptive adjective—"mean": he "looked mean"; he "looked at me real mean."

"Why did you go into the bathroom?" I asked.

"It was the first thing I could think of doing after he turned mean," Desiree answered. Later, in court, Tyson's attorneys would attempt to create a controversy over Desiree's removal of her panty shield. Even in November, it was clear that they were moving in that direction. Anyone who listened to Desiree's explanation would conclude that it was a nonissue. Desiree described how she went into the bathroom to escape Tyson, and out of habit discarded the soiled panty shield and reached down to get another from her purse, or pocketbook, as she called it. But she had left her purse behind. She decided she could find another panty shield at one of the parties she wanted to attend.

When she left the bathroom, she was shocked to see Tyson sitting in his undershorts on the edge of the bed. As she discussed what happened next, her voice developed a subtle quake, her breathing picked up speed, and her eyes got bigger.

It hurt to listen to her story, but I couldn't spare her feelings. I had to press her for the details.

Under Indiana criminal law, a rape victim cannot just say, "He raped me" or "He accomplished penetration"; she must use the correctly anatomical words. Desiree used the words precisely and without embarrassment. She described how Tyson pinned her to the bed and stripped off her clothes so quickly that she wasn't certain what was happening. Then he put his arms underneath the backs of her knees, lifted her up, and "licked me from my rectum to my vagina."

As she told this graphic and very painful story, I thought, *He knew exactly what he was doing. He knows how to rape people. He's done it before. He knows that a terrified woman is not going to lubricate, and so he's doing the job for her.* In one of the few notes I made during the session, I wrote: KNOWS RAPE. INVESTIGATE. I felt certain that when Tommy Kuzmik started digging around, we would discover another woman or two whom Tyson had raped. As it turned out, I wasn't disappointed. We would get unsubstantiated reports that he had done it before, and that he had used the same method.

Desiree's eyes welled with tears as she described the actual penetration, but she didn't break down, and she didn't stop. When she had talked with Barb about her dog, she seemed like any other teenager—her face animated, she laughed easily and was charming in a somewhat air-headed, "Oh, wow!" sort of way; she gave the impression of being capable of forgetting to put on her shoes before walking out in the snow. But as she described her encounter with Tyson, I sensed her deeper reservoirs of pride and courage and strength.

Several friends had asked me—and I had wondered myself—"How could she finish the pageant after being raped?" The implication was that if she had truly been raped, she would have been so traumatized that she would have quit. Since she hadn't quit, they assumed she could not have been raped.

I asked her about why she had stayed in the contest, and her answer surprised me. "I was determined," she said, "not to be defeated by what had happened. I didn't want to be a quitter. I didn't want to let him dictate the rest of my life."

It made perfect sense. And I knew that this one-hundred-eight-pound woman, one who looked and sounded like the sweet neighborhood girl you might ask to baby-sit for your kids (if it weren't a school night), was going to deliver a heavy blow to Mike Tyson when she took the witness stand.

As Barb and I wrapped up our conversation with Desiree, Ed Gerstein kept darting in and out of the room. He looked so nervous and preoccupied that I began to get jumpy. More than once he sidled up beside me and whispered that he had to talk to me immediately, in another room. There he would launch in, fretting about what some story in *Sports Illustrated* would say about the case or what Williams & Connolly was planning. The next step in Gerstein's method, as I learned too well in many subsequent conversations with him on the telephone, was a call to action: he would then demand that I respond, personally and forthwith, to the perceived crisis. He wanted me to counter this or that statement by Don King or some other member of Tyson's entourage.

I told Ed during our first conversation and many times again during the next month that I did not believe in trying a case in the press. I gave him two reasons. First, I had no time to respond to every wild verbal missile fired by Don King. Public posturing was King's forte, his game. He *wanted* me or someone else in the prosecutor's office to grab a fistful of mud and let fly. Then both sides would look like a truckload of professional wrestlers. The public would have no confidence in either side. Result: draw. Tyson would walk.

Second, and more important, I told Gerstein that I didn't think that the people of Indianapolis paid two cents' worth of attention to anything King said to reporters. Indiana juries had a tendency to pay attention only to what they heard in the courtroom. But Ed disagreed. The real battle, he suggested, was in the press, and during the next month he pushed and pushed constantly until his favorite sentence—"This has got to be responded to"—rang in my ears.

As far as I could tell, the only thing Gerstein succeeded in doing was dividing the Washingtons among themselves and keeping me on edge. His theme on that first day was, "You guys are going to get run over. You don't understand how these people work. The media blitz is going to be terrible." Great— just what I wanted to hear. Even worse, I could see that such talk worried and frightened Desiree. She had been through a terrifying ordeal. She didn't need her lawyer saying, in effect, *You ain't seen nothin' yet. Wait till the trial.*

On the flight back to Indianapolis that night, Barb, Kuzmik, and I compared notes of our impressions of Desiree. We had a newfound commitment to the case. We felt a sense of indignation and even outrage that such a beautiful person as Desiree could be twisted into a pretzel for somebody else's pleasure.

We also discussed Ed Gerstein. At that point I had no idea what to make of him. Barb's instincts were far better than mine. "I don't trust him," she said. "And I don't think we should confide in him."

I agreed. "We can't get rid of him, but we don't have to tell him anything important. I just hope Desiree is strong enough to survive him."

In his account of the Claus von Bülow case, *Reversal of Fortune*, Alan Dershowitz entitled one chapter "Learning the Rhode Island Shuffle." He described how von Bülow explained to him that Rhode Island lawyers played by a set of rules different from those observed in the rest of the nation. "Everybody goes to see the judges," von Bülow instructed the innocent Dershowitz. "Everybody relies on the inside track. It's the only way to practice law in Rhode Island. Any outsider who tries to win without tipping his hat to the insiders is immediately given the Rhode Island Shuffle." Judging from Gerstein's behavior—his concern about intrigue and the media—I did not doubt that there was a Rhode Island Shuffle.

As I thought about Gerstein that night and during the next few days, I felt relieved that the Tyson trial would take place in Indiana. Ed Gerstein and the Rhode Island Shuffle, I thought, were irrelevant in the Midwest. Or so I assumed.

But I had not heard the last of Ed Gerstein. Or of the Rhode Island Shuffle. Or, for that matter, of Alan Dershowitz—star pupil of Claus von Bülow.

# CHAPTER 10

# CORROBORATION

Ten thousand feet above New York in the evening darkness of November 9, en route from Providence to Indianapolis, the case against Mike Tyson began to take form. As Barb Trathen, Tommy Kuzmik, and I held a debriefing session, combing through what we had seen and heard during our discussions with Desiree, we began to plot our next moves. Only two people knew for certain what had happened on that July night in Suite 606, and they told wildly different stories. Late in January the State of Indiana would charge a Marion County jury with the responsibility of evaluating the two stories and rendering a verdict of guilty or not guilty. The defendant had the gambler's edge; in case of a draw, he won. He didn't have to prove his innocence; he didn't have to tell his story to the jury. The burden of proof belonged to the state. As prosecutor, I had to establish beyond a reasonable degree of doubt—as slippery and imprecise a phrase as there is in our legal vocabulary—that the defendant was guilty.

"Ours is an accusatorial and not an inquisitional system—a system in which the State must establish guilt by evidence independently and freely secured and may not by coercion prove its charge against an accused out of his own mouth." In that pronouncement, made in 1961, Justice Felix Frankfurter had underscored the essence of the U.S. criminal code. The State of Indiana, with the support of a grand jury, had accused Mike Tyson of a crime—an alleged assault that only the victim and the defendant could have witnessed. How could Barb and I now prove the state's contention? We had to take Desiree's story apart, break it into its component pieces, and decide which fragments could be independently corroborated. How to verify, shore up, support Desiree's story from as many directions as possible—that was the main topic of conversation as the State Police plane moved west toward Indianapolis.

One of my frustrations with the case was that I could never devote my full and undivided attention to it. Somebody forgot to stop sending me bills once I started on it, and until that oversight was corrected, I had to continue to work for a living. Every week until the trial, I had to handle dozens of other legal problems—forfeiture cases, insurance claims, civil disputes, and the usual accumulation of depositions and motions. The week after the trip to Providence was particularly hectic. I had to finish a RICO matter, then catch a commercial flight to New Orleans to interview a doctor for a health insurance company.

On Monday, November 18, Barb and I returned to our problem of how best to corroborate Desiree's testimony. The testimony of several witnesses, we agreed, would be crucial. At the top of the "A" list, in a class by herself, was Virginia Foster. She had driven Tyson to the Omni Severin Hotel to pick up Desiree, transported the two back to the Canterbury, and was the first person to talk to Desiree after the attack. What she observed, what she heard, what she sensed were of fundamental importance. Virginia Foster was a key witness, and her testimony in court was likely to help decide the case.

Kuzmik assured me that Virginia would be our chief corroborative witness—that is, if we could get her to testify. "She's tough, she has loads of information, and she doesn't like Tyson very much. However, she might like the press and the publicity even less." Since her name had been released to the press, reporters had made her life miserable by camping outside her house and hounding her for interviews. "Sometimes I'm afraid she's going to go south on us," Kuzmik observed. "The key to Virginia is Darryl Pierce. She likes him. She trusts him. If anybody can get her to testify, it's Darryl." I knew Pierce, a police sergeant attached to the grand jury, from years of working with cops. He was a tall, handsome, natty black man. He inspired confidence and trust, and since July he had served as police liaison with Virginia Foster.

Barb and I had our first meeting with Virginia in the office of the Metropolitan Drug Task Force at the Woodview Government Center. We chose that location because it was close to Foster's house on the east side. Pierce, who had escorted her to the meeting, introduced her to Barb and me. She was an attractive woman in her early forties who must have had on ten thousand dollars' worth of jewelry; gold chains and diamonds dominated her appearance. She seemed out of place in the Spartan office, and she looked uncomfortable. Her level of comfort did not improve when she met me. Although she was not unfriendly, she appeared to be guarded and cautious, and avoided making eye contact. As we talked, she seemed occasionally distracted and always uninterested, conveying an "I don't need this shit" attitude. Clearly, there was a serious chemistry imbalance between this bright, sensitive woman and me.

I wasn't sure if it was me personally or just that she was uncomfortable around white men generally. But we stood on two different sides of a cultural river, and she wasn't about to allow me to build any bridges—at least, not then.

Virginia had talked extensively with Pierce about Tyson's actions. She had told him the full story of her confrontations with the former champion. Tyson and Dale Edwards had harassed her almost nonstop from the moment they got into her limousine. "All the time, it was 'fuck this' and 'suck that,'" she had confided to Pierce. "Their language was right out of the gutter." Both men propositioned her repeatedly. One time late at night, Tyson ordered her to stop alongside a road so that he could "take a piss." As he stood, urinating, he called over to her, "How would you like to come back here and hold this big dick?" Tyson's most offensive actions, however, came after Foster delivered his overnight bag to Room 604 in the Canterbury Hotel. As she told both Pierce and Kuzmik, Tyson had made unambiguous and aggressive sexual advances, even though B Angie B was next door, in his suite. Although she was frightened, Virginia "set him straight." She banged him on the chest and informed him that she would drive a limo for him but that was all she would do. And if he wanted sex, there was a woman awaiting him next door.

I wasn't sure how much of Virginia Foster's story of her experiences with Tyson would be admissible in court, but I thought that all of it demonstrated a consistent pattern. In particular, I was interested in the way Tyson would suddenly turn mean and sexually aggressive. He had alarmed Virginia. Trapped and alone with him in his suite, she had experienced a moment of panic and fear. Even more important to my case, Tyson had seen that fear and enjoyed it. Virginia's maturity and strength of character may have saved her from an even worse experience, but what she had gone through was more than enough to give credence to Desiree's charges.

I was anxious to get every detail of her adventures with Tyson—perhaps too anxious. I am sometimes overly insistent and impatient; if a witness knows something, I want him or her to tell me without too much dancing around the point. But Virginia closed up on me completely. I don't know if I came across as too businesslike or too tactless; if I seemed too aggressive or too insensitive; if I had on too little deodorant or was just too white. For whatever reason, Virginia eyed me like a disease. I clearly saw distrust in her face, as if she thought I was ready to use every sleight-of-hand trick to get what I wanted from her, and her instinctive response was to resist. To every question I asked she gave a slow, guarded response. I was getting nowhere at about a hundred twenty miles an hour. I thought that maybe somewhere in her past she might have had to learn some difficult street lesson the hard way, that I reminded her of someone or some experience she would just as soon keep locked away. But my psychological training was limited to two foreign movies and one Henry James novel I never finished. In any event, I could see that I wasn't about to discover what Virginia Foster didn't like about me.

In our first interview, Virginia gave me even less than I had read in her initial police statement. She couldn't bring herself to repeat the vulgar words Tyson had used with her, the same words she had comfortably discussed with Pierce. Her reticence worried me. When Barb and I had divided the witnesses between us, deciding who would prepare each one and later examine that person in court, I had chosen Virginia Foster.

That meant that I had to develop a trusting, supportive connection with her, the same kind of relationship that Darryl Pierce had forged. As we talked, I stared directly at her. She seemed to be searching the floor for a can of bug spray to use on me. Never once did we make eye contact. *Great,* I thought. *One of my star witnesses doesn't want to talk to me.* I called time-out and left the room to powder my nose. I needed to talk to Barb.

She cut to the chase, wanting to know what I had done to Virginia Foster in some past life. "You know, I don't think she likes you very much." She said it looked like a "real personal thing" that I would have a difficult time overcoming. We decided to change our plans, agreeing that it would be best if Barb prepared and examined Virginia. Barb wasn't sure she could do any better than I had, but she was absolutely certain she wouldn't do worse.

The change worked. Although Virginia remained cautious for the rest of that meeting, during the next two months Barb developed a stronger rapport with her. They didn't become close friends, but they did gain a mutual respect. Eventually, even Virginia and I discovered something important about each other, something that may have affected the outcome of the Tyson trial. But that was still a few miles down the road, and even then she was never moved to pencil me in on her Christmas card list. When we ended that first interview, however, I had serious doubts about what kind of court testimony we were going to get out of Virginia Foster, the woman who had seen so much and seemed so determined to keep her distance.

Two days later, on November 20, Barb and I met in the grand jury room with another witness who we hoped would also corroborate Desiree's account. Cindy Jenkins was the police officer who took Desiree's statement on the night she visited Methodist Hospital, twenty-four hours after the rape. As a member of the sex crimes division of the Indianapolis Police Department, she had been trained to deal with rape victims, and she was thoroughly familiar with the typical behavioral patterns of women who had been raped. Officer Jenkins was as cooperative as Virginia was restrained. She remembered every detail of her encounter with Desiree; the fact that Desiree had accused a celebrity heightened her memory of the event.

Unfortunately, she informed us that during their initial interview with a victim of rape, the police ask only a few basic questions—simple questions just to get an investigation started, nothing in depth. Who were the parties involved? Where had the attack taken place? Was a weapon used? Were there any injuries? "Normally," Officer Jenkins told us, "victims are pretty upset. We try not to aggravate their condition. We listen and ask a few questions, but we never press. Often at that point we don't even know if the victim will file charges. It's up to the victim. No charges, no investigation."

I asked about Desiree's demeanor. What had Jenkins noticed? She answered that there was nothing in the way Desiree acted that was inconsistent with the typical reactions of a woman who had been raped. She was upset but quiet; very emotional, but not hysterical. She had difficulty talking and was extremely tired, but was fully aware of where she was and what she was saying. "Desiree looked like what I'm used to seeing," Jenkins concluded.

Officer Jenkins provided solid but not spectacular corroboration. Barb and I later discussed putting her on the witness stand, finally deciding to use her as much for the way she looked and acted as for what she had to say. She was an attractive policewoman, tall, slender, and feminine, but also visibly down-to-earth and steady. She reminded me of Betty Thomas, Ed Marinaro's female partner on the old "Hill Street Blues" television show. Looking at her, you could tell she was an intelligent, compassionate person; she would make the kind of witness who was certain to leave a good impression on the jury. And everything she had to say about Desiree was positive.

In preparing for the trial, Barb and I debated the value of every piece of evidence and every witness, not just Cindy Jenkins. Sitting in the grand jury room reviewing evidence and witness statements, driving or flying to and from witness interviews, or talking on the telephone during the days and nights leading up to the court date, we endlessly played the same war game. What if Fuller presented this piece of evidence; how would we react? How could we best present this witness? Where would that witness be vulnerable? Would this witness understand every question put to him? Would that witness be able to withstand the stress of a vigorous cross-examination? What would the defense do to try to compromise the evidence we introduced? Where were the weak spots of the witnesses for the defense, and how should we attack? Endless what-ifs and what-thens, back and forth, trying to prepare for the unexpected, hoping not to miss the obvious or obscure. It was a game I didn't even need a partner to play. I would rummage through so many scenarios at night in bed that I had trouble getting to sleep. Potential witnesses were reduced to vital bits of information jotted down on a legal pad.

> ### CINDY JENKINS
> — *ATTRACTIVE, POISED, GREAT IMPRESSION*
> — *CORROBORATES DESIREE'S STORY OF METH. HOSP.*
> — *DESIREE'S BEHAVIOR CONSISTENT WITH RAPE VICTIM*
> — *NO CONTRADICTIONS*
> — *NOT VULNERABLE TO CROSS-EXAMINATION*
> — *USE*

Between Virginia Foster and Cindy Jenkins—between the absolutely essential witnesses and the less important ones—ranged scores of witnesses whom Barb and I needed to meet, interview, and evaluate. Chris Low belonged in the middle ground. A bellman at the Canterbury, he had held the door for Tyson on the nights of both July 18 and 19. He had seen Tyson enter the Canterbury with two markedly different women, B Angie B on the eighteenth and Desiree on the nineteenth. He had also carried Dale Edwards's late-night snack to Room 604 and there, outside in the hallway, witnessed Desiree leaving Tyson's suite, her shoes in her hands and the look of a frightened rabbit in her eyes. From his grand jury testimony and police report, I judged Low to be an important, almost critical, witness. He seemed articulate, helpful, and scrupulously honest.

The son of a Korean mother and an American father, Chris had a slight build and a clean-cut, fresh-scrubbed appearance. He had spent several years in college. On the job, he noticed everything. He remembered stories about every famous person he had ever met while working at the Canterbury. An ideal witness, right? Not quite.

Chris had a very disconcerting mannerism: when he was thinking about his response to a question, his eyeballs would move upward and to the left until they disappeared in his eyelids. The effect was that he looked like a zombie who still had numbers across his chest from doing some heavy time in the state penitentiary. Instead of appearing thoughtful, he looked as though he was cooking up some bullshit lie. Once he showed the whites of his eyes in that way, I feared any jury would discount everything this otherwise charming young man had to say. Fortunately, Chris was easy to work with. I told him what the problem was, and he said he'd try to avoid it. Every time his eyes disappeared and he started to look like a thug emerging from an alley ready to cut someone's throat, I would snap my fingers and shout, "Stop it." He would smile and reply, "Sorry."

All witnesses, whether for the prosecution or the defense, need preparation. Most people, after all, have never testified in court. They don't know what to expect and have a tendency to freeze when answering questions. Part of preparing witnesses is acquainting them with courtroom procedure. Slowly, I walk them through what will happen. I go over every question I'll ask and work with them on their answers. I don't coach them on what to say, but on how to say it—when to take a breath and pause before making an important point, when to look at me and when at the defendant, when to substitute one word for another. I make them conscious of how they will appear and sound to the jury. If the witness is, say, a doctor, I remind him or her of the educational level of the jurors. If a medical or some other technical expert needs to use a chart or diagram to explain something, I instruct the person to talk to the jury and not to direct his or her testimony at the chart. I go through my questions and each witness's answers at least twice. Then I cover the questions that the defense will probably ask.

The object of the preparation is to eliminate surprises and sloppy answers, not to script a performance. Prosecutors and defense lawyers work on a thin wire, and both underprepared and overrehearsed witnesses will knock them off it. If one of your witnesses rushes past an important detail, the jury might miss it. If another witness's testimony seems canned, the jury might lose interest or conclude that the person simply memorized lines concocted by you. Either way, you lose. If a third witness has some mannerism that makes the jury nervous or suspicious, it might detract from otherwise solid testimony. It's a balancing act. You want the jury to see your witnesses as prepared but not rehearsed, self-assured but not overconfident, down-to-earth but not dumb. And appearing prepared, self-assured, and down-to-earth when a defense attorney is throwing bombs at your story and questioning your honesty takes practice.

By Thanksgiving week, the Tyson case was consuming most of my time. Every day there was something—study sessions in the grand jury room, witness interviews and preparation, meetings with Dave Dreyer about motions and paperwork, progress reports for Jeff Modisett. Jeff was starting to get anxious. Although I knew he trusted me, he sometimes treated me like a wild horse. He seemed to be afraid that at any moment I might start dragging him through the mud and brambles. On Monday, November 25, we talked on the phone. He was like an expectant father, and I felt like the doctor. I tried to reassure him that everything was falling into place, but nothing I said would ease his mind. He was feeling the pressure. So was everyone else connected to the case. In two months we were going to trial, and we had yet to begin the deposition process; we hadn't even met Tyson's lawyers. And there was still so much I didn't understand about Mike Tyson.

The riddle of Mike Tyson was on my mind that Monday afternoon when my partner Mike Kiefer and I talked with Phil Berger in my office. Berger was the friendly, immediately likable sportswriter for the *New York Times* who had come to Indianapolis to pump me for information about the state's case against Tyson. I agreed to the interview because I wanted to pump him in turn for information about Tyson. Throughout the preparation for the trial I gave interviews to a number of reporters who had dealt extensively with the boxer. I especially needed to understand Tyson in case I got the chance to cross-examine him. Berger turned out to be one of my best sources. As soon as we shook hands, we began to negotiate. We both knew something that the other wanted to know. The only question—and neither of us was so crass as to ask it—was, how much would I have to tell him about the case to get his read on Iron Mike? A gag rule prevented me from talking specifically about the charges, but Berger seemed content with the few other details I could give him. He needed background material on me and why I was selected to prosecute the case for an article. In return for that information, he gave me an insightful sketch of the former heavyweight champion.

Berger was the author of one of the four books that had been published on the career of Mike Tyson. *Blood Season: Tyson and the World of Boxing* was written in the late 1980s, when Tyson's public image was undergoing profound changes. But Berger had sensed that there was no glue at the center of Tyson's life, nothing to hold the fragmented parts together. "Tyson seemed lost in the universe, moving about with his compass impaired," he wrote in the summer of 1988. "The champion had always been moody, restless, needy, and romantic to a flaw about violence. . . . Added in now was a paranoiac edge—an us-against-them perspective that pervaded [his] outlook." Berger saw a clue to Tyson's personality in the words on the back of the fighter's custom-made white leather jacket: DON'T BELIEVE THE HYPE. The words were the title of a rap song that had been a hit for Public Enemy, Tyson's favorite group. The song's lyrics seemed to Berger to express how Tyson perceived himself: they portrayed a man living on the fringes of society—feared, hated, poised for violence, but also profoundly misunderstood.

Although I thought the song centered more on the difference between hype and reality, I was intrigued by Berger's take on what it meant to Mike Tyson. In the most telling paragraph in his book, Berger wrote: "There was an ominous hint in those words that [I] thought reflected the soul of the fighter. A premonition crept upon [me], and wouldn't let go, that this was another Joplin or Hendrix—live fast and die. Dead or arrested before his time—that was the creepy intuition that played in [my] mind, and when [I] told that to [Mike] Katz, of the *Daily News,* as the two of [us] flew cross-country on assignment July 4, the Wolfman, as he was known, nodded matter-of-factly, as though the same bad news had inhabited his dreams."

"Dead or arrested": half the prediction had come true, and if Berger hadn't seen it first—indeed, the same prediction had been voiced by nearly everyone involved in boxing—he had at least gotten it into print early. Berger had just finished another piece on the ex-champion for *M* in which he took another stab at solving the Tyson paradox. As we talked, he outlined the fuzzy boundaries of the paradox, revealing to me two Mike Tysons, two seemingly different personalities that inhabited the same body.

The one Tyson, Berger explained, was quiet, shy, and generous. He spoke in a lispy, sweet voice, loved animals and pigeons, hugged reporters as though they were part of the family, and helped out poor kids and broken-down fighters. The writer recalled visiting Tyson's camp before the fight with Razor Ruddock in June 1991. There he saw Scott Ledoux, a retired boxer who had fallen on hard times. Tyson had heard that Ledoux's wife had died of cancer and that the old fighter couldn't pay her outstanding medical bills, so he hired him as a $1,000-a-week sparring partner. After one training session Tyson saw that Ledoux no longer had the stamina to spar with him, but he told Richie Giachetti, his trainer, to keep Ledoux on the payroll nevertheless. "I'll tell you this about Mike Tyson," Ledoux told Berger, "he's got a lot more heart than folks give him credit for."

The other Tyson was rude, unfriendly, violent, and mean. Berger mentioned interviews he had conducted with Tyson in which the boxer's eyes and attention never strayed from his television set. He recalled press conferences where Tyson answered questions with bored disdain and belittled reporters. He reviewed Tyson's well-publicized and hushed-up scandals and legal problems—his rocket ride with Robin Givens, his street fight with Mitch "Blood" Green, his driving record, his aggressiveness with women. Berger once wrote that "Tyson was a clear and present danger to Tyson." As we talked, I became convinced that Tyson was also a clear and present danger to other people, especially women. There was a predictable pattern to his behavior: as a youth Tyson had stolen to get what he wanted; police had arrested him and authorities sent him to a reform school because he mugged people and robbed them. Although he had moved away from street crime, he still tended to resort to violence—after all, it was violence that had made him a millionaire—and take whatever he desired.

And what he desired was women. Berger said that he had long suspected that if and when Tyson self-destructed, a woman would be involved. Too many people had told Berger too many stories that had the same theme: Mike Tyson enjoyed women—

he enjoyed screwing them and frightening them and sometimes hurting them. José Torres, once a close friend of Tyson's, had told Berger that Tyson derived pleasure from hurting women through anal sex. Teddy Atlas, an early trainer, said that while he was still a teenager, Tyson had assaulted several girls in upstate New York. As he grew older, he grew bolder. During a break in a deposition for one lawsuit, Tyson approached Joann Crispi, an associate of the opposing counsel's, made a crude sign by poking a finger from one hand through a circle he had formed with the index finger and thumb of his other hand, and said, "I want to fuck you." Had he been serious, I wondered, or did he just want to shock and humiliate the woman?

During the next two months I had more discussions with Berger about Tyson. Each time I sensed that he had mixed emotions about the fighter he had covered for the previous six years, and that he had yet to resolve the puzzle. But he was moving closer in his article for *M.* Toward the end of the piece he commented, "There have always been skeptics who say the two sides of Tyson are really the same, that the sweet side simply reflects the ingenuity that certain jailhouse sorts have for ingratiating themselves, and that the real Tyson has always been mean-spirited to the core." Had Berger become one of those skeptics? I never asked, but in our conversations he hinted that he had.


As Berger and I talked, Indianapolis was getting ready for the holiday season. Christmas lights went up after the Thanksgiving parades; downtown was filled with shoppers. A stretch of Indian summer made it too warm to think of the holidays, however. As for me, the most demanding work still lay ahead, and I had little time to think about anything except preparing for the Tyson trial.

I read in the newspapers that Tyson and King were stepping up their pretrial media blasts. On November 22, the Friday before Thanksgiving, they took two busloads of reporters, volunteers, and assorted hangers-on to Brownsville, Tyson's old neighborhood in Brooklyn, to pass out free turkeys. The Team Tyson Turkey Tour, I learned, planned to pass out turkeys in eight other major cities as well. Catching the atmosphere of the tour, one reporter described Team Tyson as "King, Tyson, some thuglike bodyguards and a bunch of people in 'It's a family affair' T-shirts."

I don't know whether the Turkey Tour made its other stops, or if so, whether Tyson, King, and the thuglike bodyguards went along. I'm fairly certain that Indianapolis was not booked on the tour. But whether it was one stop, or two, or eight, the Associated Press wire service informed the nation that Mike the Good was out there somewhere, doling out turkeys to hungry Americans. And at the same time, the ex-champion took the opportunity to remind the public that "everyone knows I'm innocent."

*Well, maybe not everyone,* I thought. I knew a handful of people very close to the case who doubted Tyson's innocence very much. The day before Thanksgiving, Judge Patricia Gifford denied five defense motions seeking dismissal of the rape and related charges. During a fifty-minute hearing, Vincent Fuller argued that Gifford should dismiss the charges because they didn't mention that Tyson compelled Desiree Washington to have sex, and that compulsion was the essential element of rape. Dave Dreyer, who handled all the pretrial motions, responded that the rape charge against Tyson referred to force, implied compulsion, and conformed with Indiana law. The charging document stated that Tyson had sexual intercourse with the alleged victim "by use of force or imminent threat of force." Gifford agreed with Dreyer. The charge accused Tyson of rape, and he would stand trial for the offense.

# CHAPTER 11

# PLANES, TRAINS, AND TALK OF CHAMPIONS

**A**t eleven-thirty on the morning of Wednesday, December 11, I met Barb at the State Police hangar for a flight to Washington's Dulles airport. It had been a cold, crisp, clear morning, but the news reports predicted that the good weather would soon end. The pilot told us to enjoy the flight east because there might not be much to savor on the return home. Unfortunately, I was not in much of a mood to enjoy anything. A scene from *Butch Cassidy and the Sundance Kid* was rerunning endlessly in my mind. After robbing a train, Butch and the Kid head for the safety of the mountains, where in the past they were always able to escape posses. But this time something's different. They use all their outlaw tricks, all their practiced dodges and twists, but are unable to shake the lawmen who are after them. Time and again, Butch and the Kid look at each other and ask some variation of "Who are those guys?" Barb and I faced a slightly different problem. We knew who our legal opposition was; we just didn't know exactly what made him and his firm so good.

On the three-hour flight to Washington, I reviewed what I had learned about Vincent Fuller. Born June 21, 1931, in Ossining, New York, the son of a municipal court judge, he had graduated from Williams College in Williamstown, Massachusetts, served a tour in the navy during the Korean War, and earned his law degree at Georgetown University. In 1956 he was admitted to the District of Columbia bar and hired by Williams, Wadden & Stein. During the next thirty years he had worked closely with Edward Bennett Williams, the nation's leading defense lawyer, and after Williams's death in 1988 had become the senior partner in Williams & Connolly. Fuller, noted Evan Thomas in his biography of Edward Bennett Williams, was one of Williams's "surrogate sons." "These young men," Thomas wrote, "not only worked with Williams on cases, they lived with him, sharing hotel suites when cases were tried on the road, playing sports with him, dining with him, and drinking with him (a hollow leg was a helpful attribute when traveling with Williams)."

Over the years, Fuller had taken the second chair to Williams in a number of famous cases. They were very well matched. Williams was flamboyant and charismatic, delivering opening statements and closing arguments without notes, moving jurors to laughter and to tears, entertaining journalists with his out-of-court banter. Working with Williams, Fuller stayed in the background and made a reputation as a master of detail.

"Fuller didn't care about the limelight, which made him perfect for Ed," commented a woman who had clerked for both men. "He was content in Ed's shadow, and Ed relied on him hugely." Fuller aided Williams in both the Jimmy Hoffa bribery case and the Adam Clayton Powell income tax evasion case. On the surface both cases looked like no-brainers for the prosecution, but when the trials ended it was Williams and Fuller who emerged from the courtroom with smiles plastered on their faces.

As much as any lawyer of his era, Williams was adept at playing the race card. In the Hoffa trial, for example, he believed that blacks would be more sympathetic to his client. He used all sixteen of his peremptory challenges during jury selection, so that when he was done Hoffa's jury had eight black and four white jurors. In an attempt to ingratiate himself—and by extension, his client—with the jury, he hired Martha Jefferson, a black lawyer from Los Angeles, to aid the defense team. But Williams saved his best card to play later in the trial. One afternoon he invited former heavyweight champion Joe Louis to the courtroom, where in full view of the jury the boxer warmly

greeted Jimmy Hoffa. After the Louis incident, the government's case against Hoffa lost steam, and the Teamster boss
was acquitted. The government cried foul play, Williams protested his innocence of any tawdry tricks, and Joe Louis went
on to marry Martha Jefferson and gain employment as a
greeter in a Teamster-owned casino in Las Vegas.

The Adam Clayton Powell trial was a pure numbers case. Williams assigned Fuller to account for every penny on Powell's
complex tax returns. It was the kind of job Fuller relished, and
he worked out Powell's finances within a hundred dollars. Williams then worked them down even further and memorized the
results. As a result of Williams's and Fuller's calculations, the
Powell trial ended in a hung jury—ten to two to acquit—and
Powell had Williams named Harlem Man of the Year. "Abra-
ham Lincoln freed the slaves," Powell told a crowd in Harlem,
"but Edward Bennett Williams freed Adam Clayton Powell!"

In 1981, Fuller stepped out from behind Williams's shadow.
That was the year John Hinckley, Jr., shot President Ronald
Reagan. John Hinckley, Sr., sought advice from Maurice Bates,
a corporate securities lawyer in Dallas whose firm represented
Hinckley's Vanderbilt Energy Corporation. Bates and Fuller
had gone to Georgetown together, and he put Fuller and
Hinckley in touch. The Hinckley case was well outside the usual
range of Fuller's practice. He had specialized in white-collar
crimes—bribery, tax evasion and fraud, liquor violations. In
the Washington legal community he was well respected for his
honest, no-nonsense style and his mastery of technical issues.
He had stayed away from street crimes—murder, rape, armed
robbery. But the Hinckley trial promised to be a once-in-a-life-
time experience. Doubtless, Williams was not thrilled about
Fuller's taking the case; he had strong ties to the Reagan White
House and knew that Nancy Reagan was unlikely to be pleased
if his firm defended the man who had tried to kill her husband.
But he told Fuller to take it on. Indeed, Williams's own reputation had been built defending unpopular clients, from Joe Mc-
Carthy and Jimmy Hoffa to Frank Costello and Robert Vesco
to Bobby Baker and George Steinbrenner.

Fuller provided Hinckley with the best defense, arguing that
when Hinckley shot Reagan and three other men outside the
Washington Hilton Hotel he was insane. He convinced a jury
that Hinckley was a deeply disturbed loner, a lifelong failure

who had gradually slipped out of the here-and-now and taken up residence in a "magical" world of his own invention. He became obsessed with suicide and murder, obsessed with his imagined relationship with Jodie Foster, then best known as the child star of the film *Taxi Driver*. He became a real-life Travis Bickel (the Robert De Niro character in the movie), cruising from town to town, restless, friendless, alienated from his family and the world around him. To explore the depth of Hinckley's insanity and obsession with Foster, Fuller convinced the court to show *Taxi Driver* to the jury. In a rare moment of courtroom levity, he introduced the film to the jury by observing, "Now let's get out the popcorn and watch the movie."

Twelve jurors subscribed to Fuller's characterization of Hinckley and returned a verdict of not guilty by reason of insanity. The judgment shocked the courtroom and the nation. The *New York Times* said that even Fuller seemed surprised by the verdict. Afterward, White House officials expressed their outrage. "I think when a person stalks a leading citizen of this country, shoots him, three of the people surrounding him, and then gets off scot-free, I think that's absolutely atrocious," commented Treasury Secretary Donald T. Regan. Fuller, who had maintained an outward distance from Hinckley during the trial, was careful not to voice his own view about this landmark verdict that enlarged the scope of the insanity plea. "Another day, another dollar," he told reporters as he left the courthouse.

The Hinckley trial allowed Fuller to take his place as one of the most famous defense lawyers in America. Like Edward Bennett Williams, Fuller was among the handful of men sought out by those who were in serious trouble and had deep pockets. "The ideal client is a rich man who is scared," Williams often repeated. After Hinckley, ideal clients started coming to Williams & Connolly looking for Fuller almost as often as Williams.

In 1984, Don King turned to Fuller for help. Rudolph W. Giuliani, the United States Attorney for the Southern District of New York, announced in December that a grand jury had indicted King and his business manager, Constance Harper, on twenty-three counts of income tax evasion, filing false and fraudulent returns, and conspiracy. Altogether, Giuliani charged that King and Harper had failed to report a million dollars of income.

Even more than the Hinckley case, the King trial provided clues to the strategy Fuller would employ in his defense of Tyson. Fuller never denied that King had failed to report the income; indeed, the government easily demonstrated how King and Harper had skimmed corporate account money for private use. He argued instead that King was ignorant of all the illegal transactions, persuading the jury that King, a man who had once balanced figures from his numbers business in his head and successfully juggled three different bank accounts, wasn't aware of what Harper was doing with his money. In his closing argument, Fuller summarized King's financial empire: "The point of it is that this is not a smooth ship that's being run here, and we all recognize that King is the captain of that ship, and perhaps can be criticized for not being a more aggressive administrator. But there is no evidence to support that Mr. King has the skills to do that, that he is educated or trained to run that kind of massive ship." I had no idea of what kind of sailor King was, but anyone who had read much about him realized that he was not untrained or maladroit at handling his own money. Somehow, Fuller satisfied the jury that King didn't know that Harper was endorsing and depositing checks into his private bank account and a joint account that the two kept together. Although he did not call a single witness during the trial, in his closing argument Fuller blamed accounting errors and King's unsophisticated handling of his finances for his client's tax problems. The jurors agreed. They found King innocent of any wrongdoing. Harper, they decided, was at fault, and she served her full year's sentence in prison. King displayed his appreciation by taking the entire jury out to dinner.

How had Fuller been able to make King's past disappear? How had he transformed the wolf into the lamb? These questions occupied my mind as our plane touched down at Dulles.

Dick Chapman occupied office 5118 on the fifth floor of the eleven-story Judiciary Center, a federal office building three blocks north of the Federal Courthouse. It was a massive building, with the U.S. Attorney's office dominating the first five stories. To get to Chapman's office, Barb and I had to wind down what seemed like miles of hallways and corridors, past lobbies large and small, and through several metal detectors. I felt as though I was moving through Washington's version of Checkpoint Charlie. After passing an obstacle course of filing cabinets and secretarial stations, we finally arrived at Chapman's office, which wasn't much more than an alcove with a door. It was piled from floor to ceiling with files full of motions, pleadings, and briefs. The papers partially obscured a small window and must have completely swallowed the telephone. The office sounded one note with perfect clarity: inside was a government employee who was overworked, underpaid, and treated as if the bureaucracy pinched pennies on a tight budget. But Barb and I were interested in what was inside Chapman's head, not his office. Along with Roger Adelman and Mark Tucker, it was Chapman who had prosecuted John Hinckley, and he had agreed to talk with us about Fuller's work on the case and his bearing in the courtroom.

"Vince Fuller wins by preparation," Chapman began. "He out-prepares everybody. His people motion you to death. They discover you till you're blind. They know your case better than you do." Less than two months before, the *American Lawyer* reported that Fuller was one of three members of Williams & Connolly who charged clients $400 an hour for their services. For $400 an hour, clients had the right to expect the best preparation, the best courtroom strategy, the best defense.

A pleasant man, a former naval officer who was educated at the University of Iowa, Chapman discussed Fuller's many strengths. "He's at his best during his opening statement and closing argument, when he's in complete control of the courtroom and the facts. He's a powerful advocate, a great advocate who can weave any set of facts into a compelling, believable narrative. His style is formal and authoritative—his voice has a kind of rough growl that forces jurors to pay attention. He doesn't have Ed Williams's charm and presence, but like Williams, he has the ability to win cases that appear on the surface to be sure losers."

Would Fuller and his colleagues, backed by Tyson's vast resources, discover some small, seemingly insignificant piece of evidence that Barb and I had overlooked? Could Fuller command a county courtroom as deftly as he dominated a federal one? Chapman read my concern. After what seemed like more than an hour of praise for Fuller, he began a pep talk meant to show Barb and me that Fuller wasn't invincible. His style had a

chilly, Olympian quality; though he was pleasant enough outside the courtroom, inside he struck observers as distant. Perhaps it was the nature of the Hinckley case and its audacious
defense, but Fuller never chatted with his client, never demonstrated anything that could be interpreted as a personal bond.
Apparently he just plain didn't like Hinckley very much. And
Chapman doubted that Fuller would show any more warmth
toward Tyson. Furthermore, he believed, Fuller would be uncomfortable cross-examining Desiree Washington on the details of the rape. It was a gut feeling on Chapman's part, maybe
a premonition, that Fuller's patriarchal aloofness, his federal
style and to-the-manor-born air would not go over well with a
Marion County, Indiana, jury.

"I don't know how Vince would handle a rape case," Chapman said. "I'm not sure he's ever defended a man accused of
rape. It certainly isn't white-collar stuff; it's not about numbers
or a failure to pay taxes. Frankly, the entire Potomac bar is
wondering why he accepted the case. It doesn't fit the Williams
and Connolly profile; they just don't do street crimes. Never.
Not even in the D.C. area."

Two and a half hours after entering Chapman's office, I had
convinced myself that Barb and I were better suited for the
Tyson case than Fuller and his Williams & Connolly associates. I
was having trouble imagining Fuller with his Montblanc pen,
gold cuff links, and tailor-made shirts down in the mud and
blood and beer of what was essentially a run-of-the-mill street
crime. Perhaps he was only being kind, but Chapman agreed.
"The Tyson case is going to be about personalities, not just
Tyson's and Desiree Washington's but also Fuller's and yours.
And you're much more likable," Chapman said. "You ought to
be able to take the courtroom away from him," he went on. I
liked what I was hearing. "You ought to be able to win the
personality contest. You ought to be able to hammer his ass.
But you've got to be ready, because he's going to have everything in the world lined up against you, and he'll spare no cost
and no energy. In his polite, calm way, he'll try to shoot you
between the eyes. Don't be fooled by his patrician manner.
Vince Fuller doesn't like to lose."

Outside the Judiciary Center the weather had turned nasty.
Low gray clouds sprayed Barb and me with a cold drizzle. We

hailed a cab and went back to our hotel rooms to change into more comfortable clothing, then walked from Foggy Bottom to Georgetown for dinner. We found a small, quaint restaurant on the main drag that was having a slow night. Seated in front of a huge fireplace, we watched a burning gas log, drank a couple of glasses of wine, told a lot of lies, and got to know each other better. It was our first extended, informal experience together. Although we were roughly the same age and had known each other for ten or twelve years, we had never worked on the same case or socialized with one another. Since Barb had come onto the case, I had wondered how we were going to get along when we were stuck together for a long time. Were we going to discover that each of us had quirks and idiosyncrasies that drove the other nuts? Would there be underlying tensions? Gender conflicts? Would we go around tinkling on bushes to claim territory in a contest to see who was going to be boss?

The dinner resolved everything. Barb was completely without guile, sincere and honest. There were never any tensions or unresolved conflicts. We talked about our families and friends, planned how we would attack the case, and discussed the problems we faced. But we didn't contest turf—not then, and not ever. It was our case; we were co-counsels. Barb trusted me to make the final call if we disagreed on any major issues, but we didn't. I valued Barb's judgment of people, which turned out to be better than mine. We agreed on so many things, it seemed silly to look for areas of contention.

The rain had stopped, so we took a long walk after dinner, visiting the Lincoln Memorial, the Washington Monument, the Capitol—the usual tourist locations. Barb had never seen the Vietnam War Memorial, so we stopped there. Finally we looked for a cab to take us back to Foggy Bottom. It was then that it occurred to me that in some ways Washington wasn't so very different from Indianapolis. When it got close to midnight, most of the city was asleep, and we struggled without avail to find a cab. Finally an off-duty driver agreed to give us a ride. He talked about the same things an Indianapolis taxi driver would talk about—the fear of violence, the cost of living. If taxi drivers were the same, then perhaps the lawyers were also. The not four but five hundred dollars an hour Mike Kiefer had told me Tyson was paying Vince Fuller was way too high by

Indianapolis standards, but then hotels, meals, everything was far more expensive than at home. More expensive; not necessarily better.

The studio of the Black Entertainment Television cable network at 1899 Ninth Street in northeast Washington was tucked away on a low patch of land between two railroad tracks and surrounded by a ten-foot chain link fence with strands of barbed wire running across the top. It looked like an urban Fort Apache stuck in the middle of rough industrial territory, ready to repulse an enemy assault. It seemed odd that any building whose stated purpose was communications should appear so unapproachable.

BET was the country's only cable network aimed at African Americans. Robert Johnson, a Washington cable lobbyist, launched the network in 1980 with the help of a $15,000 loan. Although Johnson encountered problems attracting mainstream advertisers, BET became part of the boom in cable broadcasting during the 1980s. At the beginning of the decade it offered a two-hour-a-week service for 3.8 million cable subscribers in 350 markets; by 1990 it had become a twenty-four-hour, seven-day-a-week operation serving 27 million subscribers in 2,200 markets with a variety of programs ranging from soul and gospel music to news, sports, entertainment, and children's programming. Several of the country's leading media corporations, including Home Box Office and Tele-Communications, Inc., had supported Johnson in his enterprise.

Johnson had tapped into a growing consumer market—the black middle and upper classes. During the 1980s the income of black families, adjusted for inflation, shot up 40 percent. And demographic studies reported that blacks watched nearly 50 percent more television than the general population. Between the rising incomes and the heavy viewing stood BET. Two months before Barb and I visited its studios, BET went public, selling on the New York Stock Exchange at $17 a share. The price of a share quickly rose 50 percent. "It's incredible," Johnson told the press a week before our visit, "how a company with $9 million in earnings in 1991 could leave Wall Street with a market value of $475 million."

In researching BET, I had one question: How strong was Don King's pull with the network? Like Johnson, King had interests in all forms of black-oriented entertainment. Was he tied in to BET? Although I learned that the boxing promoter Butch Lewis and Johnson had joined together in a pay-per-view television deal, I found no direct ties between King and BET.

Barb and I went to the BET studio to talk with Charlie Neal, the handsome spokesman and announcer for the Miss Black America pageant. Meeting us in the lobby, Neal escorted us to a well-appointed conference room. After some small talk, which Neal excelled at but Barb and I had little time for, I began asking him about his career, including the short time he had spent with Mike Tyson at the Miss Black America pageant rehearsal on the afternoon of July 18 in the Omni Severin's Allison Ballroom. Barb and I knew from other sources—Tyson's own grand jury testimony among them—that Neal had been talking with Tyson as the boxer ogled the Miss Black America contestants. And Desiree told us that she had seen Tyson and Neal looking and motioning in her direction as they conversed. After talking with Neal, Tyson had walked over to Desiree and said, "I hear you're a good Christian girl. That's good. I like that." Tyson's opening lines and show of respect had immediately put Desiree at ease with the former champion.

Neal was a thorough professional—poised, articulate, and relaxed. He told us that he had met J. Morris Anderson in 1974 in Philadelphia, and that Anderson had asked him to be the master of ceremonies for the Miss Black America pageant. The pageant was run on a tight schedule. In 1991 Neal arrived in Indianapolis on the morning of Monday, July 15, met and talked with each contestant that afternoon, and worked the swimsuit and projection preliminaries that evening. Talent rehearsals and other preliminaries occupied most of Tuesday and Wednesday, and by Thursday everyone was rushing to get ready for the weekend finals. "No time to relax," Neal said, "for anybody, especially myself." To host the event properly, Neal spent hours interviewing the contestants, asking them questions about their hometowns, parents, high school or college activities, likes and dislikes. He prepared cards on each contestant and studied the cards during the week.

Neal recalled Desiree: "She seemed like a nice, well-behaved young lady—bubbly, pleasing personality; bright. Met her entire family. Nice, nice people." As he sat drinking coffee, Neal considered in turn each question Barb and I asked. Occasionally, before returning a polite, thoughtful answer, he looked outside at the early winter sky that was now threatening rain.

Moving closer to the heart of the matter, I asked him how well he knew Mike Tyson. He knew both Tyson and King only professionally, he said. He had interviewed both a number of times, most recently at King's house in Las Vegas, but it was strictly a professional relationship. He knew neither the boxer nor the promoter well, but he liked Tyson. "Mike's very respectful. He always addresses me as Mr. Neal. He's always been a gentleman when I interviewed him."

I asked about his conversation with Tyson at the rehearsal. Neal answered that when he arrived, Tyson and Johnny Gill were already there. Tyson was preparing his rap number and Gill was sitting in a chair with an amused look on his face. The two men appeared to be at ease, and the contestants were obviously excited. After Tyson finished his promo, Neal chatted with him briefly.

"Did Tyson ask about Desiree Washington?" I asked.

Neal thought for a moment, then replied, "No, I don't think so. Not that I can remember."

"Did you at any time tell Tyson that Desiree was a 'good Christian girl'?" We had heard that when Tyson asked about Desiree, Neal had told him, in effect, that he wouldn't be interested in her, and that she was a "good Christian girl"—said in a way meant to discourage Tyson from approaching her.

Neal denied that he had ever said anything like that. He had no knowledge of Desiree's religious beliefs or church activity. He explained, however, that such a statement has a special meaning in the black community. "It's a sign of respect," he said. "It means you think the girl is something special." According to Neal, recognizing a woman as a "good Christian girl" didn't necessarily limit what you might do with her on a date; the point was that no matter what happened you would respect her in the morning.

Moving the focus back to what happened on July 18, I asked him what he remembered about his talk with Tyson. He recalled very little. "It was just general conversation. Small talk . . . But I'm sure we didn't discuss anything about any specific contestant."

Barb and I inquired next about Tyson's behavior at the open-ing ceremony for Black Expo. Everyone we talked to had said the same thing: all Tyson seemed interested in was the contes-tants. He had moved from one to another, talking, touching, laughing, feeling, and more than one civil suit had resulted from his behavior. Watching Tyson trolling among the contes-tants that afternoon, Jeff Modisett had had a sense of impend-ing trouble. The Reverend Jesse Jackson must have had the same feeling. Several people, including Modisett, overheard Jackson tell one of the Expo organizers, "Get him the hell out of here before he hurts someone."

Neal, however, remembered nothing unusual about Tyson's behavior. Yes, he had seemed interested in the contestants, and they were apparently thrilled by his attention. Neal himself, how-ever, had seen nothing inappropriate, and certainly had experi-enced no premonitions. Tyson was just a famous celebrity being treated like a famous celebrity. Nothing out of the ordinary.

In fact, as far as he knew at the time, the entire pageant went as planned. While other officials for Black Expo and the Miss Black America pageant had heard about the alleged rape, the rumors completely bypassed him. Not until that next Friday, when he was in the Bahamas watching CNN, did he learn about the charges. They took him by surprise. During the pageant, he hadn't noticed any change in Desiree's behavior. She seemed the same on the last day as on the first.

At all times during our visit, Neal maintained the same friendly, polished tone. But what he had to say boiled down to *I didn't see nothin', I didn't hear nothin', I don't know nothin'.* The interview was a flat-assed bust. It was clear to me that he must be thinking that these honkies weren't going to get a thing from him against a brother. He never said as much, of course, but the attitude was there. I wasn't surprised by his response; we had met with it before. Half a dozen people had heard Jesse Jackson's comment, but when asked about it by Dave Dreyer, Jackson de-nied ever saying such a thing. The enclave mentality was at work. Some witnesses wouldn't turn on Tyson no matter what he had done, and regardless of whether the victim was white or black.

We had reached an impasse. Barb and I thanked Neal for his time and help, and left. We had to catch a train to New York City.

Sweeping north from Washington to New York's Penn Station, I saw a part of the East Coast that isn't described in any of the travel literature. Trains seldom wind through high-priced neighborhoods. Some of the scenes reminded me of snapshots of Dresden taken after the war: buildings that looked as if they had been bombed were now hollow shells where winos and drug addicts wasted their lives. Young kids played games around trash can fires and overflowing garbage. Whether in the outskirts and outback of Washington, Wilmington, Philadelphia, Newark, or New York City, the landscapes were identical. I kept thinking that if the East Coast and the area surrounding our nation's capital were rotting from the inside like this, we must be in one hell of a shape.

Looking out at these squalid cesspools where people struggled just to stay alive, I thought about Mike Tyson. One point that Charlie Neal had made bothered me. Toward the end of our talk, I asked him if he thought there had been a rape. "Something happened, sure," he answered. "But I don't know what. Only two people know that. But I know one thing. Mike had his pick. He could have had lots of women. Now why would he have to rape one?"

Why? The same question would be in every juror's mind. *Why?*

"Only in America," as Don King constantly said, did these poor youths I saw from the train window, darting between the winos and addicts, have a chance. Maybe it wasn't a good one, but there was a chance. Mike Tyson came from the same mean streets, yet at twenty-five he had everything material America glorified—success, wealth, fame. He had made it. So why would he throw it all away and rape a girl when women were cruising the Canterbury looking for him? It made no sense.

The question was central to *State* v. *Tyson*. Without a good answer, I had no working motive. Desiree's tale presented an unflattering portrait of Iron Mike Tyson, a man described by some as America's most misunderstood superhero and by others as a sociopath in hot pursuit of his own destruction. One thing was certain: jurors demand a motive for a crime. To convict Tyson, Barb and I had to demonstrate beyond a reasonable degree of doubt that he was the man Desiree Washington said he was. To reach that end, we had to cut through a lifetime of lies and a career grounded in hype and deception. That's why we had come to New York, to visit José Torres, former protégé of Cus D'Amato, world light-heavyweight boxing champion, and friend of Mike Tyson.

Barb and I arrived at Penn Station in the early afternoon. Our combined knowledge of New York was limited to one senior field trip in high school and a few crime movies. Walking out of Penn Station onto West Thirty-first Street, we were warmly greeted by an old drunk who, standing with imperious dignity, was taking a piss on the sidewalk. *Welcome to New York,* I thought.

We didn't look like natives. I'm not sure what gave us away; it might have been the fact that each of us was carrying a large suitcase, a hang-up bag, and an overstuffed briefcase, or it could have been our never fully suppressed tendency to gaze upward and exclaim, "Gosh! Look at that!"

Before we left Indianapolis, Jeff Modisett had impressed on us the need to economize, so we decided to take the subway to Torre's office in lower Manhattan, working under the assumption that a taxi ride would cost about the same as an airline ticket to Paris. We got on the subway, and ninety blocks and a half dozen stops later, Barb and I started fumbling around with a map and asking each other where the hell we were. A woman sitting next to us with a mildly exasperated but sort of friendly look on her face said, "You're going the wrong way. You need to stop. Here's what you do: the next time this thing stops, get off, turn around, and go back." She gave us the name of another stop, which turned out to be exactly right. It was enough to revive my faith in the basic decency of humanity.

Sitting on the subway, now heading south, 90 percent asleep and dead-dog tired from dragging around a hundred pounds of luggage, I saw something that made me bolt to attention. Across from me a man was reading the *New York Daily News.* The paper was open so I could see the front page. In a banner headline eight inches high, the paper announced the result in the William Kennedy Smith trial: PROSECUTOR BOTCHES CASE. On the previous day, December 11, a jury in Palm Beach had returned a not guilty verdict. I shook my head and looked again just to make sure I wasn't having a bad dream. PROSECUTOR BOTCHES CASE. A cold chill ran through me that made me want to throw up. I nudged Barb awake and pointed to the headline. "That's not going to be us!" I hissed. If we had to sacrifice every ounce of energy and self we possessed, and even if we were beaten, they'd at least know they'd been through it. We certainly weren't going to *botch the case*. That headline probably drove Barb and me harder than anything else to prepare, prepare, prepare.


"**S**tart with a simple assumption: boxing is lying for a living. The best boxers are the superior liars. From that point all else follows as logically as a fist at the end of a right cross."

José Torres sat in his office in the shadow of the World Trade Building. Barb and I had finally located the place, a rickety old high rise with an off-price record store on the first floor and a group of seedy-looking deadbeats standing around in the front. Even in midafternoon it seemed like dusk, as if the buildings never permitted sunlight to reach the street. But the neighborhood had a vital, energized feeling. Working women in business dresses wearing white socks and running shoes strode along between streams of bicycles and taxis. Honking horns and shouting construction workers kept time with the music pouring out of the record store. This seemed like the right place to come to learn about a New York boxer.

Torres had a classic boxer's face—permanent scar tissue and puffiness around the eyes, flattened nose, ruddy complexion. He was a handsome man, not tall but trim and fit, with the erect posture and graceful movements of an athlete. His shoulders displayed an inner confidence, and his gnarled, rough boxer's hands were expressive. Except that his face and hands bore the marks of his former career, I would have guessed him to be a Latino businessman. He spoke with an accent, but his English was perfect, his diction as crisp and sharp as his jab had once been. He said each word as if it was followed by a period, and pronounced Tyson with a hard emphasis on the second syllable: Ty-*son*.

Tyson was twelve when Torres met him, an introverted, troubled youth with two shiny gold teeth, a lispy voice, and a sheepish smile. Constantine "Cus" D'Amato, the legendary boxing savant who had guided both Torres and Floyd Patterson to world championships, introduced Torres to his latest protégé.

"This boy," D'Amato told Torres on a raw day in February 1979, "is going to be the heavyweight champion of the world someday." Tyson had yet to enter the seventh grade, but D'Amato had already set up the training regimen that would make him a champion.

But then, Tyson had always been precocious. As Torres discussed in *Fire and Fear,* his biography of Mike Tyson published in 1989, by the age of nine he was a criminal. A product of the streets of Brownsville and Bedford-Stuyvesant, two Brooklyn slums, Tyson grew up fast and mean. At first he just stole candy from grocery stores and fruit off produce trucks, but the level and nature of his crimes quickly escalated. He quit going to school, smoked marijuana, drank Mad Dog, Bacardi, Don Q. He started to hang around with pimps, thieves, and drug dealers who passed as role models. He carried a gun. He would snatch groceries and purses from women, mug grown men, and pickpocket people for sport. "Shit, we were wild," he once told Torres. "We didn't fuck around, man; we were a bunch of maniacs. Sometimes we got really crazy, nuts, got guns and just started shooting in the neighborhood."

In his world, violence was as common as hot summer nights without air-conditioning and cold winter mornings without heat.

"His mother lived off and on with a guy named Eddie Gillison," Torres said. "Eddie tried as best he could, but occasionally he and Lorna would go at it pretty hard. One time he punched her in the mouth and knocked out her gold tooth, which is a status symbol in the slums. She went wild. Tried to throw a pot of boiling water on him. Tyson and his sister saw the whole fight—even got some water thrown on them."

In Tyson's neighborhood, violence was simply the way you settled problems. Kids laughed at Tyson's lispy voice and glasses, called him "faggy boy" and "sissy." So he hit them—hard. He was good at hitting. "I didn't give a fuck who was my opponent," he told Torres. "I beat up friends and enemies the same way. I even had fights with guys I was afraid of because I was so short and young, and I still kicked their asses."

School officials put him in one of New York's "600" schools for troubled children, which was about as meaningful as giving a starving man a subscription to *GQ.* Juvenile authorities sent him to Spofford, a youth detention center in the Bronx.

Spofford scared him until he realized that everyone there followed the same basic law that governed life on the outside: if you were tough enough, you got respect.

"If you got into a fight with a guy fair and square, then you would get no help," Tyson explained to Torres. "I fucked up a bunch of people that way and I got my ass kicked in once. Some guy hit me in the eye. I think he was a boxer, a Puerto Rican. . . . I said, 'Motherfucker, I'm going to kill you.' . . . So I waited until one morning when he was brushing his teeth, and when his brush was in his mouth, I hit him and he was fucked up. We became good friends after that. It's funny how some people get respect. . . . I got my respect by fucking them up."

The courts would send Tyson to Spofford for a few weeks at a time, but as soon as he got out he would commit a robbery or two and get sent back. Spofford became his country club, a place to go see old friends and make new acquaintances. He was a regular. His crimes were serious, but all the courts could do was slap him on the wrist, about the same as a friendly kiss in Tyson's world. Once he turned eighteen the slap would have more sting, and he would have to do real time in a real prison.

But Tyson got a break, or at least what seemed like a break at the time. Before he was thirteen, the courts shipped him off to the Tryon School for Boys, a reform school in Johnstown in upstate New York. One employee at Tryon was Bobby Stewart, a former National Golden Gloves champion who had enjoyed a short, relatively successful professional career before joining the Tryon staff. Stewart ran a boxing program. During one of Tyson's stays at Spofford, Muhammad Ali visited the institution. Ali and boxing represented an alternative to crime, a socially respectable way for Tyson to channel his rage. Stewart gave Tyson a chance. They sparred and Stewart hit him with a few hard shots, made him look foolish in front of the other inmates, waited for him to get frustrated and quit. "Humiliation . . . that's what I felt," Tyson later told Torres. But Tyson didn't quit. He kept coming back for more punishment and more instruction. Stewart was impressed—with Tyson's drive and especially with the twelve-year-old's punch. Stewart had been a professional, but within several months he couldn't keep Tyson from hurting him in the ring. Tyson, Stewart concluded, was special.

Stewart brought Tyson to D'Amato's attention. Some people believed Cus D'Amato was a genius; others thought he was crazy. Actually he was a little of both. In 1980, when he met Tyson, D'Amato was seventy-two years old, blind in one eye, color-blind in the other, and had difficulty smelling, tasting, and hearing. During the 1950s and 1960s he had been one of the most successful managers and trainers in boxing, while at the same time convincing himself that the underworld was out to get him. One sportswriter dubbed him the Neurotic Napoleon. Age only increased his paranoia. Montieth Illingworth, another of Tyson's biographers, captured the flavor of D'Amato's strangeness: "D'Amato enjoyed food and drink on the town, but he feared that someone would spike his beer, so he stopped going out. He was afraid that someone might drop drugs in his pocket, so he sewed up the pockets of his jackets. When the phone rang, he never spoke first, choosing instead to listen until he could identify the caller. He kept a hatchet under his bed and an ice pick in his pocket." By the end of the 1960s he had fled New York City and lived in semiretirement in a rambling Victorian house in Catskill, New York. There he continued to dabble in boxing, training local fighters and kids.

As Stewart later told Torres, "When Cus first saw Mike spar with me he seemed to be in shock. 'This boy cannot be twelve as I've been told,' Cus said. 'Not with those moves; not with that quickness.' You could see that he was doubtful but hoping to be wrong." He was wrong. Tyson *was* twelve, and he *was* that talented. In Tyson, D'Amato saw raw material he could mold into another heavyweight champion of the world: an angry, distrustful, violent kid who had the reflexes and power of a great athlete.

Torres emphasized that the whole business about "Cus and the Kid" was pure bunk, public relations hype for Charles Kuralt's "Sunday Morning" crowd. D'Amato didn't want to transform Tyson into a kinder, gentler person or reform him into a model citizen. The anger, the suspicion, the brutality— in D'Amato's world, these were desirable characteristics. Balanced psyches are not the stuff of champions. Torres used an odd word when he talked about D'Amato's relationship with Tyson. "Cus," he said, "wanted to engineer a champion." He tried to teach Tyson how to control and channel his violence in the ring. He told him what he told every fighter he worked with: "Boxing is a sport of self-control. You must understand fear so you can manipulate it. Fear is like fire. You can make it work for you: it can warm you in the winter, cook your food when you're hungry, give you light when you are in the dark, and produce energy. Let it get out of control and it can hurt you, even kill you. . . . Fear is a friend of exceptional people."

At first Tyson was suspicious of this old white man and his philosophy, but he listened because he wanted to become a boxer. He figured that he could use D'Amato while D'Amato used him. There were benefits for Tyson. D'Amato convinced the New York State Corrections Department to release Tyson into his custody, and the youth moved from the worst slums of Brooklyn into D'Amato's comfortable rural home. He had a room, enough to eat, spending money, a place to train, and one of the best teachers in the sport. There were also benefits for D'Amato. He was never interested in money—"Money is something to throw off the back of trains," D'Amato liked to say—but he did relish the chance to get back into the action one last time. Over the years D'Amato and Tyson undoubtedly developed a real affection for each other. A common goal united them: the title. And if Tyson's violence and anger spilled out in public every once in a while—if he grabbed a woman or intimidated a teacher or returned for a week to his old Brooklyn haunts and practices—D'Amato chose to overlook the slips, all the time focusing his one eye on the goal.

"Ty-*son* had all the physical abilities," Torres explained. "Cus taught him technique, but more important, he talked philosophy with Mike. Boxing is ninety-nine percent mental and one percent physical. Most boxers are quick and powerful and strong. It's what's here," Torres said, touching his head, "that separates them. It's all mental."

The lies boxers tell had consumed most of Torres's adult life. He himself had lied his way to a championship, mastering D'Amato's art of deception. "Champions and good fighters are champions and good fighters because they can lie better than the others," he wrote in *Sting like a Bee,* his 1971 biography of Muhammad Ali. "The first thing you learn in the gym is that you have to have a double personality if you are to become a good fighter. Basically, you must have the discipline to lie when you're hitting the heavy bag, the speed bag, or human flesh.

"What's a feint? What's a left hook off the jab? What's an opening? What's thinking one thing and doing another? . . . A feint is an outright lie. You *make believe* you're going to hit your opponent in one place, he covers the spot and your punch lands on the other side. A left hook off the jab is a classy lie. You're converting an I into an L. Making an opening is starting a conversation with a guy, so another guy (your other hand) can come and hit him with a baseball bat."

Bad fighters are as simple as a *Dick and Jane* reader; great fighters are as complex as the classics. Judged by Torres and D'Amato's critical standards, Mike Tyson was *Ulysses*. No other boxer, Torres was convinced, lied with the complete conviction of Tyson.

Torres recalled visiting Tyson in Las Vegas during the summer of 1986 when the boxer was preparing to fight Alfonso Ratliff, a six-foot-five-inch heavyweight who could bang with both hands. Vegas was rife with rumors that if Tyson won he would be matched with Trevor Berbick for the heavyweight title. Tyson's camp was electric; their man was a fight away from being the youngest heavyweight champion in history. Torres, who was helping to prepare him for the fight, told Tyson to forget about Berbick and the history books and concentrate only on Ratliff. Tyson appeared to listen. Although Torres knew he was boiling inside, outwardly he appeared so cool. "Man," Torres told him, "you are a much better liar than I ever was. You can hide that anxiety and fear much better than I could ever do." Tyson gave him a tiny, deceptive smile.

In the ring Tyson was brilliant. He hit opponents with punches that came from nowhere. He appeared in places where he wasn't, almost a momentary mirage of himself. Torres was in awe of Tyson's prowess as a fighter, but he had a lower opinion of Tyson as a human being. For a time, Torres and Tyson were very close. He helped D'Amato keep the fighter in line. "Mike was always headstrong," Torres said. "He was impulsive and prone to sudden mood changes. He was easily frustrated and felt dislocated in the white environment of upstate New York. One day he would be Cus's perfect fighter, and the next he'd be gone." He would leave the comforts of D'Amato's Catskill home and return to Brooklyn and his Brownsville haunts, where he would drink a few beers, smoke grass, and run with his old friends. Familiar with the streets, Torres would locate Tyson and persuade him to return to Cus. Back in Catskill, Tyson would hug and baby-talk Cus and the manager would melt. Torres saw several such reunions: "Normally Cus was very disciplined with his boys. He allowed no bullshit. But he treated Mike differently because Mike *was* different. He knew Mike was going to be heavyweight champion of the world. And that promise carried privileges and excused behavior." More than once, Tyson himself admitted to Torres that he was a spoiled brat.

When Barb asked Torres about Tyson's attitude toward women, José shook his head from side to side. He drew in and expelled a deep breath, then confessed, "Mike *always* had a problem with women. Maybe part of it was his mother. You know, she never came to see him during his stay at Tryon School. She never called or wrote him a letter. Not even a Christmas card. Or maybe it was the men around his mother. Mike didn't know his father, and he remembered some bad fights between Eddie and his mother. Or maybe it was just something in Mike that wasn't anybody else's fault."

During his early years in Catskill, Tyson was frustrated by girls. Some laughed at him, calling him "big head" and "fat boy," or ignoring his interest in them. "I'll kick all your asses," Tyson said several times when his frustration had spilled over into anger. "One day when I'm champion, I'll get you." It was almost as if winning the championship would grant him some special authority to punish everyone who had hurt or humiliated him in the past.

D'Amato encouraged this line of thinking. One day D'Amato gave Tyson a baseball bat. "What's this for?" the boxer asked. "For the women," the manager answered. "When you're the champion, you're going to need something to beat them off you."

Although D'Amato's intention was to bolster Tyson's confidence and ego, I thought about the message he was sending: *Win the title and women will desire you. Win the title and then swing away. Win the title and you'll get everything you want. Win the title and you can do anything you want.* It was the privilege of success, the dispensation of the famous.

Torres told Barb and me about Tyson's run-in with Teddy Atlas, his first trainer. Atlas was a disciplinarian who believed that all of Cus's fighters should have to follow the same set of rules. It bothered him that D'Amato used one standard for the other fighters and another—or none—for Tyson. In 1982, Atlas's twelve-year-old sister-in-law told him that Tyson had fondled her. As Torres tells the story, Atlas confronted Tyson in the gym. Aiming a gun at Tyson's head, Atlas told the sixteen-year-old boxer that if he ever touched his sister-in-law again, he was dead. Several weeks later, D'Amato dismissed Atlas. Again, the message to Tyson was clear: *Do what you want. You're special.*

In November 1986, a week before Tyson won his first heavy-weight crown by knocking out Trevor Berbick in the second round, Torres watched Tyson batter sparring partners in Johnny Tocco's Ringside Gym in Las Vegas. Tyson was edgy, mean, impossible for his trainers to get along with. But he seemed genuinely happy to see José. After the workout, Tyson and Torres walked the two or three miles from the gym to the Las Vegas Hilton. At first they talked boxing—technique, strategy, movements. Then Tyson changed the subject to women: "You know something, I like to hurt women when I make love. I like to hear them scream with pain, to see them bleed. It gives me pleasure."

"Why?" Torres asked.

"I don't know."

"You want me to believe that you always thought this was just natural behavior? You're full of shit."

"José, I am that way and I don't know why."

"Well, did it ever occur to you that men who behave that way probably hate women; that deep down they simply don't like them?"

"You may be right. You're the first person to tell me that. . . . You know, you may be fucking right. Holy fucking shit!"

Tyson was intrigued by the conversation. He pressed Torres to continue, to explain to him why he might hate women. "Some men who dislike women at an unconscious level could be considered latent homosexuals," Torres speculated. Tyson listened, now and then shaking his head or asking for more details. No, he decided; he liked women, just women and sex and the sight of pain.

Torres claimed that only two things really interested Tyson: fighting and sex, and in recent years he had even grown bored with the first. Tyson and his Albany friend Rory Holloway once regaled Torres with tales of Tyson's sexual prowess. There was the time in Pennsylvania when Tyson had sex with twenty-four prostitutes in one day. It was nonstop, they told Torres. " 'You—now you—you're next,' just one after another, from five in the afternoon till one in the morning," Holloway told Torres. "He was fucking [one] bitch so hard that the bitch hit the wall and Mike said, 'I made the bitch faint! I made the bitch faint!' " Tyson nodded his agreement. He only liked it better when he inflicted pain.

On another occasion, Tyson told Torres about a fight he had had with Robin Givens, who was then his wife: "She really pissed me off, so I hit her with a kind of backhand punch. José, she hit every fucking wall in the room. It was a great punch. And then she wanted to call the cops from my own fucking telephone. My own telephone! She had some balls. She wanted to call the fucking cops from my own phone."

It was clear from what Torres said about Tyson and how he said it that the two were no longer doing lunch together. Torres had been with Tyson at the start of the fighter's career. And he had stayed with him. He was there to comfort Tyson in early November 1985, when Cus D'Amato died. Torres was there again in late March 1988 when Jim Jacobs, the man who had replaced D'Amato, died. Cus had been old and frail, and Tyson was saddened but not really surprised when he died. Jacobs was different. Tyson didn't know about Jacobs's eight-year battle with leukemia and was devastated, just blown away, by his death. After both deaths, Tyson actually cried on Torres's shoulder. Torres was there too during Tyson's stormy relationship with Robin Givens. Whenever Tyson was hurting, emotionally wounded, Torres was there. Tyson came to his house, ate at his table, talked with his wife, was accepted as a member of his family.

All that changed after Don King moved into Tyson's life. For King, Torres was a link with Tyson's past management, to Cus D'Amato, Jim Jacobs, and especially Bill Cayton, Tyson's manager-of-record whom King wanted to replace. King's goal was to cut Tyson loose from his past and secure the champion in his own kingdom. One after another, the members of Tyson's older support team were fired: Steve Lott, a longtime friend of Jacobs's and the day-to-day manager of Tyson's training camp, went in June 1988; Kevin Rooney, Tyson's trainer and the most visible link to D'Amato, followed in December 1988. Torres's turn came a few months later. A week before Tyson fought Frank Bruno in Las Vegas in February 1989, Torres showed up at the champion's training quarters. Dale Edwards met Torres at the door and told him that the day's workout was private. Torres refused to leave; he had been invited personally by Tyson. Edwards pleaded; he had orders. Finally Rory Holloway came by. "What gives?" Torres asked. "Mike said specifically: 'No José,'" Holloway answered.

"No José." If Tyson had not said that, Torres would never have talked to Barb and me. He was a man of great pride and very much a one-way street. He was devoted to Tyson, but when the boxer publicly turned him away from the gym, that was it. Since that day, Torres told us, he refused to speak to or meet with Tyson. Several times Tyson called him, but Torres hung up the phone when he heard the fighter's voice. If Torres saw Tyson, he turned away. But as he talked there was great sadness in his voice, the kind one hears in the voice of a father talking about a dead son. Torres described Tyson as a low-rent Macbeth, a tragic character because he was unable to control his lust for power, sex, and money.

Toward the end of our conversation, I asked Torres if he thought that Tyson was guilty, if he believed Tyson was capable of rape. "Oh, yes. Absolutely," he answered. Sliding into Freudian jargon, he talked about Tyson's inability to control his libido and the domination of his id. "He takes what he wants. He always has," Torres concluded.

The saddest part was that nobody had much interest in teaching him anything else—not D'Amato, not Jacobs, not King. In fact, Torres observed, they each had a vested interest in keeping Tyson in a childlike state. "If Tyson ever matured, if he ever gained control over his own life, what would he do? I'll tell you. He would get rid of Don King. And King knows that; he's the most intelligent man in boxing. He knows that as long as Mike doesn't grow up he can control his career and fortune. It's that simple. If Mike became his own man, he would be his *own* man."

I asked one final question: "If Tyson takes the witness stand, what can I expect?"

Torres shook his head in doubt. "What would you expect from a spoiled child? Anger? Rage? I don't know. Maybe he'll try to be nice. In the past he's often been able to sweet-talk his way out of trouble. Maybe he'll get mad and try to intimidate you. He's used that tactic before too. Maybe he'll cry. He's easily moved to tears. I just don't know. But one thing is for sure, he'll try to out-think you and give the jurors what they want. Remember, boxers are liars. And Tyson's the best."

On the last page of *Fire and Fear*, Torres tells about a conversation he had with a Jewish survivor of a Nazi concentration camp. "I know what it is to survive," the man said. "I cheated and I lied and I robbed; I became the master of deception and I wounded and killed people. I had six nice, nonviolent, decent brothers and sisters, and they all went straight to the ovens. I was the only one to survive. But I have never recovered." The man compared his past with Tyson's, his amoral struggle to survive with the fighter's. "Only a very few ever recover, and Tyson is not one of them."

The night had turned raw by the time we left Torres's office. The State Police had told us to meet them in Teterboro, where the big corporations with New York offices quarter their Lears, Cessna Citations, and Mitsubishi high-wing jets. We took the subway to Hoboken and then a train to Teterboro, which turned out to be a commuter pimple in New Jersey, a train stop and a small parking lot about two miles from the airport. It was after ten o'clock and just above freezing, and the wind blew a cold rain in our faces. In the distance we saw the lights of the airport. Still hauling our briefcases and other assorted luggage, we headed for the lights, walking along a poorly lit but heavily used section of highway.

The state troopers were waiting for us in a twin-engine Beach Bonanza, which is a slow, unpressurized airplane. Facing us was a sixty-knot head wind. "Settle in," the pilot said. "It's going to take awhile. We may have to stop for fuel because of the wind. I'll let you know later." Barb and I were too tired to care.

Barb stayed awake for about three minutes, then she was gone. I was asleep for nearly an hour when the plane started bouncing all over the sky. It was rough, and we were making very little headway. At one-thirty we had to land in Columbus, Ohio, to refuel.

The trip from Columbus to Indianapolis took an hour. It was my worst plane ride ever. The pilot kept changing altitude, trying to go around the winter storm. The wind buffeted the plane back and forth, and streaks of lightning cut through the darkness. I thought, *This is wonderful. I'm going to die in this airplane because of some street chump who commits a rape in my town.* At times the plane was bouncing so hard that I didn't think at all. I simply recited the Twenty-third Psalm more times, and faster, and the Lord's Prayer more times in a row without taking a breath, than I had ever done in my life.

After we landed I asked the pilot, "How bad was it?" He answered, "Well, on a scale of one to ten, it was about a seven. And if it had been an eight, I wouldn't have wanted to be in that airplane."

The long day was over. My records show twenty-one billable hours for the day of December 12, 1991. Twenty-one hours, including a plane ride that seemed to last a week. But the season of flights had just started. And there were still a few bumpy trips ahead.

## CHAPTER 12

# "ARE SPERM VISIBLE TO THE NAKED EYE?"

**D**esiree Washington arrived in Indianapolis for her deposition early on December 17, 1991. The streets were lined with Christmas wreaths, most of them plastic, a few real. Christmas music tinkled out of the department stores, and the shop windows downtown had that warm feel that made me want to buy something. An army of Santa Clauses had been deployed on every corner, ringing bells and collecting money for soup kitchens. Everything, as my daughter informed me, was "warm fuzzies." Everything except the weather. December was being its disagreeable midwestern self—cold, wet, and uncomfortable.

Ed Gerstein had joined Desiree on the trip from Providence. The only thing that had changed about Ed was his wardrobe. Somewhere he had picked up an oversize scarf that trailed behind him like a kite's tail. Opinionated as ever, he talked nonstop, his monologues dominated by the subjects of the media and the ability of the lawyers from Williams & Connolly. Ed had also acquired the services of an Indianapolis lawyer, Dave Hennessy. As far as I could tell, Hennessy's only function was to provide color—to give geographical directions, intercede with the locals (presumably Barb and me), and disrupt everything now and then with an unintelligible objection—always from left field, and usually without legal authority.

Barb and I spent the morning and afternoon preparing Desiree for the next day's deposition. We walked her through those fateful days in July again, trying to help her anticipate the tone and direction that Vincent Fuller would take. We explained how Fuller or one of his colleagues would approach the more difficult and touchy issues. Repeatedly we went over the cardinal rules of testifying: "Don't guess. Don't argue. Don't volunteer. Answer only the question asked. Tell the truth."

By late afternoon, Desiree was dead tired. She had just finished her first semester at Providence College, completing her exams and then promptly boarding a plane to Indianapolis. She looked even thinner than before, and she seemed worried. Then, of course, there was Ed Gerstein.

Ed was nervous, and I believed that his fears were well founded. During the previous month, as would later be reported in *Sports Illustrated*, influential African-American leaders made a concerted effort to persuade Desiree to drop the case. Sometime in November, several Baptist ministers, including the Reverend T. J. Jemison, head of the eight-million-member National Baptist Convention USA, called Desiree and suggested that for the sake of African-American unity she should not press forward with the trial. Jemison also hinted that Desiree would be generously compensated for such an action.

Desiree told her father Donald about the offer, and he reported the conversation to Gerstein. Ed immediately contacted the FBI. During the next few weeks, the FBI taped several conversations between Donald Washington and Jemison, and it wired Donald for sound when he met with Jemison and several other ministers in a Newport, Rhode Island, hotel room. According to *Sports Illustrated*'s Lester Munson, Jemison initially offered Washington $250,000 if his daughter would drop the charges. In the auctionlike atmosphere, Jemison quickly upped the ante to $500,000 and finally $1,000,000. What Jemison did not know was that an FBI agent and Desiree were sitting in a parked car outside the hotel listening to the auction.

When Desiree and Gerstein arrived in Indianapolis, the investigation of the offers was still underway. The FBI wanted to know who was bankrolling the money, and it was organizing an elaborate sting operation, which ultimately collapsed. Desiree and Gerstein were both visibly shaken by all the cloak-and-dagger goings on.

"Come here," Ed would say to Desiree, "we need to talk." Then again, fifteen minutes later: "Des, how are you doing? You need a break?" Occasionally he would call me out of the room, only to inform me one more time: "I'm telling you, these assholes don't play fair—you don't know what they can do. They're out there saying things to the media right now. This thing is going to get ugly. You don't know these people. They'll stop at nothing." "Like what, Ed?" I would ask. "I'm telling you, these motherfuckers play for keeps. They're dangerous. They do whatever they want. This is really going to get messy." He had me imagining everything from a bomb hooked up to my car to the appearance of a surprise witness who would testify that she was in the suite with Tyson and Desiree. By the end of the day I was as jumpy as an inbred dog, and I could only wonder how Desiree felt. I noticed at lunch that she ate as though she was getting ready for an operation.

The deposition experience turned out to be worse than I anticipated. After agreeing to meet Barb and me at 9:00 A.M. at the prosecutor's office in the Municipal Court section, which was in Market Square Tower, the same building as the court reporter's office, where the deposition was scheduled for 9:30, Gerstein and Hennessy, with Desiree trailing behind, showed up *late*. When Gerstein was late for several other meetings, I realized that timing was part of his power play: show up late; get lost or delayed coming back from lunch; argue over the location of the next meeting; interfere with scheduling based on some fanciful concern over media coverage, or on Desiree's supposed need for rest. It was always the same. By keeping everyone guessing, keeping time by some hidden clock, he maintained control.

When we arrived at Associated Reporting Services, the Williams & Connolly people had already set up. Vincent Fuller, whom I had yet to meet, stood at the far end of a long table, peering out of the ninth-story window at the City Market below. A quiet man who had recently turned sixty, conservatively but expensively dressed, he was shorter than I expected. He glanced at me without turning his body in my direction, then looked back out the window.

For over thirty years, Fuller had lived the life of a defense lawyer, often living out of a suitcase, eating in hotels, and working late into the night. His face showed the years of flannel combat; beneath the neatly trimmed gray hair, deep lines intensified the expression of his pale blue eyes—eyes that had seen more courtrooms and more drama than had those of all but a small handful of other American lawyers. Looking at him from across the room, I felt not intimidation, but excitement and admiration. Out of respect, I made the first move. As I walked toward him, I watched his face reflected in the window for some sign of who he was or what he felt. Nothing.

His handshake was firm, a cross between *Good to meet you* and *Don't fuck with me.* I looked squarely into his eyes, which were open and friendly, but then again a bit shy. I made some small talk, wanting to observe him, hear his voice, engage him. He responded in kind about the weather, the hotel, the trip from D.C. Then we moved toward our seats to begin work, both, I think, satisfied with the cut of the other.

I also said hello to James Voyles, the local lawyer Tyson had retained in the case. Voyles was one of the most highly regarded defense attorneys in Indiana. We had been working different sides of the street for several decades, but I admired his integrity and liked him as a person. We smiled and shook hands and played grab-ass for a while, talking about the Indy 500 or some such thing. I had heard that Voyles would spend most of his time in this trial sitting and watching, and that worried me. If the Williams & Connolly people could afford to stick Voyles at the end of the bench, they must be some kind of lawyers.

Before settling down, I walked over to Fuller's co-counsel, who sat at the middle of the table, fidgeting with a two-hundred-dollar Montblanc pen. She sensed my approach without looking up, becoming rigid, motionless, and feigning preoccupation with her notes. Thirtysomething, wearing no makeup, she had a haircut that looked as though it came out of Fort Benning. She had on some sort of boring suit that was supposed to look businesslike. She was either terrified or angry; probably the latter, since her ears were red, her neck blotchy, and her hands shaking. I said, "Hi, my name is Greg Garrison," and stuck out my hand. She didn't even raise her eyes. I waited a few seconds, then decided to keep standing there with arm extended, a statue to the legal profession, until she acknowledged my presence. I was beginning to wonder how long I could keep my arm outstretched, feeling as though I was holding a dumbbell straight out from my shoulder, when finally, without looking up, she slid a wet hand across mine. It felt like a freshly caught mackerel in cold water. And that was that. She didn't say a word, and quickly returned to her papers.

I had been informed that her name was Kathleen Beggs, "Kate" to her friends, though I was not one and it was difficult for me to imagine who they might have been. The circumstances of her first affiliation with Fuller, as I learned later, made an interesting story. Fuller had once defended her father, James Beggs, a former NASA administrator whom the government had charged with defrauding the Department of Defense. Fuller won a complete dismissal of the charges and an official apology from the government. I don't know if there was any connection between that case and her joining Williams & Connolly, but by the time of the Tyson trial she was a full partner. Barb also picked up some gossip from reporters for the *New York Times* and the *Washington Post,* who had observed Beggs and Fuller together at private dinners. Beggs, the reporters claimed, constantly looked after Fuller in the manner of a loving older daughter.

That was what Barb had heard, but I never had a chance to judge what psychological wires bound the two together. I knew only one thing for certain: from the get-go, Kathleen Beggs disliked me, and my feeling for her was not cordial. During the next two months we didn't exchange five minutes of conversation that could by any standard be judged pleasant. Every time we were thrown together, categorically every time, she never failed to pick a fight. More than any lawyer I had ever known, she had a singular knack for being disagreeable, argumentative, and rude. Perhaps her function was to get under the skin of the opposition attorneys, to distract them with her rudeness from her client's crime. She had the gift. I certainly didn't think she had been brought along for her legal abilities, which were, at the least, mismatched for this case. In this first and all subsequent engagements, she seemed obsessed with discovering signs of collusion or impropriety but ignorant of important aspects of the case. At any given moment she was liable to charge Gerstein or Hennessy with signaling the witness or Barb and me with not saving her a copy of something. Then she would say something absolutely off the wall. My personal favorite was when she asked a physician, "Are sperm visible to the naked eye?"

Pleasantries out of the way, the deposition started. Surprise: Kathleen Beggs, not Vincent Fuller, asked the questions. The accuser, one of the case's two primary figures, was not deposed by the defendant's top gun. Beggs immediately sent a negative ion charge through the proceeding by complaining that Desiree, Barb, and I had arrived late and that wasn't right and we had bad manners and *blah, blah, blah.* "Well, fine," I responded. "You made your point. Now ask your questions."

Oh, no, not yet. She wanted to know what the other two lawyers, Gerstein and Hennessy, were doing at the deposition. Before I could answer—not that I had a good response—Gerstein waded in: "Well, we're here on behalf of Miss Washington." Beggs: "Well, do you represent her?" Gerstein: "No, we're here as observers. We're not involved in the criminal case." Beggs: "Well, what is your function? Are you going to observe or are you going to be on the record? And if you will be on the record, we object." Gerstein: *Blah, blah, blah.* Beggs: *Blah, blah, blah.* I looked at my watch, scratched my head, and leaned back in my chair. Shutting my eyes, I listened to two people say more about nothing than I had ever heard before in my life.

When Beggs and Gerstein had finished pissing on the ground to mark their territory, Beggs turned on Desiree—and I mean turned on her. Accusatory, arrogant, unkind, and mean-spirited—Kathleen Beggs began to fry Desiree Washington. I had never seen anything like it in a deposition in a criminal case. From a strategic standpoint, such an attack was stupid. She should have been sweet and kind and all-understanding, at least at first, and tried to finesse information that would help strengthen Tyson's case against Desiree. Instead, she knocked Desiree into a defensive shell. Desiree sat frozen, occasionally fighting back tears, one moment intimidated and afraid, the next hurt, even angry, at Beggs's condescending manner. But beyond being ill-conceived, Beggs's approach was just one of unvarnished, inexcusable rudeness.

So it continued. Beggs picked on Desiree, talked down to her, smarted off to her, and generally treated her badly. I objected some, but it's difficult to charge someone with behaving

abominably during a deposition. After ten minutes I had a bel-
lyful of this particular Williams & Connolly lawyer, and I had to
struggle to keep my mouth shut. By the time we broke for
lunch, my arms ached from the tension of the morning.

I hoped things would get better afterward, but no such luck.
Gerstein and Hennessy had taken Desiree to lunch with them,
and they returned late for the afternoon session. Beggs complained, and there was another battle over some trivial point.
When she resumed her questioning of Desiree, it became clear
to me that she was operating on the basis of ineptitude rather
than according to some devious strategy. She would tiptoe beyond an issue, beside it, or just short of it without ever managing
to step on it. When she asked questions about the rape itself, she
demonstrated a supreme insensitivity to the woman whose
nightmare she was dissecting. As Beggs posed her questions, I
kept my eyes on Desiree. Some of the questions hurt her deeply,
while others simply mystified her. Beggs's cumbersome, clumsy,
and generally inarticulate queries led me to wonder if she had
any idea how sex is actually performed. There were times when
Desiree would look at her in a searching way, as if to ask *Where's
this person coming from? What planet was she raised on?*

Jim Voyles could have taken Desiree's deposition in three
hours, but Beggs just kept circling and circling. And every so
often Gerstein would stretch his vocal cords. I should have told
him to get out, but he had half convinced me—though not
Barb—that without him Desiree would leave the case.

The deposition had to be resumed the next day, and if Fuller
had not had a plane to catch, it might have lasted even longer.
Not that it would have helped their case any; Beggs seemed far
more intent on insulting Desiree than on gaining an understanding of the facts.

The result was a discovery effort where nothing was discovered. The deposition should have helped Tyson's case, but instead it aided Desiree's. Because of Beggs's rough, boorish,
assault-ridden deposition, neither she nor Fuller had any idea
of how good Desiree would be on the stand. Beggs would make
other significant errors before and during the trial, but none
was more egregious than her brutal treatment of Desiree in
that deposition.

Barb and I walked out of the conference room tired, angry,
and a lot more knowledgeable about our opposition. "If this is

any indication of what they're going to throw at us, we're going to win," Barb said. I agreed. I couldn't imagine Kathleen Beggs presenting her witnesses and cross-examining ours without alienating every member of the jury.

Only once was Vincent Fuller a force during the deposition. On the second day I lost my temper and shouted at Beggs. Fuller put on his best Daddy face and said, "Keep your voice down! Keep your voice down! Don't yell." "You want someone to keep quiet, you tell her to be quiet," I shot back, much to my own surprise. He suppressed a smile, and we went on. That night I wondered what was behind that half-smile. Had he allowed Beggs to run the deposition so he could concentrate on us? Was she there simply to get on our nerves, to show how we functioned under stress? As I struggled unsuccessfully to get to sleep, I wrestled with the idea that I had unknowingly taken a critical test. And I was not at all certain that I had passed.

Christmas came a few days early for Mike Tyson—or perhaps for J. Morris Anderson. On December 18 Anderson held a press conference to announce that after meeting with Tyson's lawyers he had decided to drop his $607 million suit against Tyson and Black Expo. He talked about everything except whether or not any money had changed hands. "I really, really, really investigated this thing," Anderson told reporters. When all the facts were in, he concluded that he had been lied to by the women who had accused Mike Tyson of all those bad things. Tyson was not the "serial buttocks fondler" Anderson had maintained in his lawsuit, and the Reverend Charles Williams had not brought Tyson to Indianapolis "to feast on the flesh of the Miss Black America Pageant Queens."

Anderson claimed that Miss Black America of 1990, Rosie Jones, and several others had fabricated stories about Tyson to attract attention to themselves in order to get on television talk shows. They "were telling outright lies specifically for the purpose of obtaining publicity." Anderson was shocked—shocked and hoodwinked—by their actions. In addition, he had entertained "second thoughts about participating in the crucifixion of a black role model."

I was both amused and angered by all the posturing. Once again, a black man was calling black women liars. No one had forced Anderson to sue Tyson; as old George Washington Plunkett used to say, he had just seen his opportunity and taken it. But after the settlement he used the contestants in his own pageant as scapegoats. And comparing Tyson to Christ a week before Christmas was obscene. I didn't care if Anderson had succeeded in obtaining a small piece of Tyson's fortune, but to suggest that the boxer was being crucified went too far.

If Anderson was in a Christmas mood, so were Tyson and Don King. The boxer and the promoter gave Indiana Black Expo a check for $17,000 to buy two thousand Christmas turkeys and all the fixings to distribute among needy families in Indianapolis. Al Hobbs, vice president of WTLC-FM radio and one of the sponsors of the We Can Feed the Hungry Program, said that the gift was in no way prompted by Tyson's upcoming trial. In 1989 Tyson and King had paid for three hundred turkeys; they had upped that number to five hundred in 1990. In 1991 they just happened to be in a 300 percent more giving mood. "For people to suggest that Tyson is trying to buy favors is a low blow," Hobbs commented.

When contacted for a comment, I noted the "striking coincidence" between the timing of the Tyson giveaway and that of the start of the trial. Jeff Modisett agreed, saying, "I think it is transparently obvious" why Tyson and King donated the turkeys. "I am sure the people of Marion County are wise enough to see through this." When Modisett took some heat from the Indianapolis black community, including Black Expo, WTLC, and the Interdenominational Ministerial Alliance and the Concerned Clergy, he apologized for his remarks. It was one of those times I was glad I never went into politics. Modisett had been perfectly correct; the motive for the giveaway was transparently obvious. But *bon appetit*. The gesture did not affect the case, and two thousand people received Christmas turkeys.

Barb and I bought our turkeys in the supermarket as usual and tried to pretend that our lives were normal. Barb took Christmas Eve and Christmas day off—the only two days between November 1 and the end of the trial that she didn't work on the case. My parents and family gathered at my house, where we fed the fires in an attempt to keep out the cold blowing in from the fields. Talk of the trial was unavoidable. Tyson should have joined us for dinner to answer all the questions my father wanted to ask him. In any case, the boxer's presence was felt as surely as if he had been sitting at the table.

I had to feed the horses anyway, so my cousin David and I decided to take a ride. We have always been as close as brothers, and he knows my moods, understands intuitively when to talk and when to remain silent. He left me alone with my thoughts. The trial was scheduled to start on January 27, and Judge Patricia Gifford had made it clear that it would begin on that day. More than two weeks earlier, she had denied Fuller's petition for a sixty- or ninety-day delay. I knew that the next six weeks would be the busiest of my life. Williams & Connolly would try to stretch the prosecution to the snapping point with motions, petitions, and depositions. They would pull Barb and me across the country to depose or watch them depose scores of potential witnesses. Although Deputy Prosecutor George E. Horn, Jr., had recently joined the trial team and was working as hard as anyone to prepare the case, the January 27 deadline loomed like Mount Everest on the horizon. As I rode, I doubted we would be ready.

At some point between Christmas and New Year's I stopped dreaming. When my head touched the pillow each night, it was as though I was hit by a six-foot wave. I slept like a dead man, sound and deep, but never for long. Each night for the next month and a half I would waken two or three times and imagine arguing this point or presenting that witness. I anticipated the dramatic portions of the trial, rehearsing the words I would use and the tone of voice. I planned when to get tough and when to soften, how to introduce a piece of evidence and how to create a particular mood. Gradually I became familiar with what I would ask and what each witness would answer. But there were important parts of the trial that would not speak to me in the nights, and that worried me.

Dreamless at night, I moved through the daylight hours of the next month as if in a nightmare: I would run as fast as I could but never seemed to get anywhere. I was in a race, running in waist-deep water, and my opponent was speeding across dry land. Williams & Connolly had scheduled depositions from one end of the country to the other. We tried to overcome our lack of resources with organization. Barb and George Horn, occasionally accompanied by Jeff Duhamell, attended depositions west of the Mississippi River; Tommy Kuzmik and I attended those to the east. In twenty-seven days the two teams took fifty-two depositions in fifteen different states. In Indianapolis Dave Dreyer, aided by research assistants Kim Devane and Erika Roach, contended with the stacks of motions and petitions generated by Williams & Connolly. And Dave Wagner, the paralegal for the prosecutor's office, filed and organized the results of everyone's efforts.

Between depositions I interviewed and prepared witnesses I planned to use in the trial. It didn't take a rocket scientist to predict which witnesses would be the most important. A rapist has only three defenses, each one of which is powerful. He can claim that there was no sexual intercourse, that the woman consented, or that it was not him. Tyson had confessed that he did have sexual intercourse with Desiree, thus eliminating two of the three defenses. He based his plea of innocence on consent, banking that in the absence of witnesses Desiree could not prove he raped her any more than he could prove he did not. Scattered across the country were dozens of Miss Black America contestants, women who would occupy most of my energies during the month before the trial, who knew nothing about what happened in Suite 606 in the early hours of July 19. The most important witnesses lived in Indianapolis. Virginia Foster's testimony was essential because she had seen Tyson in action in the hours leading up to the rape and had seen Desiree minutes after the rape. But Virginia's testimony, regardless of how effective it was, would not be enough to overcome Tyson's consent defense. From my first full day on the case, I knew that the trial would swing on the doctors' testimony.

At eight o'clock on the morning of December 27, I met Dr. Thomas Richardson in Modisett's office in the City-County Building. Richardson had just come off a twenty-four shift in the emergency room, and he was still in his scrubs, tired, and ready to go home. He didn't have the Hollywood profile of Vince Edwards or Richard Chamberlain, but Richardson's job description was straight out of "Ben Casey" or "Dr. Kildare." He saw the critical cases coming into his hospital, men and women who had been shot, stabbed, peeled off telephone poles, and snatched from fires. As part of the Lifeline helicop-

*Mike Tyson was never short on support. Even though he was on trial for rape, hundreds of people were always waiting to shake his hand.*

*Before she met Mike Tyson, Desiree Washington dreamed of being elected president. She was a high school athlete, an honor student, and a contestant in the Miss Black America pageant.*

*Jeffrey Modisett (center) was elected prosecutor for Marion County less than a year before Mike Tyson raped Desiree Washington. A Democrat, he had received strong support in Indianapolis's African-American community. Modisett chose Barbara Trathen from the prosecutor's office (left) and J. Gregory Garrison from outside his office to present the State's case.*

*Tommy Kuzmik (left) and Greg Garrison discuss the case. Kuzmik, an investigator in the Indianapolis Police Department's sex crimes division, coordinated the case.*

*Tyson (center) was presented by Vincent Fuller (left) and Kathleen Beggs (right) of the Washington, D.C., firm of Williams & Connolly. Fuller, one of the nation's leading criminal attorneys, had gained national attention with his defense of John Hinckley, Jr.*

*Indianapolis attorney James Voyles (left) and F. Lane Heard III of Williams & Connolly also provided legal aid for Tyson. Heard examined many of the beauty contestant witnesses. Voyles seemed closer to Tyson than the other attorneys.*

*Judge Patricia Gifford made several controversial rulings during the trial. The daughter of an army colonel, she had a firm sense of justice and a chilly courtroom demeanor.*

*The jury was instructed to judge the case on the presented facts and to forget that Mike Tyson was one of the most famous men in the world.*

*Tanya Levette St. Clair-Gills, one of the Miss Black America contestants, suggested that Desiree Washington was after Mike Tyson's body and money. Her stories, however, struck most listeners as pure fiction.*

*Dale Edward, Tyson's bodyguard, testified before a special grand jury. What he said supported Tyson's account of the episode, but his testimony wildly differed from that of a half-dozen other witnesses. He did not testify during the trial.*

*Support for Tyson was visible and vocal before,
during, and after the trial.*

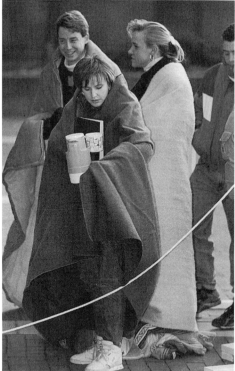

*Despite the winter cold, spectators waited
throughout the night in long lines for
one of the seventeen public access tickets
to the trial. Surrounding the proceedings
was a rock concert atmosphere.*

*Mike Tyson (left) watched as the Reverend T. J. Jemison, head of the eight-million-
member National Baptist Convention USA, speaks at a Tyson rally at the Christ
Missionary Church in Indianapolis. It would later be alleged that Jemison offered
Desiree Washington one million dollars to drop her case against Tyson.*

*Tyson moved through the halls of the Indianapolis City-County Building as if he were pushing toward a prize ring, surrounded by photographers, well-wishers, and bodyguards. Camille Ewald (front), Tyson's stepmother, had been his most faithful supporter for more than a decade.*

*Don King, Tyson's flamboyant and controversial promoter, was no stranger to the courtroom. He had served time for killing a man but, with the help of Vincent Fuller, had escaped conviction on income tax evasion charges.*

*No longer a free man, Mike Tyson prepares to enter the Reception Diagnostic Center in Plainfield, Indiana. Although some boxing analysts had suggested that the trajectory of his life pointed toward prison, the road from the championship to incarceration seemed remarkably short.*

*Alan Dershowitz, whose clients have included Claus von Bülow, Michael Milken, and Leona Helmsley, took on Tyson's appeal and demanded justice for the fighter. By upholding Tyson's conviction, the Indiana Court of Appeals dispensed that justice.*

*Greg Garrison, worn down by death threats and lack of sleep, was satisfied after the verdict in* State v. Tyson *that Desiree Washington and Mike Tyson had received justice.*

ter team at Methodist Hospital, he treated life-threatening coronary and neurological cases, and he examined far too many women who had been raped.

Richardson was a young man with a pleasant voice, and we hadn't talked very long before I knew that he also had quiet but genuine compassion. Although at the time Richardson examined Desiree in the early hours of the day after she had been raped he had been busier than a lawyer at a public draft card burning, he remembered her and vividly recalled her demeanor.

She was scared and withdrawn, agitated but not confrontational, Richardson said. Carol Orbison, a sex crimes specialist from the prosecutor's office, interviewed Richardson with me, and she nodded in agreement as Richardson described Desiree's behavior. She had heard it all before, this nightmare of the rape victim. Struggling mentally between outrage and denial, the woman asks one moment, "How could he do this to me?" and the next moment finds herself hoping, "None of this is real. This didn't happen to me."

The exam only extended Desiree's nightmare. She had been required to disrobe, lie on her back, place her feet in stirrups, spread her legs apart, and allow a complete stranger, a man, to examine her. Part of the problem was immediately obvious to Richardson: she had two small but visible vaginal abrasions. Richardson noted her discomfort but continued the standard "rape kit" examination, which involves some vaginal exploration with various swabbings, scrapings, and combings for evidence. Richardson said that when he touched the metal speculum to the introital area of her vagina, Desiree cried out in pain and almost backed off the table. At that point he decided to end the examination. He knew that she had showered and washed repeatedly in the more than twenty-four hours since the rape, and the chance of discovering any evidence was minimal. Richardson believed that her emotional and physical discomfort from the examination outweighed any possible evidentiary discoveries. He was right. The rape kit was meaningless; we didn't have to prove that Tyson and Desiree engaged in sexual intercourse. The issue was consent.

And the injuries spoke to that issue. I asked Richardson if he had ever seen the sort of injuries Desiree had suffered that had resulted from consensual sex. Twice, he answered, twice in the up to three thousand pelvic exams he had conducted. Of those two, he believed that one woman was lying because she was afraid of how her husband would react, and the other told him a story that involved large quantities of alcohol and a rugby team.

As we spoke, I tried to evaluate the impression Richardson would make on the witness stand. What he had to say, the evidence he had to offer, was powerful. But I had been in the trial business long enough to learn one thing: evidence doesn't win cases; witnesses win cases. I saw both strengths and liabilities in Richardson as a potential witness. He was compassionate and friendly, and he had an important story to tell, but the idea of testifying with the lens of the international media focused on him made his hands sweat. He was unaccustomed to legal proceedings and had no experience testifying in a high-profile case. Several of the forensic pathology people I knew, physicians for whom testifying in major trials was almost part of their job description, worried that Richardson might get beaten up in cross-examination because of his lack of experience. But I sensed a real strength of character. Richardson was a journeyman physician, good at his job, and tested panic-proof. With some preparation the jury would see him for exactly what he was—the man who saves your life when you are already over the edge.

Looking for an expert to support Richardson's generalizations, I talked with Dr. James Nocon, an associate professor of medicine in ob/gyn at the Indiana University Medical Center with whom Dave Dreyer had discussed the case. Nocon had the credentials of the perfect witness: aside from being a doctor and a former flight surgeon in Vietnam who had also flown an F-4 Phantom, he was a card-carrying lawyer with litigation experience. He had a manner, self-confident with a touch of swagger, that would impress any juror. I took one look at him and thought, *Man, he's going to be one King Kong of a witness.*

But when I reviewed the facts with him and asked his opinion, suddenly the swagger disappeared and he started crawfishing. "Naw, you know, it can happen both ways," he said. "I just don't know. You know, you can't say."

I had a woman who said she'd been raped; I had clean proof of vaginal abrasions, and a doctor who said that when he tried to examine her she almost jumped off the table; I had blood on her panties at spots consistent with where those abrasions were located. In short, I had a damn good case, and Nocon was try-ing to poke holes in it.

Finally I cut to the chase: "Now, look," I asked him. "What gives here? This is good evidence. You know it is; you said as much earlier to Dave Dreyer. And I need you." It took awhile, but eventually I caught on. Nocon, for all his swagger, didn't want to testify. His tenure decision at the medical center was pending, and he was a lobbyist for an Indiana medical associa-tion. He was concerned about both appearances and his own availability, since the legislature would be in session during the trial. With the issue of whether he would be asked to testify out of the way, he relaxed and agreed with my interpretation of the facts, saying he would help as much as he could. He advised me to talk to Dr. James Akin, another member of the staff who was a reproductive endocrinologist and infertility specialist.

No sooner had Nocon mentioned the name than who should walk past the door but Akin, a young doctor with a baby face and a voice that hadn't quite finished changing. Nocon called him in and quickly reduced the case to a medical question: "You do postcoital exams all the time on women trying to get pregnant. Abrasions located at twelve and three o'clock. Is that consistent or inconsistent with consensual sex?" Akin answered without hesitation: "Yeah, I've done thousands of postcoital examinations. I've never seen a woman with a vaginal abrasion, ever, who wasn't raped."

I could have kissed him. I asked if he would testify to that in the Tyson trial, and he gave a nervous yes. Not only would he testify, he would do so for free, even though it was the normal practice to pay expert witnesses for their time and expenses. The more we talked over the next few weeks, the more my con-fidence grew in Dr. Akin. So what if he was nervous and his voice cracked; like all gifted teachers, he could make a complex subject seem simple. And as a specialist on infertility, he would wow the jury. Most female jurors were familiar with one woman or another who was profoundly grateful to a reproductive en-docrinologist. They were the storks of the medical profession.

**B**etween talks with the chief prosecution witnesses, I roamed the East Coast and the South taking depositions. Slowly, almost imperceptibly, it began to dawn on me that the prosecution and the defense were preparing to try different cases. What I believed was important didn't seem to interest the lawyers at Williams & Connolly, and what they thought was important seemed trivial to me. The doctors' stories were the prime examples of this failure to connect. Akin's testimony had the potential to put Tyson in prison, or at least it seemed so to me. But when Beggs and Fuller deposed Akin, they treated him like the redheaded bastard at the family reunion. They had to go through the motions and be in the same room with him, but they seemed uninterested in what he had to say. Once again Beggs asked the questions, and I suspected that she had not done her homework. Her questions hit everything but the mark, and she seemed singularly unimpressed with the fact that Akin had performed twenty thousand postcoital examinations and never seen vaginal abrasions that resulted from consensual sex.

I didn't treat the defense's physicians so lightly. My life had been spent in the company of physicians. My father was a country doctor who over the years had delivered babies on our family pool table and sewed up farmers who had misjudged the mendacity of tractors. My cousin David, too, was a doctor. And as a homicide prosecutor I had always depended on forensic pathologists to help me piece together what happened, how it happened, and when it happened. I respected physicians, and liked most of the ones I met. In fact, my opinion of physicians was almost as high as their opinion of themselves.

Doctors are used to being listened to, accustomed to giving orders and passing judgments. The younger ones rarely admit to ignorance of any subject, and when in doubt they resort to a language that few understand. They know that people, lawyers and jurors included, will believe anything phrased in language they do not understand. I've seen the reaction: "Ah, well, I don't know what that doctor just said, but it sounded right. He must know what he's talking about." I don't know how many times I've wanted to interrupt some medical explanation by a physician by simply saying, "Bullshit. You know it is, and so do I."

To protect myself and my victims from their medical mumbo jumbo, I learned to speak a bit of physicianese. And before interviewing, deposing, or cross-examining a doctor I would do enough homework to acquaint myself with the issues and vocabulary involved in the particular case. As long as you never challenge their professionalism, most doctors don't mind if you politely disagree with them.

Williams & Connolly placed two physicians on their witness list, both of whom I deposed. The first was a doctor based in Washington, D.C., who admitted during the deposition that it was highly unlikely for a woman to sustain visible introital abrasions during consensual sexual intercourse. Once he had made that confession, his effectiveness as a witness was undermined, and he was never called to testify. The other physician was Dr. Margaret Watanabe, an obstetrician and gynecologist who was an instructor at the Indiana University Medical Center. Peggy Watanabe was a delightful person, a woman who had earned a doctorate in microbiology and immunology before entering medical school. Williams & Connolly had chosen her to testify because she was willing to say that the abrasions that Desiree had sustained could have resulted from consensual sex.

It doesn't take long to depose a doctor because everyone knows what he or she is there to say. After reading the medical literature on the subject—which is vague about the relationship between introital injuries and consensual sex—I knew that Watanabe would not be able to support her opinion with any firm scholarship. When I asked her about the incidence of such injuries, she resorted to anecdotal evidence. "I've seen it before," she said. "I've seen introital abrasions on women who attributed those to consensual sex."

"How many times?" I asked.

She said she had seen one just the other day, a woman with an abrasion the size of a thumbnail

"Well, how many others?"

"Well, I don't know. I mean, they happen."

"How many?"

She finally answered that she had seen two or three—two or three in about twenty thousand pelvic exams. Bingo! Peggy Watanabe had just become more my witness than the defense's. Attempting to hide the importance of what she had just said, I started to pick on her gently. "How could that be?" I asked. "What are you talking about?" "I know," she openly responded. "I don't understand. I wasn't there, but that's what the women told me."

And that is the issue. Physicians have to take at face value what they are told. The more experienced ones are suspicious, but only the woman can say she was raped. My guess, based on the medical literature and talking with physicians and sex crimes prosecutors, is that women get raped by their husbands, raped by their boyfriends, raped by an acquaintance or a stranger, and they just don't want to tell anybody what happened. When their doctors ask about the cause of their abrasions, they say it happened during normal sex.

After deposing Watanabe, I was sure that all the physicians who testified during the trial would tell essentially the same story. And that story would nail Mike Tyson.


By mid-January, deep winter had set in from Indianapolis to Boston to Atlanta, the kind of winter that made you doubt the eventuality of spring. Everywhere I traveled to take a deposition, the weather reports were the same—cold with more cold to come. But the anxiety that my time was running out kept me warm enough to sweat. The closer we got to January 27, the more certain I was that we would not be prepared when the trial started. It seemed as if I was spending most of my time on airplanes and trains and accomplishing nothing of substance. Half a dozen times a day I panicked. Just as many times a day, Barb and I would discuss the case on the phone, comparing results of depositions and adding lines to our list of things to check. The list seemed to get longer, not shorter, as we moved closer to selecting a jury.

Part of the reason that the list kept growing was that several of the beauty contestants who had supported Desiree's story in their statements to the police and the grand jury had begun to have second thoughts. Somehow memories that they had suppressed for six months were returning with unnatural clarity. I was particularly concerned about Pasha Oliver, Desiree's roommate who had been a stalwart supporter in her grand jury testimony and her early conversations with Kuzmik, Barb, and me. She seemed different in her deposition, more distant and guarded, as if she was trying to soften the ground for her own suit against Tyson. I suspected that several other contestants had come under the influence of people who supported Tyson, perhaps friends from home, perhaps just friends of Tyson's. Suddenly stories surfaced reporting that Desiree had said that she was going to get her share of Tyson's fortune or that Tyson had the kind of ass she liked. Most of the statements now being attributed to Desiree would have made a streetwalker blush; everyone who knew Desiree said that she simply didn't use that sort of language. But the new stories concerned me, adding to the suspicion that we needed more time to investigate the potential witnesses.

Frank Valentine was the most mysterious person on Williams & Connolly's witness list. A relative of Aleta Anderson and a close friend of Parquita Nassau, a contestant from Georgia, he had helped out with the Miss Black America pageant. According to several people, Valentine had said that he had a conversation with Desiree in which she said that she was going to be the next Robin Givens. We wanted to depose him before he took the stand, but we couldn't locate him. The address we had for him was no good. His telephone had been disconnected. The defense lawyers, particularly F. Lane Heard III at Williams & Connolly, said they too had had trouble reaching Valentine. Heard said he would try to set up the deposition, but it never happened. Finally, a few days before the start of the trial, we tracked him down in a small town in southern Georgia.

George Horn flew down to take the deposition. Lane Heard, a charming young lawyer with a Texas drawl and an unassuming manner, showed up for the defense. George pinned Valentine down on what he had heard and when, and in the course of the deposition, he asked Valentine how he kept in touch with Williams & Connolly. Valentine looked surprised, as if George had asked a stupid question, then answered, "Tyson's lawyers have my pager number." I wondered how many more tricks might have been played along the way. Williams & Connolly's lawyers were used to battling with big boys in the federal courts, where the procedure is basically trial by ambush. They weren't accustomed to the wide-open discovery rules of the county courts, and they weren't in a big hurry to be friendly.

As the pace became more frenetic, I worked longer hours, slept fewer, and worried more. Ten days before the trial I caught a chest cold that moved up to my head—sore throat, plugged-up ears, runny nose, the works. During a flight to Atlanta in an unpressurized State Police airplane, my ears began to hemorrhage. I felt like a human guinea pig in an endurance test. The cold contributed to the stress as I imagined myself in the courtroom not being able to hear or speak and blowing my nose every ten seconds. Justice was supposed to be blind, not deaf, dumb, and sick. An ear, nose, and throat specialist prescribed some huge horse pills for me to take, and luckily I regained my voice and hearing a day or two before the start of the trial.

By then we had done all the major depositions and were back to follow-up interviews and preparation of our witnesses, particularly Virginia Foster, Chris Low, McCoy Wagers, Thomas Richardson, and James Akin. We had also moved into a new set of offices in Superior Court V. Security changed the locks and keys and posted guards twenty-four hours a day outside the rooms. We covered the walls of the main office with construction paper summarizing all our exhibits and what each witness, ours and theirs, was likely to say. Across the top of a matrix grid were the names of the various witnesses; running down the side were the exhibits. The idea was to allow Barb and me to see quickly which witnesses would talk about which exhibits. Looking at the grid, we could follow the line of any one exhibit and find out which would be the most or least discussed. We did the same thing with the elements of proof. The grid showed the elements we wanted to stress—state of mind, physical injuries, corroborative testimony. By the first day of the trial the room looked like an air traffic control tower, with strings and wires and tape and lines running from one grid to another.

There was one defense exhibit, however, that we couldn't place on our grid. Someone at Williams & Connolly had hired a local craftsman to build a three-dimensional scale model of Suite 606 at the Canterbury. It was a piece of dollhouse perfection. Everything in the room had been faithfully reproduced, down to the chairs, lamps, bed, television set, and the colors of the draperies and carpet. The model must have cost a thousand dollars. We couldn't figure out what the hell they were going to do with it. What was it about the layout of those rooms that was so important? We speculated and scratched our heads but got nowhere.

We never discovered why it was important because the model never left Jim Voyles's office. Williams & Connolly didn't use it, mark it, or bring it to court. Maybe it was just an effort to spook us into worrying about some nonissue. If so, it worked.

On Saturday and Sunday, January 25 and 26, we finished the last details. Jury selection would begin on Monday. After working on the case all day Saturday, I took my wife out for dinner to a small gourmet restaurant in Noblesville. Stacy was dressed beautifully in clothes she had received for Christmas, and I bought flowers to mark the occasion. We had a wonderful bottle of wine, ate too much, then drove home and did what a husband and wife can do if they like each other. Two weeks later, the trial would be over. And so would my marriage.

# CHAPTER 13

----

# VOIR DIRE

"**G**ood morning, ladies and gentlemen, my name is Greg Garrison and I am a deputy prosecutor in Marion County." It was always the same text, used when I first address potential jurors during the pretrial selection process called voir dire. The same text, and beneath it the same subtext, which begins before I speak and is expressed in a hundred subtle ways, and which continues as I talk to the men and women in the jury box. The subtext runs: *Good morning, ladies and gentlemen, I'm the boss here. Listen up because I'm about to tell you what's going to happen.*

**O**ver the weekend, Barb and I had prepared to pick a jury. We spent the two days buffing and shining our case, taking care of last-minute details, pouring over the questionnaires of potential jurors, and following the beginning of the media circus in the newspapers. As expected, the journalists were treating the story as a morality play, a tack that combined sensationalism with human drama and was fairly close to the truth. Holed up in the exclusive suburb of Carmel north of Indianapolis in a house owned by a local entrepreneur, Mike Tyson was being portrayed as "the leading character in his unraveling." Already, more than 150 journalists had arrived, all looking for a different angle on the story. Many combed the William Kennedy Smith trial for signposts. The *New York Times* writer E. R. Shipp commented that "there is some concern that an acquittal in the Tyson case would persuade women to remain silent about an offense that . . . remains vastly under-reported."

This concern, however, was not voiced, and perhaps not shared, by leading feminist organizations. Such groups as the National Organization of Women, which had played an active public role in the Smith case, remained largely silent during the Tyson trial. Had the leaders of NOW and similar groups decided that they would speak out when the victim was a white woman and the accused a white man but ignore black-on-black cases? I sensed a quiet racism seeping from their silence, and the level of hypocrisy made me all the more determined to fight for Desiree.

If Desiree's defenders were few and silent, those supporting Tyson were loud and vocal, charging the citizens of Marion County with every sort of racism. On the streets outside the City-County Building, vendors hawked T-shirts at $12.50 a pop picturing a blindfolded Mike Tyson holding a scale of justice above the words CAN MIKE TYSON GET A FAIR TRIAL? Tyson's spin doctors were already portraying the boxer as a victim—the victim of a white county prosecutor, of white deputy prosecutors, of a gold-digging black woman, of his own wealth, his own fame, his own sexual accessibility. From listening to one call-in show, you might think that the state had gotten the victim and the accused mixed up.

Behind the comments I sensed that Indianapolis and the white Midwest were also on trial. Could a black person, any black person, find justice in the land of corn and pigs and basketball hoops nailed to the sides of barns?

The last Indiana trial that had grabbed the interest of the country took place in 1925. Early in that year D. C. Stevenson, the pudgy Grand Dragon of the Ku Klux Klan in Indiana and the leader of the Klan in twenty-two other northern states, drugged and abducted a white women named Madge Oberholtzer. Then on a train bound for Chicago, Stevenson assaulted and raped her. Remembering the nightmare, Oberholtzer stated, "He held me so I could not move. . . . He chewed me all over my body, bit my neck and face, chewing my tongue, chewing my breasts until they bled, my back, my legs, my ankles, and mutilated me all over my body." The next day she bought a box of mercury bichloride tablets and swallowed a few in an attempt to commit suicide. Stevenson made her drink milk and ginger ale but refused to take her to a doctor. Almost a month later, Oberholtzer died, and Stevenson was charged with rape and second-degree murder. He was tried, convicted, and sent to prison, but not before it was revealed that 30 percent of the native-born white male population of Indiana belonged to the Klan and Stevenson had ties with almost every influential Republican in the state, including Governor Ed Jackson.

The Stevenson trial shocked the nation, helped to break the back of the Klan, and exposed the shoddiness of Indiana politics. For a generation it branded Indiana as Klan country, on a level with Alabama and Mississippi. Now the Tyson trial unfairly revived the echoes of racism in Indiana.

But if the Klan symbolized Indiana's past, basketball served as the state's present token. Bobby Knight, not D. C. Stevenson, had become Indiana's modern Pied Piper; sneakers and gym shorts, not hoods and robes, were the state's uniform.

Indianapolis had been a fly-over city, a dot on the map between one's point of origin and point of destination. Locally dubbed "Indian-no-place," it battled not so much a bad image as no image. At least Detroit and Cleveland inspired jokes: Cleveland was "Newark without the glitter"; for a good time in Detroit, people got on a plane. Indianapolis was just *out there,* somewhere between the cornfields, with an identity so white-bread that even comics wouldn't touch it.

But in the 1970s and 1980s, funded by money from the Lilly Foundation and tax bonds, Indianapolis rebuilt its downtown as a living memorial to Vince Lombardi, John Wooden, Major Taylor, and Reebok. The goal was to use amateur and professional sports to turn Indianapolis into a center for tourism, conventions, and recreation. From 1974 to 1989 the city spent $142.8 million building a sports infrastructure, all but $16.4 million of the total between 1979 and 1989. Market Square Arena was built for a professional basketball team, the Hoosier Dome for a professional football team. World-class facilities were constructed for soccer, rowing, swimming, track and field, bicycling, skating, and tennis. Overnight Indianapolis had a velodrome and a natatorium—though I'm still not sure of what takes place inside a natatorium. The plan paid off. Attendance at events rose above even the original optimistic predictions. Indianapolis hosted national sports festivals, the Pan-American Games, NCAA basketball championships, and other national and international sporting events. The *Wall Street Journal* called Indianapolis the Star of the Snowbelt; *National Geographic* ran a feature article on the city's revival.

The Tyson trial, however, was one sporting event the city hadn't competed for. And it occurred during a time of economic retrenchment in Indianapolis, when many residents were beginning to question the wisdom of the Sports First strategy. The money spent on changing the profile of downtown could have been used to upgrade the city's poorer neighborhoods. Social services lagged behind the triumph of the central city. In 1988 a national health survey listed Indianapolis among the ten cities in the country having the highest rates of infant mortality. Indianapolis blacks complained that sports construction had made many white developers and real estate dealers rich but had delivered only a few custodial jobs to them, jobs that left no money to buy tickets to Pacers or Colts games. For them the Tyson trial became a symbol of the city's retarded racial progress.

In an effort to advance their case, the lawyers of Williams & Connolly threw gasoline on the smoldering embers of racial resentment. During the months before the trial they had filed a series of motions on Tyson's behalf, ranging from a protest of the prosecution's use of the FBI to aid in the search for witnesses to requests to have an expert testify about the size of Tyson's genitalia and another expert to translate the fighter's street language. But the motion they pushed hardest aimed at excluding the entire jury pool on the grounds that the selection system used in Indianapolis was racially biased. Indianapolis, like other cities, made a random computerized drawing of registered voters to select a jury pool. The system had been tested and upheld by the Supreme Court, which judged it a perfectly fair way to select prospective jurors. To suggest that it led to racially unbalanced juries or precluded justice was simply not correct. But the strategy worked to introduce the notion in the public mind that the jury selection process was tainted by racism.

Several days before the start of jury selection, I had a long discussion of Williams & Connolly's tactics with my partner Mike Kiefer. I was nervous and wired from too much coffee and too little sleep, but Mike seemed strangely relaxed and calm. His Buddhalike serenity implied either that he was about to join some Tibetan monastery or that he knew something I didn't.

"Have you been following Williams and Connolly's motions?" he asked me.

"A bit," I answered. Dave Dreyer had handled most of them but I knew their general content.

"Well, that's their case. They've taken their best shot. We'll own the trial."

Although I couldn't be as calm as Mike, I believed that when the bell rang on Monday, Barb and I would be prepared to present a strong case. If the jurors listened, if they forgot about Tyson's celebrity status and the media hype, we had a chance to win. One newspaper article I read gave me hope that an Indiana jury would make its decision on the merits of the case. Harry Alford, the founder of the Hoosier Minority Chamber of Commerce, told a reporter for the *Chicago Tribune*, "Palm Beach is indulgence; people there have seen it all. Washington is a city full of compromise and political deals. Everybody plays an angle there. This is Indianapolis and we don't play about crimes like rape. Mike Tyson is in serious trouble." Other interviewees, black and white, expressed the same opinion.

"Mike is a hero to our kids," commented a black minister. "But the girl wasn't a drunk, she wasn't a barfly." If the jurors were as open-minded as the city residents the *Tribune* reporter talked with, then the trial would be honestly contested.

The jury consisted of twelve people who would make the final decision, but Barb and I would play a part in selecting that jury. We would be given an opportunity to meet and talk with the potential members, to eliminate any we believed to be biased, and to accept the ones we thought were capable of rendering an impartial verdict. There were 130 potential jurors in the jury pool, all strangers: men and women, black and white, wealthy, middle class, poor; Indianapolis citizens united only by the mathematics of a random drawing.

Over the weekend, Barb and I studied the questionnaires each person in the jury pool had filled out. Erica Roach, a young local lawyer who provided invaluable research assistance during the case, tore the questionnaires apart line by line, evaluating how each person would likely lean in a closely contested trial. The questionnaire provided information about a would-be juror's age, health, education, occupation, religious beliefs, family, military record, experience with the legal system, opinion of lawyers, knowledge of the case and witnesses, and interest in sports. A portion of the seventy-eight-question survey written especially for the Tyson case asked about knowledge of Black Expo, the Miss Black America pageant, the William Kennedy Smith trial, and the charges against Tyson. Other questions concerned the books and magazines jury candidates read, the news shows they watched on television or listened to on the radio, the people, living or dead, they most admired, the image they had of themselves. One juror noted that he most admired Pope John Paul II; another felt a certain sympathy for Charles Manson. Some thought of themselves as thinkers and leaders; others judged themselves to be primarily feeling people and followers. Some liked to work within groups and make decisions; others asserted that they were loners and hated making difficult decisions. Reading through the questionnaires and studying the notes made by Barb and Erica, I knew which members of the pool I wanted to see in the jury box, and I knew that my picks would not be the same as those made by Tyson's lawyers.

Carol Orbison, the lead sex crimes prosecutor for Marion County, and George Horn, who was experienced in trying rape cases, advised Barb and me on the selection of the jury. The central issue was not so much getting those we wanted on the jury as it was keeping others off. Carol gave us a short course on rape prosecution. First, she emphasized, psychologists and rape trauma experts maintain that women fear rape more than any other crime, including murder. They fear it so much, in fact, that the mere thought of it triggers an unconscious survival mechanism. Instead of blaming the rapist, which would amount to a stark admission that they had no control over the crime, they blame the victim, searching for things the victim did that caused the rapist to act. Psychologically, by blaming the victim they assert control over the crime. They scrutinize the victim for some vital defect in her character or actions: maybe it was something she wore; maybe she was in the wrong part of town at the wrong hour. By rationalizing the crime in this manner, they reassure themselves that it couldn't happen to them. They wouldn't dress the way the victim did. They would never be drawn into an early morning visit to a man's hotel room. They insulate themselves from the psychological threat entailed by the utter powerlessness of the rape victim.

On top of this, Carol said, women tend to be critical of each other. Barb agreed: "Men accept each other's behavior; women look for flaws." This tendency is more prominent in older women who have been housewives for most of their adult lives. "They just don't have an appreciation of the different lifestyles of younger women," Barb explained. "They have formed, hardened opinions. Women don't go to men's hotel rooms. They don't wear tight clothing. It goes back to what their mothers once told them: 'You don't go there'; 'You don't wear that'; 'You don't talk that way.' And if you do, you're a bad girl and you get what you deserve."

With those assumptions in the minds of jurors, any young rape victim is in trouble. She probably did do something foolish, say something she shouldn't have, make an unwise choice. But that doesn't mean she provoked the rape. I've never had a robbery case where a juror thought, *Well, you know, that victim, maybe he shouldn't have had so much money in his wallet;* or *Maybe the victim should have had a tighter grip on her purse.* The blame-the-victim mechanism comes into play only in rape trials. I wanted a jury that would focus completely on one question: Did that man rape that woman? I didn't want jurors evaluating the victim's morals or lifestyle. Sartorial miscalculations and poorly thought-out decisions did not mitigate rape.

Unlike the process in the federal courts, where the judge conducts the voir dire, in county courts lawyers for the prosecution and the defense speak directly to the potential jurors. *Voir dire,* a French phrase that translates "to speak the truth," is an ancient and honored part of the legal system. It permits lawyers to examine the biases and opinions of the members of the jury pool so that they can choose an impartial jury that will weigh only the evidence presented in the trial in rendering a verdict. Prosecution and defense attorneys can eliminate jurors by peremptory or cause challenges. A peremptory challenge entitles lawyers representing either side in the suit to eliminate a potential juror by fiat; no reason or justification has to be given. In a cause challenge, a justification must be advanced. Either side can eliminate candidates who confess to a prejudice against one of the litigants, who have a personal relationship with or are sympathetic to someone involved in the case, who express their inability to understand the issues in the trial, or for any one of a number of other reasons, but no cause challenge can be based on race, age, or gender.

Since the basis of a peremptory challenge is not given, it can be based on almost anything, including the color of a person's hair, his or her tone of voice in answering a particular question, the look in a person's eyes when he or she glances at the defendant. In Indiana, each side is allowed ten peremptory challenges, limited only by race. Neither side, but particularly the prosecution, can use peremptory challenges to dramatically alter the racial composition of the jury. Although this notion had been modified and reinterpreted in half a dozen Supreme Court decisions, in Indiana it plays out like this: the prosecution can use one peremptory challenge against a black, any further challenges against blacks must be for cause.

The peremptory and cause challenges were our tools for fashioning a group of young to middle-aged jurors whose minds were open about lifestyles. And like all prosecutors, we wanted jurors who held firm opinions about what was right and what was wrong. No prosecutor likes jurors who are in the forgiveness business—ministers, social workers, professors, schoolteachers—who are often too quick to look for moral qualifications and shades of innocence and guilt. Prosecutors look for decision makers, men and women who hire and fire employees, make tough calls, and don't measure guilt with teaspoons.

During the week before the trial we heard rumors about the Williams & Connolly annex that had been set up at the downtown Hyatt Regency. Several reporters told us that the firm had taken over monstrous sets of suites and had trucked in its own desks, furniture, computers, fax machines, filing cabinets, law libraries, and everything else, including bottled water coolers. Barb and I imagined what was going on inside the state-of-the-art hotel *cum* law office complex. What sort of jury selection procedure had the defense lawyers devised? We heard hints that they would use the same jury selection expert who had been called in in the William Kennedy Smith trial. In that trial, a six-person jury, including four older women, found the defendant innocent of all charges.

January 27, 1992, began for me at zero dark-thirty on a frost-bitten Monday morning. As on most days, I read the Bible awhile and said some prayers that were hard to get out because what I wanted to say was *Please, God, let me win this case,* which somehow seemed inappropriate. Instead, I just asked him to work his will. Then I read from the Book of Matthew, for no other reason than I had just begun one of my periodic attempts to work my way through the New Testament. Time and again I would start with good intentions, and once I had even sailed through the three synoptic Gospels, gained speed in John, struggled through the letters of Paul, only to sputter out in boredom somewhere in Revelation. This time I had promised myself that I would finish.

I tried to tell myself that the only thing I had to accomplish that day was to pick a jury, something that I had done scores of times, even taught seminars on. I thought about the questions I would ask, simple questions that, except for a death penalty case, do not vary five degrees between a Roselyn Bakery holdup and the Iran-Contra affair. Picking a jury was picking a jury, but though I knew that was true, I experienced an anxiety I hadn't felt since my first real date.

At six-thirty A.M. Jack Geilker, a tough, experienced police officer who had been assigned as my driver and bodyguard, picked me up, and we headed through the early-morning darkness for the City-County Building. Jack told me that he had reached a definite decision concerning his New Year's resolution. "I'm going to lose more hair and gain twenty pounds," he proudly announced. When I asked why he wanted to go bald and gain weight, he answered, "I like something I can accomplish."

Jack's resolution was a perfect start of the day. I listened to the radio, which was full of hype about the trial. I leafed through the *Star,* trying to relax, but the paper too was awash with hyperbole about the case. A Tyson biographer was in town, presumably peddling his book. The Guardian Angels were marching in front of the Canterbury, holding signs offering such advice to the former champion as KEEP IT CLEAN, DON'T GET MEAN and DON'T GET MEAN, DO THE RIGHT THING. One newspaper column presented a media guide to the trial, comparing the credentials of the various expert commentators and listing the plans of "A Current Affair," "Hard Copy," and "Inside Edition" to cover the case. Managers and promoters discussed the effect the trial would have on boxing. Pundits covered the meaning of the trial for black Americans. Politicians postured and tried to please their constituencies. Ministers talked about morals. *Sports Illustrated* called the trial "an event so extraordinary as to be without precedent. . . . No athlete of Tyson's celebrity and stature has ever faced criminal charges of such gravity as those confronting him in Judge Patricia J. Gifford's courtroom." "Sports, Sex, Sleaze," *Star* columnist John Shaughnessy said, the trial—"the hottest ticket in town"—had it all. "It could make *The Bonfire of the Vanities* seem like a cozy campfire."

Jack dropped me off at the Delaware Street entrance to the City-County Building and I was suddenly in the middle of the show. It was as if God had said, "Let there be light" all over again. Sun guns lit up the sky; videotape started to spin; paparazzi went nuts and shot whole rolls of film of me walking into a building surrounded by flashbulbs and flashguns as though I was on a movie set.

For the next two weeks, through snow, rain, slop, or whatever other crap was falling out of the sky, I was met every morning at seven A.M. by the same group of journalists and photographers who asked questions and took my picture as I walked the hundred yards from the curb to the elevator. They must have taken a hundred thousand useless pictures, hoping that one would record some noteworthy event. When I started to receive death threats, I figured out what that event might be.

In the war room on the fifth floor I met Barb, swallowed a few cups of coffee, and tried, as Eliot wrote, "to prepare a face to meet the faces that you meet." Barb and I then walked down the six flights of steps to the second floor, emerging outside the doorway of Criminal Court IV. Boom! The sun gun flashed on again and the cameras started clicking. It was time to go to work.

From the time they sit down in the back of the court-room, subpoenas clutched in their hands, potential jurors search for a source of authority, someone who seems to know the ropes. I want to be that person. At the start of the session, I try to be the first lawyer in the courtroom. I can feel the eyes of those twenty-five, fifty, seventy-five, one hundred people who have been summoned to jury duty watching me as I open my briefcase and prepare for the voir dire. I can sense them wondering which side I'm on and what the case is all about. I'm sure that from the first they start picking up on nonverbal, subliminal, and probably even metaphysical clues about my personality. I want them to read one thing: confidence—in myself, but most of all in my case. Whether I'm shooting the shit with one of the bailiffs, or exchanging views on the weather with a lawyer in the other camp, I'm aware that the members of the jury pool are watching, absorbing, interpreting. I want them to see that I'm not loaded with venom or ready to throw rocks at anyone, that I do not regard the lawyers at the other table as enemies.

As I walked around the courtroom, shaking hands with friends and bantering with a few local reporters, I glanced once or twice at Fuller and his associates. I knew that Fuller and Beggs would be unaccustomed to this phase of a trial. They worked federal courts, where the judge conducts the voir dire and the first time the lawyers address the jury is during their opening statements. I doubted if Beggs had ever conducted a voir dire, and I suspected that Fuller was out of practice. Ironically, the greatest unknown on Tyson's defense team was the one person Barb and I knew best: Jim Voyles. Jim had worked the City-County Building his entire career. He was an outstanding defense lawyer, adept at handling street crimes and skilled at picking juries. We had no idea, however, if Voyles was there merely as a consultant, to make sure motions were properly filed and to offer advice about Indiana law, or if he was going to play an active role in the trial. The voir dire would answer that question. If he spoke, he was a player. If he didn't, he was one more extra carrying Perrier.

After a short conversation with the defense attorneys, I knew that Voyles was only along for the ride. I knew him well enough to read his expression and his tone of voice when we shook hands. His smile expressed outward confidence but lacked the spark, the indefinable edge, of a person who was about to take center stage. That was welcome news. But not for the first time I wondered, if Voyles's talents were expendable, how much better must the Williams & Connolly people be?

Tyson joined his lawyers at the defense table. It was the first time I had seen him "up close and personal," and he was massive—heavier, I suspect, than his normal fighting weight by thirty or forty pounds, but not fat, just thick, like a roughly formed slab of granite, a sculpture that had yet to be refined. He was dressed conservatively in a dark suit, white shirt, and red tie, but I knew you couldn't buy a dress shirt off the rack with a collar to fit that neck. It seemed as wide as a normal man's shoulders, and I had trouble imagining a punch that could knock back a head so well anchored. In front of him on the table was a pen and a notepad. It was an old defense trick— but perpetually recyclable since juries are always fresh. The idea is that the accused takes notes, as if he is participating in his own defense. Occasionally a practiced defense attorney will consult with his client, and together they will discuss the content of some jotting. In truth, the only object of the note-taking is to keep the defendant's hands and mind occupied. It helps to prevent him from looking bored or making hostile eye contact with potential jurors, who constantly cast furtive glances at the person in the hot seat.

Judge Patricia Gifford, gray-haired and black-robed, walked into the courtroom, sat down, looked sharply about the room, and pounded her gavel to start the proceeding. People who knew her well said that in private she was a warm, gentle person who liked "Wheel of Fortune," "Jeopardy," a good book, and gardening, but as a judge she maintained a cool demeanor, not exactly unfriendly, but distant. The daughter of an army colonel, she had been a schoolteacher before going to law school, and she had worked in the Marion County prosecutor's office, where she was one of the first female prosecutors in the nation to handle sex crimes. She had also helped draft the new Indiana rape law, which prohibited questioning a rape victim about her past sexual activity. During thirteen years on the bench she had gained a reputation for stern but fair decisions. Four times she had sentenced murderers to the electric chair, and although she was commonly regarded as tough on sex crimes, her sentences were actually lighter than those of the other criminal judges in Marion County.

Judge Gifford skipped the pleasantries and went to work. She identified the parties, introduced the attorneys, described the nature of the case, estimated the length of the trial, and then turned the proceedings over to me. It was my duty as prosecutor to read the statute and charges and then to define the nature of "burden of proof" and "presumption of innocence." It was also my job to tell the prospective jurors what we were all here to do.

I told them that it was not their job to find the defendant guilty. We were not there to convict anyone. We were in the courtroom to present evidence and let the evidence do the work. All they had to do was listen to the evidence with open minds, weigh the testimony of the various witnesses, and use their God-given common sense. That's all the state asked. If at the end of the trial they did not believe the evidence conclusively proved that the defendant was guilty, then they should not convict him. They should allow him to walk out of the courtroom a free man. *But* (here pause a few seconds, count to three) . . . on the other hand, if the evidence convinced them that the defendant had committed the crime, it was their duty to return a guilty verdict. If the evidence convinced them that Mike Tyson had raped Desiree Washington, it was their job to convict him.

What I wanted—what I quietly demanded—was the same thing Don King was calling for in the press: a level playing field. Barb and I were after jurors who could say, "I don't care what I've read, I don't care what I thought I knew, I don't care if the defendant is rich and famous. I'm going to treat him like any other John Q. Public charged with a crime."

Which was easier said than done. The reality was that stars were difficult to convict, especially if they played their cards right. People want to believe heroes; they like to think that Mickey Mantle never drank much more than a sociable beer and that Michael Jordan only gambles for small stakes. Before I could effectively try Tyson, I had to strip him of his celebrity status.

I asked each prospective juror, "Does the fact that this man is a person who is famous mean to you that the laws apply differently to him than they would to you or me if we committed the same crime?" Of course, everyone said no, even if he or she thought differently.

"Does the fact that the defendant is a famous man mean that you should hold him to a higher standard of conduct than you would if he were not famous?" I continued. Again, everyone replied, "No, it doesn't."

"You understand that the law does not require more of him than it does of you or me. He is entitled to all the same privileges and immunities that you and I have as citizens of Marion County. Do you agree with that statement?" In turn, every head nodded agreement, every person said, "Yes, I do."

"On the other hand, does the fact that he is a famous man, that he has been heavyweight champion of the world, entitle him to have special privileges that you and I would not have if we were similarly charged?" "Absolutely not," each would say. And I could see that the very notion made many of the prospective jurors a little mad. Several flinched slightly as I asked the question, a few faces reddened. I knew from a lifetime of experience that the plain folk of the Midwest just don't cotton to privilege at all. It's something that might figure in New York or Boston, Palm Beach or Hollywood, but not here.

"Do you understand that the law says this man is to get exactly what you or I would get, no less and no more? Do you agree with that?" "Yes, I do."

All this took no more than a minute or a minute and a half for each person, but I could see it made the prospective jurors think, *Screw this guy. He's just an ordinary mope. He's not going to get a special deal here. I'm going to treat him like anybody else. That's the only fair way.*

Watching how prospective jurors react is fun. I see expressions on their faces that seem to say, *Wow, this is just like Civics class—just like that teacher taught us in high school.* They look at me as though I'm Clark Kent. I see them thinking, *Did I hear that guy right? Did he say that if we didn't think the defendant was guilty we should send him out the back door, tell him to go home? Yep, there he just said it again, even though his job is to convict the man. What a guy.*

Of course, as I'm telling them they should send the defendant home if the evidence doesn't prove him guilty, I'm sending out another message loud and clear: *Who are we kidding? There's no fucking chance. Would I be standing up here telling you all this if I thought there was any way in hell that this guy was innocent? No way. He's dead meat. He's mine.* That's the part you never say, but that's what I want to be going on in their minds when they nod their heads.

"Do you understand that?" I asked that January morning. It's a question I've asked hundreds of times. If a potential juror says no, then he or she is gone, excused, thrown out of the pool. But if jurors say yes, then they're on, not because of some snake oil I sold them or spell I cast over them, but because they believe in me. They like that good old-fashioned, Ray Nitschke style: *Ladies and gentlemen, we're going to stand up here and knock this defendant unconscious. That's what we're going to do, but we're not going to use any sleight of hand. We're going to do it because the man is just flat guilty.*

And when I talk about "the defendant," I give a quick side-long glance over to the defense table to let the potential jurors know exactly who I'm talking about and that I don't like him very much. You want them to know that what the defendant did—rob, shoot, stick, or rape an innocent person—makes you sick. In the Tyson trial I labored to make the men and women in the jury pool understand that Mike Tyson wasn't a hero in my eyes, that he had hurt a young woman badly and for no other reason than to satisfy a fleeting sexual urge. I wouldn't even accord him the honor and dignity of using his name. For me, he was "the defendant"; if I ever did say "Mr. Tyson," I did it with a sneer to indicate that I did not have much respect for him. He might have won respect in the boxing ring by knocking people down, but that behavior was unacceptable in civilized society.

When I teach how to pick death penalty juries, I tell my students that their job is to take twelve ordinary, timid citizens and turn them into fanatics who can disregard the stomach acid and pucker factor they feel when they think about the juice in the electric chair, and to try the case strictly according to the evidence and the law. If I can vaccinate a jury with that serum, I'll have half a dozen commitments before the opening statements—commitments not to me, but to the system. "Do you understand that oath?" "Yes, I do." "Do you understand what you have to do if the evidence proves the defendant guilty?" "Yes, I do." "Do you understand what you have to do if the evidence does not convince you beyond a reasonable degree of the defendant's guilt?" "Yes, I do."

I watched the potential jurors sneak peeks at Tyson. When Barb was conducting her portion of the voir dire, I searched his fighter's face for any sign of what he was thinking, but he was like a sphinx, his face a mask. Occasionally he would yawn or look bored, but mostly he seemed divorced from what was going on around him, as if he was watching a plodding movie about the problems of another person. "Boxers lie for a living," José Torres had said. "The best can look you directly in the eye and tell you an absolute lie. You'll never know what they are thinking or what is the truth. And Tyson is the best."

The one important person who was not there with us in the courtroom was Desiree Washington, and I knew the potential jurors would be thinking what I had once thought: *What was she doing in his room at two in the morning?*

"Imagine that you drive into a bad part of town at night," I said. "A section you know you shouldn't be in, but it's a shortcut and you think you'll be fine. But everything doesn't go as planned. Instead you get a flat tire. As you are changing the tire, some guy hits you over the head with a tire iron and takes your wallet. Is that your fault?" Everyone answered no.

"So bad judgment does not excuse criminal behavior?" No, the prospective jurors repeated. I was planting a seed, one that I wanted to allow to grow for two weeks. If all went well, I would harvest the crop during my final argument.

I also kept an eye out for the seeds Fuller was planting. I searched for clues to the strategy he would use in the trial. As I suspected, both he and Beggs seemed uncomfortable with voir dire. Fuller appeared stiff, asking his questions from behind a lectern in a formal, slightly patronizing manner. Perfect. Instead of talking with the prospective jurors and treating them as friends and equals, he was lecturing them. His clipped eastern accent and machine-gun style of elocution grated on midwestern ears. I could see that the people in the jury box were struggling to understand him, and when they asked him to repeat something, he spoke even faster. His failure to connect with the members of the jury pool seemed to rattle his rhythm. He kept putting on his glasses and taking them off, and as he stood behind the podium, there wasn't much sticking out for people to focus on. The jurors strained to watch and listen, became frustrated, and finally just checked out mentally.

Fuller's questions didn't help to maintain their interest. He asked them legal questions, inquiring if they knew the difference between expressed and implied consent. "Do you appreciate that consent can be given impliedly or expressly?" he asked one member of the jury pool, who stared at him as though the question was in Hindustani. Fuller tried again as the man scratched his head in what seemed to be an attempt to stimulate his brain. "Do you understand that the facts and circumstances between two people can give rise to express or implied consent?" One journalist commented that Fuller used the word "implied" so often that he once slipped and asked one woman how long she had been implied in her job.

Fuller repeatedly asked what the potential jurors knew about Tyson and Don King, whether they followed boxing or had read any biographies of the fighter. Had they heard about Tyson's relationship with Robin Givens? Did they know anything about his emotional problems? The defense then used its peremptory challenges to exclude from the jury those who knew most about Tyson.

Beggs further complicated matters. If Fuller failed to connect with the people in the jury box, she positively alienated them: talking over their heads, condescending to them, using big words. She seemed to regard them as a bunch of hicks. She asked one person if something or other would "give you pause." *Give you pause.* Tommy Kuzmik, who was sitting to my left, looked at me and held both hands up like dog's paws as I struggled to control my bladder.

As we moved into the second day of voir dire, Barb and I became perplexed about Fuller's and Beggs's tactics. Except for the fact that they didn't want anyone on the jury who knew much about Tyson, we weren't sure what type of jurors they were after. Generally, defense lawyers try to exclude professional management types from juries. They dislike decision makers, take-charge people who make hiring and firing decisions and tend not to buy the smoke and mirrors. They also avoid CPA types who like life to add up like a column of numbers. But Fuller allowed a few management people onto the jury. The biggest surprise was juror number 9, an ex-marine who was a marketing manager with IBM. He was a prosecutor's dream, a jury foreman waiting to be elected—steady, forceful, with a strong personality, he was a natural leader, a man who could make a difficult decision himself and help others arrive at theirs. Evidently Fuller, a navy veteran of the Korean War who was deeply interested in naval history, believed that he could communicate with the former marine. After that, we stopped trying to guess Fuller's strategy.

Jury selection becomes a numbing process, asking each person the same questions, explaining jury duties again and again. But voir dire is too important to allow it to become boring for the jurors. If a prosecutor loses a good case, it is typically lost during jury selection. I'm convinced that that's what happened in the first Rodney King trial. To ensure the jury would be strong, I worked to engender the same passion, the same commitment to the legal system, in each prospective juror. On the first day we questioned twenty persons and chose five. Of the two blacks questioned, the first, an elderly man who was hard of hearing, indicated that he would have a difficult time coping and asked to be excused on medical grounds. The second was seated.

On the second day we questioned eighteen more prospective jurors and chose six, two of whom were black. For nine hours we talked and explained and asked, trying to get a read on everyone. Sometimes I discussed law; at other times I asked would-be jurors questions about themselves—where they lived, who they worked for, what they thought about Bobby Knight and Indiana basketball. I wanted them to relax, to open up and show me how their minds worked. If at all possible, I sought to weed out anyone who was too dumb to understand the legal issues in the case and any nut with some hidden agenda. Occasionally, however, an off-beat answer relieved some of the tedium. When Fuller asked one elderly woman what she knew about Don King, she replied, "I just call him Mr. Hair." The comment was almost—but not quite—enough to keep her on the jury.

On the third day we talked with six more people and chose the final juror, then concluded the process by picking three of the ten people we questioned for alternates. Although several of the older women struck alarms in Barb and Erica, only one prospective juror bothered me. A younger black man, he sat through most of the proceedings in silence, but listened closely to my questions and the different answers. When I began to question him he said all the right things, answering yes when he was supposed to and no when he wasn't. Something about him seemed calculated: he glanced at Tyson too often; he seemed too anxious to get on the jury. An invisible sign over his head read HUNG JURY. A gut feeling that his mind was already made up wasn't enough to justify a cause challenge, but it was sufficient to win my only peremptory used against a black. It was a gamble. The rules set down in *Batson* v. *Kentucky* prevented me from using another peremptory strike against a black. From then on there was no way we could alter the racial composition of the jury.

But we didn't have to. There were no more red flags. Of the twelve members of the jury, eight were male and four female. Three of the twelve, 25 percent, were black. At the time, 21 percent of Marion County residents were black. Of the seven black men and women who were questioned, three were seated, three asked to be excused for health, educational, or religious reasons, and one was struck by the prosecution.

Looking over the results of our labors, Barb and I believed we had about as good a jury as we were likely to get. Most of the members were young enough to appreciate a lifestyle that would permit a young woman to go on a date at 2:00 A.M.; two were in their twenties, eight in their thirties, one in his forties, and one in his fifties. All except one, a man, had jobs. The ex-marine described himself as a conservative. A truck driver listed Bobby Knight and Richard Nixon as two of the people he admired most. As much as any jury we could impanel, the twelve men and women represented a fair cross-section of Indianapolis. Whether Tyson liked it or not, we knew they were capable of rendering a just decision.

# CHAPTER 14

# THE STATE'S CASE

**A**fter the trial, reading the press reports was an ego massage. William Nack in *Sports Illustrated* wrote that during my opening statement I "roamed the well of the courtroom as [I] told a seamless, compelling story." A few reporters commented on my "folksy" delivery, which I assumed meant that I didn't have an Bos-Wash accent. Several others singled out the fact that I spoke without notes, as if after six months on the case I should need something to remind me of the facts. The reporters created the impression that I was in total control, as if I had rehearsed every word, staged every movement. I wish I had. In truth, when I began my opening statement, I was nervous, unsure what my first, let alone second, sentence would be, and not at all certain that I would be able to string two thoughts together.

**A**s Barb and I had settled on the order of our witnesses during the previous week, we were forced to confront the uncomforting fact that neither of us knew much about how to try a rape case. Homicide we knew; rape was a different story. As a prosecutor in a homicide, I always planned to come in the courtroom breathing fire, get right in the jurors' faces, show the pain and suffering that had resulted from the murder, and not give anyone, jurors or defense attorneys, a second to sit back and take a deep breath. I wanted to just grab the jury by the throat and not let go until it returned a guilty verdict. To achieve this result, I usually front-loaded my witnesses. Normally the first witness is a scene-setter, perhaps the first officer at the scene of the crime who can set the stage by describing what he or she saw. The second witness is the centerpiece, perhaps an eyewitness to the murder or someone who can testify as to motive or intent. From then on it is all corroboration and support. I put one witness after another on the stand who can shore up the testimony of the primary witness.

The classic pattern for prosecuting a rape case, as Carol Orbison and George Horn explained it to me, is different. The central witness is the victim, the living person who is absent in murder cases, and the governing idea is to build toward her testimony. You start on the outside of the case, presenting witnesses who can corroborate the whereabouts of the accused and the victim at a particular time, and work toward the center, toward what the victim saw or experienced. Along the way, you build the jurors' expectations until—*ta-da*, the pièce de résistance.

Neither Barb nor I was comfortable with the classic approach. It was too cold, too slow in development, and we feared that the jury might check out before the closing act. As a former music major, I thought of Ravel's "Bolero," with its powerful ending built up from a slow, calm beginning. We opted for the homicide approach. *Bang!* Grab the jurors' attention in the opening statement. *Bang!* Give them the victim. *Bang! Bang! Bang!* Corroborate, support, shore up.

Our approach was not without its risks. Our greatest fear was the time that separated Desiree's testimony and the jury's deliberations. Desiree's testimony might sear the hearts of the jurors on the first and second days of the trial, but by the time the defense rested, her testimony might have lost its heat. To guard against, if not eliminate, this problem, we decided to put Desiree on the stand twice—at the start and at the end of the prosecution's case. Early on in the trial, we would present the flesh-and-blood victim, a young woman who had suffered and was continuing to suffer because of the actions of the defendant. Before we rested our case, we would present Desiree's

911 tape, the recorded voice of a person in pain. Of course, there was a chance that the defense would be able to prevent the jury from ever hearing the tape, but we figured we had a way to get it heard.

**W**ednesday night—less than twelve hours before my opening statement—was a circus, three rings of chaos, confusion, and intrigue. The problem once again was Ed Gerstein and his local troubleshooter, Dave Hennessy. A story about the case had just broken in Chicago. Bob Hammerle, a friend and local defense lawyer who had conducted a mock cross-examination of Desiree to help us prepare her to testify, had given an interview on a Chicago radio station in which he discussed his assessment of the strengths and weaknesses of Desiree's account of the rape. He never anticipated that his views would rebound back to Indianapolis, but they were picked up by a local station. We had no idea what influence, if any, the story would have. Would it help the defense prepare for the cross-examination of Desiree? Would it make Desiree's testimony seem too practiced, too rehearsed? Gerstein and Hennessy were totally absorbed by the speculations.

Holed up in the conference room in my offices, I tried to focus Desiree on her testimony the next day, simply running through once more what questions I would ask and where she should pause to emphasize some particularly important point. Anxiety, I told her, would make her want to rush through her testimony; she would want to get it over with as soon as possible. She had to fight that urge, take deep breaths, relax her neck muscles, and seem calm when her stomach was tight with fear and her shoulders ached with tension.

Desiree, however, was already a bundle of cut nerves. She stumbled over answers and was clearly shaken about the prospect of facing both the man who had raped her and the representatives of the world's media on the same day. The latest story out of Chicago only added to her worries. Ed, at his disruptive best, wouldn't let either of us alone. He stalked outside the room, pacing back and forth in the hallway and bursting into my office at the most inopportune moments. He seemed to be working on a fifteen- or twenty-minute rotation—pace the hall, come into the room, sit down, move around, interrupt what we were doing, ask Des how she was, start to leave, stop, call me out into the hall to tell me some terrible thing that was going on, and then repeat the sequence. He kept mumbling the same old conspiratorial mantra: "You have no idea of what these people are capable of doing. You have no idea of how bad they are. You have no idea of how powerful they are. You have no idea of what it's going to be like. Those D.C. lawyers are going to tear into Desiree." Just what Desiree wanted to hear, and for that matter, just what I wanted to hear. All the while, Hennessy was on the phone talking with every media person he could find in an attempt to organize a special televised press conference. Even more than Gerstein, Hennessy seemed never to have met a camera he didn't want to stand in front of.

Before long, Ed and Dave started to irritate the hell out of me, mostly because I could see that they were frightening Desiree. But slowly she began to change. Gerstein's activity picked up speed. He would erupt into the room, spill thirty seconds' worth of lava, then disappear for a short period of dormancy. When he left, Desiree would roll her eyes in that prototypical expression of teenage exasperation that any parent recognizes. Eventually she began to say what she was thinking. "I don't trust him," she told me. "I don't know what he's doing. I don't think he has my best interests at heart. I don't know what he's after. Whose side is he on?" Barb and I tried to calm her, telling her to concentrate on the subject at hand. When she asked for our opinion of Gerstein, we told her that our job was to prosecute her case, not to interfere or pass judgment on her relationship with her civil lawyers.

Finally, after another violent eruption, Desiree turned to me and said, "He's got to go." There was a note of finality in her voice; she had reached a decision and nothing was going to alter it. I turned my palms upward and raised my shoulders, a gesture signifying, "That's between you and him." But I thought, *Ed Gerstein is history. Thank God.*

It was almost midnight when I returned home, and I had yet to organize my thoughts for my opening statement. I tried to jot down an outline. On one level, an opening statement is simple. It's the prosecutor's job to tell the jurors what they're going to see, what they're about to hear, why the evidence will convince them that the defendant committed a crime. It's a statement, not an argument; if you argue, the judge will sustain any objection. It's also a storyteller's dream. There is no legal requirement that the prosecutor tell a good story. He or she can simply say, "The evidence will show that on the nineteenth day of January 1991, John Smith did walk into a bar and shoot and kill Sam Jones, and he meant to do it because he said, 'You're a dead son of a bitch,' then fired three times and walked out." Simple, to the point, and enough to satisfy the law. But a storyteller will relish the moment and give flesh to the factual skeleton. He or she will describe the event in graphic detail in an attempt to re-create the color and drama of the crime. If the prosecutor has talent, by the end of the statement the jurors will be so mad that they'll be ready to convict.

But Desiree's brief, brutal encounter with Mike Tyson was a complex story, one that began years before the event and was rooted in the personalities of the Beauty Queen and boxer. The central thread of the story was easily lost. As I worked on the outline, I got jammed up in Desiree's and Tyson's backgrounds. I couldn't get it right. I couldn't find the balance between the crime and the personalities of the central figures. Sometime shortly after one, I gave up and went to bed.

Three hours of restless sleep later, I was back at the kitchen table, sipping coffee and trying to make some sense of the notes I had written down a few hours earlier. They looked like the jottings of a lunatic. I tried again, with no better result. *This is stupid,* I thought. I was a wreck, an emotional mess. I was getting ready to say something that people all around the world would read in their newspapers, and I had no idea what to say. I could see myself standing up there like a damn fool, babbling in a confused, disjointed manner that no one, nowhere, would be able to make any sense of. When I sat down, the jurors would look at each other and mouth, "What'd he say?" Reporters in the media room would ask, "What'd he say?" Americans watching their evening news shows or reading their morning papers would scratch their heads and wonder, "What'd he say?" The same question would be asked in a hundred countries and a hundred languages.

So I quit, got my Bible, and began reading the tenth chapter of Matthew where I had left off the morning before. It is the section where Jesus sends his twelve disciples out to work among the people, instructing them, "Do not go in the direction of the

Gentiles, nor enter the towns of the Samaritans; but go rather to the lost sheep of the house of Israel. And as you go, preach the message, 'The kingdom of heaven is at hand.' Cure the sick, raise the dead, cleanse the lepers, cast out devils. Freely you have received, freely give. Do not keep gold, or silver, or money in your girdles, no wallet for your journey, nor two tunics, nor sandals, nor staff; for the laborer deserves his living." I read on until I came across this passage: "Behold, I am sending you forth like sheep in the midst of wolves . . . and you will be brought before governors and kings for my sake, for a witness to them and to the Gentiles. But when they deliver you up, do not be anxious how or what you speak; for what you are to speak will be given to you in that hour. For it is not you who are speaking, but the Spirit of your Father who speaks through you."

It was as close to a visitation as I'd ever experienced. It was as if God was saying, *Would you calm down? Do you think I would stick you in the middle of this mess and then cut you loose and turn my back on you? You just go show up and I'll handle what you're supposed to say.* With that, I put away my useless outline, drank the rest of my coffee, took a shower, put on a new suit, and waited for Jack to pick me up. I was still as nervous as a cat, but I was through worrying. I figured that if I couldn't tell the story that had dominated the last five months of my life, I didn't belong in the courtroom.

Shortly after nine o'clock, Judge Gifford called *State of Indiana* v. *Michael G. Tyson*, number 91-116245, swore in the jury, cautioned the jurors not to talk about the case or pay any attention to news reports, read the charges, and then gave a short lecture on the nature of reasonable doubt. It was essentially the same discussion I had had with each prospective juror during voir dire. The defendant, she said, was under no obligation to testify or to prove his innocence, but the state had to prove his guilt. In evaluating witnesses and evidence, each juror should follow the dictates of common sense: "You are the exclusive judges of the evidence, the credibility of the witnesses, and the weight to be given to the testimony of each of them. In considering the testimony of any witness, you may take into account his or her ability and opportunity to observe, the manner and the conduct of the witness while testifying, any interest, bias, or prejudice the witness may have, any relationship with any other witnesses or interested parties, and the reasonableness of the testimony of the witness considered in the light of all the evidence in the case." Her initial instructions completed, she asked for the state's opening statement.

It took me forty-five minutes to tell the simple story of a young, beautiful woman whose life was dramatically changed during her short stay in Indianapolis. It was important for me to introduce the jurors to the accomplishments and personality of Desiree Washington. All they knew from reading the newspapers was that the victim—whose name was normally withheld—was a black beauty queen from Rhode Island. To them she was a faceless, nameless plaintiff, hardly a person at all. If I did nothing else, I wanted each juror to understand that Desiree Washington was a very real person who was the victim of a very brutal crime. I discussed her church service and her educational accomplishments; I talked about her family and about how her father and brother had followed Mike Tyson's career; I explained how thrilled she had been when the famous boxer expressed an interest in her.

She was no match for Tyson, who was able to read her innocence and use it to get closer to her. He was polite, even a bit shy. He called her a "good Christian girl," wore a TOGETHER IN CHRIST button, and asked her out on a date. He was a gentleman, and his presence and soft words livened up the otherwise dull activities. I explained the numbing schedule that the pageant contestants had to follow—the hours on their feet, the grueling timetable, the boredom of the official gatherings. Meeting Tyson was a great antidote to this discomfort.

As I moved the narrative closer to the rape, I occasionally looked toward Tyson. Several times I pointed at him, indicating to the jury that Desiree had been raped and injured by the man sitting at the defense table. Step by step, I walked the jury through the events during the night of the rape, from the time Tyson called Desiree and pleaded with her to join him on a date to the time she left the Canterbury and returned to her own hotel room. In graphic, painful detail, I described the rape, shifting at times from past to present tense: "He's grinning at her. His voice is low, different than before. And he pulls her legs apart and sticks his fingers into her. She cries out in pain. The medical, anatomical, physiological miracle of human

sexuality that causes the female of the species to become lubricated when she's sexually excited ain't working, and she's terrified. So when these big fingers go into her, it hurts a lot, and
she cries out, 'Don't.' "

As I described the rape, I watched the jurors in an effort to
gauge their reaction. Every once in a while, one of them would
look over at Tyson; a few jaws were tightened in anger. They
were following what I said because I was speaking to them—
not lecturing, not condescending, not throwing around fifty-
cent words or Latin phrases, but talking directly to them in
unvarnished English: "She hops up from the bed and puts her
clothes on fast, wiping her tears, getting her clothes on, trying
to find her dignity along with her clothes, and says, 'Is the limo
still down there?' He says, 'Oh, you can stay if you want.' She
says, 'Why? So you can do that again?' "

I told the jurors not only what they would hear from Desiree,
but what the other prosecution witnesses would tell them. I
outlined our case, highlighting the victim's story and the witnesses who would corroborate important elements of that
story. Chris Low, McCoy Wagers, Virginia Foster, Kycia Johnson, Dr. Tom Richardson—each person, none of whom was a
friend of Desiree's, would buttress some part of her testimony.
They were honest people, hard-working people without an ax
to grind and with no financial or emotional stake in the trial.
They were ideal witnesses, and I asked the jurors to listen to
what they had to say. I explained that a trial was like a puzzle, a
collection of pieces that the jury had to order and arrange. But
once the pieces were in place, I was certain that they would
present a powerful and convincing picture, not only of a person but of a crime. The defendant had raped Desiree, and the
evidence would prove it.

As I sat down, Vincent Fuller rose and moved toward his
podium. He adjusted his glasses, glanced a moment at his
notes, and then tried to claim the courtroom. I leaned forward
in my chair, ready to see what all the fuss was about. William
Nack had written in *Sports Illustrated* that "Fuller is one of
those rare trial lawyers whose very presence in a courtroom
changes the complexion of the place, making it his own." An
attorney commented, "When Fuller walks in, things are done
at a different level. The clerks, the bailiffs, the judge and everyone else will deny it, but they behave differently with a guy like

Fuller around." Fuller's voice seemed stronger and more compelling than it had during voir dire. It was a voice that "would
crack the flooring in gymnasiums," an attorney who had opposed him once observed. But his style was still stiff as he began
to lecture the jury on the facts of the case.

What occurred in Tyson's hotel suite was consensual sex,
Fuller emphasized. "We believe the evidence will demonstrate
that to you to your satisfaction and leave little doubt in your
mind about it." Once again, he revisited the idea of implied
consent; that is, "consent which a reasonable person might in-
fer from the actions, the conduct of the young lady with whom
he's making advances." Fuller spoke in quick, loud bursts, in
that style unfamiliar to many of the jurors. I could see a few
struggling to follow his discourse, but they were all paying close
attention to his words.

Like any good defense attorney, he gave them another interpretation of the facts of the case. In his narrative, Mike Tyson
was as unskilled outside the ring as he was skilled inside: "He's
not a high school graduate. He's never attended college. He's
never been trained in public speaking. He's never been trained
in the skill of projecting himself, acting, if you will. He's been
trained to do one thing, to defend himself in the ring and to go
to battle in a ring.

"Desiree Washington, on the other hand, presents a stark
contrast in her background." Fuller described a woman who
was a stranger to me, but a version that the jury might accept.
Miss Washington, he said, was sophisticated beyond her age,
poised, self-assured, mature, trained in the art of projection,
comfortable around world leaders. She knew what Tyson
wanted; indeed, Tyson was crude and explicit in voicing his
desires. She went out with Tyson, went to his room and had
sexual intercourse with him, because she hoped for a more lasting relationship.

Leaning forward, listening, I looked for an opening to interrupt the flow of Fuller's narrative. When he speculated on what
Desiree was anticipating, I objected. Fuller had crossed the line
from making a statement to voicing an argument. My objection
was sustained, and it seemed to disrupt Fuller's tempo—not
much, but enough to make him speak a shade faster.

He returned to his story of love on the rocks. But his story
was constructed not on the facts, but on his interpretation of

Desiree's behavior, which again was not a permissible tack in an opening statement. I objected. The court sustained. Fuller returned to his story, portraying Desiree as a gold digger and a woman who was angry at being treated like a one-night stand. But my objections had altered the mood of the jury. Instead of leaning forward in rapt attention to Fuller's story, I saw several jurors begin to look back and forth from Fuller to me, probably wondering what all the legal maneuvering was about.

Then Fuller said something that no juror could ignore. Discussing the "money motive" in the case, he informed the jury that Desiree had hired Edward Gerstein after she returned to Rhode Island, and Gerstein in turn hired an Indianapolis lawyer to work with him. "In fact, they are here today in the audience following the case with great intensity," Fuller said, looking over toward Gerstein and Hennessy. "Why? Because if Mr. Tyson were convicted, these lawyers would bring a lawsuit on behalf of Desiree Washington that stands to make her a very wealthy woman."

I tried not to flinch, but even if I had no one would have noticed. It seemed every set of eyes in the courtroom was trying to get a look at Gerstein and Hennessy. Fuller had everyone's attention, and he preceded to point out several inconsistencies in Desiree's statements to contestants that the defense planned to call. Had she screamed, or hadn't she? Did the alleged attack take place on the floor or on the bed? Did they kiss before the attack or not? And if Miss Washington fought her attacker, where were the bruises and contusions and lacerations? Tyson was big, she was small; but there were no bruises.

Fuller closed by asking the jurors to have open minds. I saw several nod their heads. Fuller had accomplished his primary goal: he had raised a few doubts. But he had also created certain expectations in the jurors' minds. Like me, he had presented an interpretation of Desiree Washington. For Fuller she was the sophisticated gold digger out to take poor Mike's money. His Desiree had been compromised but not victimized, and now in a calculating manner she was out to get her hand in Tyson's pocket. It was a portrait that the jurors might buy in the abstract, but not once they saw Desiree, not once she told her story. As Fuller finished, I sensed that he had just blown up a balloon that I could pop that afternoon.

Kycia Johnson took the witness stand to set the stage. Tall and beautiful, she had come to Indianapolis in July representing Oklahoma in the Miss Black America pageant, and she had been assigned a room with Desiree Washington and Pasha Oliver. Desiree and Pasha had checked in before her and claimed the two beds in the hotel room; Kycia was stuck with the cot. That was fine with her. Unlike some of the other contestants, she was a veteran of beauty contests, and she had come to Indy not to sleep or see the sights but to win the pageant. Although she was shy and had a soft demeanor, she seemed more mature than many of the other contestants. She hadn't socialized much with the other contestants, even her roommates. She just quietly went her own way, showing up on time, competing to the best of her ability, and remaining detached from the excitement around her.

Kycia's position at the pageant and her personality made her an ideal opening witness. She wasn't Desiree's pal; she wasn't particularly interested in Tyson; she had no reason to be biased in one direction or the other. But as Desiree's roommate, the last person to see her before her "date" with Tyson and the first to see her when she came back to the room, Kycia could tell the jury that the Desiree who left the hotel that night was not the same one who returned. The before and the after— that's what we hoped to get from Kycia.

Barb handled the direct questioning. Resisting the impulse to ask too many questions, she led Kycia through the events in Indianapolis. Kycia had attended all the important public events, seen Tyson at the Omni rehearsal hall and the opening ceremony of Black Expo, and watched the boxer's behavior. At all times, she said, Tyson was civil to her, and she didn't see any unusual physical contact between Tyson and Desiree. But it was clear to her that Tyson was interested in Desiree.

Kycia attended the Johnny Gill concert the night of July 18 and did not return to the hotel room until after one. Desiree and Pasha were asleep, and the room was dark except for a light left on in the bathroom. She was getting ready for bed when the phone rang, which she raced to answer so that it wouldn't disturb her roommates. It was Dale Edwards calling on behalf of Mike Tyson, and he wanted to speak to Desiree, although he mispronounced her name. Desiree took the phone, and Kycia heard her run through a series of excuses for not leaving the hotel: "But it's late. I'm in bed. . . . I've rolled my hair. . . . I've taken off my makeup, and I'm not dressed." Obviously someone was pressing her, for after she repeated her excuses, she said, "Well, why don't you come up here to our room?" But Pasha, now awake also, overruled the suggestion because they weren't dressed. "Can I just see you tomorrow?" Desiree asked. Pause. "Oh, you're leaving tomorrow?"

Finally Desiree turned to Kycia and Pasha and asked, "What should I do?" Neither roommate had much advice to offer, so Desiree said, "Give me a few minutes to get ready, and I'll be down." As Desiree went into the bathroom, Kycia got in bed; a few minutes later she heard the door open and close. Not long after that she was asleep.

Kycia's cot was close to the door and she was awakened later that night when someone entered the room. It was Desiree, mumbling something to herself. Kycia listened: "He's such a creep. He's such a jerk," Desiree said. "What happened?" Kycia asked. "He tried to rape me," Desiree answered before she disappeared into the bathroom.

When Kycia awoke the next morning, Desiree and Pasha were in the bathroom whispering about something as if they didn't want Kycia to hear. All Kycia could make out was the splashing of water. Later in the day she detected a change in her roommate. Discussing the change, Kycia told Barb, "When she first arrived, she was a very energetic person. She loved to talk a lot. And after that happened, supposedly happened, she was just real, real quiet. She was kind of distant, and she looked like she was always staring, and she was totally different, much quieter."

On Saturday, Kycia discovered that Desiree had gone to the hospital and asked her what was wrong. "Mike . . . raped me, and I was in shock," Desiree responded. "That's why I said last night that he tried, because I was scared, and I didn't think anyone would believe me."

Kycia believed her, and the jury believed Kycia. As an opening witness, she was superb. She confirmed Desiree's reluctance to go on the late-night date with Tyson, her effort to get Tyson to come up to her already crowded room, her attempt to get Pasha to go along on the date. Everything she said suggested that Desiree had not anticipated a night of sex with Mike Tyson. And even more important, Kycia testified that

Desiree was a different person after her encounter with Tyson. Fuller's cross-examination did nothing to alter Kycia's account of the episode.

**D**esiree was scheduled to testify after lunch. That morning I had received reports that she was still stressed out from the night before, and Barb, Jeff Modisett, and I agreed that we wanted to keep her away from the media for as long as we could. Our major concern was getting her into the City-County Building, which was besieged by an army of television, newspaper, and magazine reporters. Armed with microphones, cameras, and tape recorders, they went into a feeding frenzy whenever anyone even remotely newsworthy walked into the building.

We decided to use a decoy, hardly a novel idea; John Grisham had used the device in *A Time To Kill*. Jeff instructed a young woman who worked in the prosecutor's office to cover her head with her coat and walk into the building through the Market Street entrance accompanied by two well-known detectives. It worked perfectly. The reporters swarmed around her, shouting questions and flashing pictures, stopping only after the elevator door shut. The woman then removed the coat, got off on the fifth floor, and returned to her desk. In the meantime, Desiree, dressed casually and unaccompanied by detectives, slipped into the building through a back door. Later, journalists attacked Jeff as if he had single-handedly subverted the Constitution and the principle of freedom of the press. Only Jack Rinehart and Channel 6 filmed Desiree's entrance into the building. As usual, Jack knew the right people.

At lunch in the prosecutor's office, Desiree was nervous but upbeat. She had heard good comments about my opening, which made her feel encouraged. In addition, she had avoided Gerstein and Hennessy, giving instructions to the detectives assigned to her that she did not want to see the two lawyers. She had refused to take Gerstein's phone calls at her hotel overnight, declined to talk to him in the morning, and requested that he not be allowed to eat lunch with the rest of us. I later learned that Gerstein and Hennessy were frantic. They didn't understand why they couldn't find anybody.

After lunch I took Desiree up to our war room next to Superior Court V, where Gerstein and Hennessy eventually showed up. They needed to see Desiree. Charles Washington, Desiree's brother who was representing the family, went out into the hall to talk with the lawyers. Chuck was angry when he left the room, and I feared he might take a swing at Gerstein. But I could hear him through the door, saying in a calm if not especially friendly voice, "You guys are off the case. Your services are no longer necessary." Just like that. In essence, the family decided that it didn't like what Gerstein and Hennessy were doing. *Bang! You're dead. Give us your courtroom passes and credentials and get out.* The two slunk off like a couple of scalded dogs.

The trial was about to resume; Kycia Johnson had not quite finished her testimony. I wanted a chance to get a couple of quiet minutes alone with Desiree, so we ducked into the jury room of Superior Court VII and closed the door. I told her about my sojourn into the book of Matthew that morning. She was a very spiritual person, one who would have no trouble relating to the scriptures, particularly in a time of stress and difficulty. I showed her the passage in the Bible. She sat on a wooden jury chair and read it through. When she finished, her eyes opened wide and a big kid's smile animated her face and she said, "Oh, wow. That's awesome." I realized now that there was something to be said for representing a live victim after all, and I gave her a little hug and sent her out the door.

In the hall her family surrounded her—Mom, Dad, brother, sister locked arms with Desiree in the middle. It was powerful to watch. They all embraced her and then quietly said the Lord's Prayer. I looked around, and there were all these mean, nasty cops, hardened investigators, and cynical lawyers just standing there, frozen in place, watching. The back hallway was as silent as a cathedral. I glanced at Kim Devane, a paralegal who had worked tirelessly on the case. Tears were running down her cheeks. Erica Roach, who had carried so much of the research burden, seemed transfixed, overwhelmed at the sight of this family from the Ebenezer Baptist Church in Coventry, Rhode Island, surrounding their daughter and sister with so much love. When the long embrace ended, Desiree and I moved toward an empty room to await her call to testify.

**V**ery few people sitting in the courtroom had ever seen Desiree. Her charges, not she, had been the center of media speculation. When the recess ended and the jurors resumed their seats, I stood, faced the judge, and announced, "The State would call Desiree Lynn Washington."

Desiree stepped in the back side door behind the jury box. She was wearing a gray silk suit, conservatively cut with a high front but fitted to her form. Her hair was all fixed up, and she looked beautiful. Here was an eighteen-year-old kid ready to jump into a pressure cooker with the world's media watching her. She was shaking when she walked through the doorway.

An audible gasp came out of the gallery. When I asked several people about it later, they said that the jurors, reporters, and spectators were simply shocked at how little and slight Desiree was. I saw a few jurors' heads swivel—from Desiree to Tyson, back to Desiree, back to Tyson. Sitting at the defense table was this 260-pound hulk of a man; walking into the courtroom was this hundred-and-a-couple-pound young lady who looked more like a girl than a grown woman. At that moment anyone with half a brain was thinking, *What are we talking about? Sex? Wait a minute.*

Barb saw that Desiree was shaking and took her by the left arm and led her to the witness stand. It was a sweet spontaneous gesture, and of course it played well, showing that her love and concern for Desiree went beyond the victim-attorney relationship. Judge Gifford looked down from her bench and said, "Would you raise you right hand, please." The witness was then sworn in and we immediately went to work.

It took an hour and a half for Desiree to tell her story. To me it seemed like only a minute and a half before I said to the defense, "Your witness." In twenty years as a trial lawyer, I have never been so absolutely immersed in what I was doing, so completely consumed by the business, the style, the presentation of a witness.

What happens in a courtroom is not theater; it's real and it's serious, not fictional or contrived. But when I present a witness, I observe certain rules of the theater. Rule number one is that action takes precedence over words. No matter what my witness is saying, if I cough, pick my nose, or fall on my ass, the jury is going to watch me rather than listen to the witness. Therefore, I try to remove myself from the jurors' range of vision. I want their focus on the witness stand. The art is to get your witness talking and then drop out of sight, intervening only to move the witness from one point to the next or to keep the witness from moving off the central subject.

My fear with Desiree was that her voice would shrink to fit her tiny frame. Rather than move close to her, where she could have answered my questions in a whisper, I stood at the opposite end of the jury box. To see me, she had to look at the jury. For me to hear her, she had to speak to every member of the jury. Although she was frightened when she began testifying, she soon warmed up to the task, sitting up straight, opening her posture to the jury, and making solid eye contact. I could see that the jurors were captivated by her beauty, innocence, and integrity. As she spoke about her life it was obvious that she had worked hard, accomplished much, and was proud of who she was and what she had done. She was proud of her race, referring to African Americans as "my people." The thought of attacking a successful black man in court obviously bothered her. But she asserted that she should be able to go out with any man, at any time, without fear of being raped.

I wanted the jurors to see her and remember her, so that when the defense started to trot out witnesses who were going to claim that Desiree had said this nasty thing or suggested that vulgar thing, the jurors would think, *Just a second. I listened to Desiree. I learned something about her background. She's a young woman of deep faith who works with disadvantaged children and studies hard. I don't believe she said what those people are accusing her of saying.*

Moving toward the rape, she told the same story about meeting Tyson as she had in her original police report and grand jury testimony. The rehearsal—"You're a nice Christian girl, right?" The Black Expo opening ceremony—a quick glimpse of Tyson praying with Jesse Jackson and the TOGETHER IN CHRIST button. The early morning telephone call—Tyson pleading, almost begging, "Can you come out? We'll just go around. I just want to talk to you. Can you come out?" A chance to see the town; an opportunity to meet celebrities; an adventure. Desiree threw on some foundation, grabbed her camera to record her adventure, and raced out the door, down to the waiting limousine. The stop at the Canterbury—"He said something about he had to stop to pick something up. And he said something about a bodyguard. And I was looking around to try to figure out where we were. And he opened the door or the door was opened. I don't remember. And he said, 'Come on.' And I said, 'Okay.' And I got out and went with him." They walked into the Canterbury, Desiree a few steps behind Tyson, who shook the bellman's hand and smiled at a few well-wishers.

In Suite 606—no hand holding, no kissing, no signs of affection, just a friendly talk about Rhode Island, foster children, pets, pigeons, families, life. A talk about everything and nothing. Friendly. A western on TV provided background noise for the conversation. Then Tyson changed—"You're turning me on." Just like that; it came out of nowhere. "And I just got really nervous and started babbling. And I said, 'I need to use your bathroom. When I come out, I want to see Indianapolis like you said.'" Tyson touched his face with both hands and said, "Okay. Okay."

When she came out, Tyson was sitting on the bed wearing only his underpants.

Q. What was your reaction?
A. I was terrified.
Q. What did you say?
A. I said, "It's time for me to leave."
Q. Like that?
A. Yeah.
Q. And his response?
A. "Come here." And he grabbed my arm; and he was like, "Don't fight me. Come here." And then he stuck his tongue in my mouth.
Q. How did you react to that?
A. He was disgusting.

Going through the painful business of the rape itself was not easy for Desiree, especially in front of a room full of strangers. But the law required it. She had to describe how Tyson ripped off her clothes. She had to verify every charge in the indictment—"He put his hand into me, his fingers into my vagina"; "He grabbed my legs, and he lifted me up . . . and he licked me from my rectum to my vagina"; "He pulled his penis—exposed his penis. . . . He jammed it in my vagina."

As she talked, I stayed out of the way. It gave me a chance to observe the effect of her testimony. Everyone in the courtroom was riveted by Desiree's story. It might be a cliché, but it was literally true. The jurors sat captivated, hardly even blinking. The reporters and spectators watched as if they were viewing the horrible act itself, grimacing and wincing as she described the rape. Even Vince Fuller sat slack-mouthed, transfixed, I think, by Desiree's testimony.

She had the guts and courage to say what the law required. At one point, as she described the physical and emotional pain of the rape, I thought she was going to start to cry. But she sucked it up hard, paused, took a couple of deep breaths, and continued. Her eyes moistened, but they didn't flood; she never broke down and no tears ever got outside the confines of her eyelashes. She just blinked them back and continued to march. Later a few reporters suggested that she was too stoical, that a normal eighteen-year-old rape victim would have broken down. One journalist commented that she seemed "a little prissy" and "almost too perfect." I agree. Desiree Washington was special. A kid with less courage than she had would have folded up like a cheap card table. In fact, a person with less courage than she had would never have made it to the trial. The pressure, the million-dollar bribe attempts, would have ended the whole thing long ago. She had the courage to say no to a million dollars, the courage to say yes to the challenge. As tiny as she was and as fragile as she seemed, she was too tough to fold.

She continued. After the rape, Tyson told her, "You're just a baby. That's all. You're just a crybaby. You're crying because I'm big." She left. She saw Dale Edwards smirk. She told Virginia Foster, "He's just a bad person. He's just a bad person." She "zoned out."

The physical pain continued for days, but she remained in the pageant. I asked why. "I played softball for about twelve years. I've had fractured ribs and fingers and stuff like that, and I always make the play and finish the game before I quit. I mean, I just don't quit. I was in pain, and I just [bore] it. If I was a quitter, I wouldn't be here now. . . . I finished what I started." But the emotional pain lingered long after the physical pain had disappeared.

When Desiree returned tó Coventry, she slept with her mother every night until she left for college in late August. She was having nightmares and was afraid. When she went to Providence College that fall, the nightmares continued. She would call her mother: "She'd read to me and stuff until I was really, really tired, and I'd just fall asleep."

Q. How long did you continue to have that problem?
A. I still do, sometimes.

I waited a few seconds. No one breathed. Then I said, "That's all, Judge." It was the most powerful moment in direct examination and presentation of evidence that I had ever experienced as a lawyer.

Fuller did his job, and I didn't envy him for a moment. It was his duty to try to poke holes in a story that I think every objective observer, including those twelve people in the jury box, knew was true. He began his cross-examination late Thursday afternoon and finished it on Friday. He attacked Desiree's credibility, suggesting that she was after Tyson's money. He asked if after meeting Tyson she began to sing, "Money, money, money, money, money" from the song "For the Love of Money." She answered, "No, I didn't." He asked if Tyson said "I want you" at their first meeting. Again she answered no.

Switching directions, Fuller focused on minor discrepancies between her original statement to Detective Thomas Kuzmik and her testimony. Had she seen Dale Edwards before or after going into the room with Tyson? How was Tyson sitting at a particular time? "I certainly was in a very traumatized and frightened state of mind," Desiree explained. "Little details. I'm sorry if I left them out at the time."

In a final attempt to discredit her testimony, Fuller began to explore the nature of her legal relationship with Ed Gerstein. This relationship, which later would become a major issue in Tyson's appeal, was not a central part of Fuller's cross-examination. For the most part the legal nature of Fuller's questions passed over Desiree's head.

Q. Do you think [Gerstein] has some retainer arrangement with your parents?
A. I don't know what "retainer" means.

Q. Do you think he had some fee arrangement with your parents?

A. I don't know.

Q. Have you heard them explain or discuss with you a contingent [fee]?

A. What's "contingent" mean?

Q. Fee payable on a contingent that he's successful in some way.

A. No. The only thing I know, they have to pay for his flights out here.

After a few more such questions, Fuller moved on to an area he explored in more depth—the alleged vulgar language Tyson used with Desiree and other contestants and Desiree's designs on Tyson's fortune. "Did you hear Mr. Tyson say to any other contestants, 'Why don't you come to my room for a kiss and sex? Sex would be better'?" "Do you recall Mr. Tyson saying to several contestants, 'You going to give it up? You going to give it up?' " "Did you comment to any of the contestants . . . 'There's twenty million dollars'?" "Do you recall . . . one of the contestants saying to you, 'Desiree, here comes your husband. Too bad he can't talk'?" Desiree: no, no, no, no. Fuller seemed less interested in her confirmation than in suggesting an alternative interpretation to the jury.

Fuller finished in time for lunch. After over four hours of cross-examination, Desiree's story remained rock solid, and the press reports echoed my beliefs. The *New York Times* reporter wrote that "the woman and her account emerged unshaken" from Fuller's attack. Alison Muscatine, the *Washington Post*'s legal correspondent, agreed: "Neither [Fuller] nor co-counsel Kathleen Beggs was able to expose any serious contradictions in her testimony that Tyson . . . had pinned her to the bed, ripped off her clothes and raped her even though she pleaded with him to stop." As much as the hometown reporters, the journalists from the East Coast had been won over by Desiree's integrity. Desiree had moved the jury several long steps toward that elusive standard—beyond a reasonable doubt.

**D**esiree's testimony was the heart of our case; the rest was merely buttressing. Since the rape, Kuzmik and the detectives who worked with him had investigated every lead. Barb, George Horn, and I had conducted over fifty depositions. We had spent hundreds of hours with our key witnesses. Over the next three days of testimony we had to demonstrate that at every confirmable point Desiree's story was true.

Chris Low, the night bellman at the Canterbury, turned out to be an excellent witness. He was bright, observant, and completely impartial. For some reason Chris had dropped out of college because he wanted to do something fun, and his idea of fun was working as a bellman in a fancy hotel. He liked to observe the behavior of the stars and other wealthy people who spent a night or two at the Canterbury, and he was a good people-watcher, paying close attention. He could describe the walk and mannerisms of a hundred guests he had seen come into the hotel. He vividly remembered Tyson's entrance with Desiree. Tyson had strolled several steps behind her; smiling, he walked the walk of a man who was famous. He did not hold Desiree's hand or talk to her or even attempt to hold the door for her. Instead, he stopped to shake Low's hand, an action that impressed the young bellman. Low's observations added credibility and credence to Desiree's claim that she and Tyson were just stopping at the Canterbury for a minute while Tyson picked something up. Low had seen plenty of famous men come into the Canterbury with women hanging off them. This was not the case with Desiree and Tyson.

Chris Low also verified Desiree's story of how she had departed Tyson's suite—confused, scared, her shoes in her hands. He repeated what he had earlier told police investigators: he was delivering an early morning snack to Dale Edwards in Room 604 when Desiree emerged from Suite 606. As he pushed his service cart into 604, he saw Edwards smirk. He turned his head in time to see Desiree leave 606: "She was looking around like she was lost." It was just as Desiree had testified.

Unfortunately for Tyson and Dale Edwards, this was not the scenario they had described in their grand jury testimony. Both men had claimed that Edwards was in Suite 606 during Tyson's tryst. As was made clear during Tyson's testimony, Edwards had claimed that he heard Tyson and Desiree engaging in vigorous, consensual sex, and that as she walked by him on her way out of the room, her shoes in one hand, she gave him her address and phone number on a slip of paper. Good story; and if true, irrefutable confirmation of Tyson's account. But it was a bullshit lie. Edwards wasn't in 606; he was in 604. The only part of Edwards's story that was true was that Desiree was carrying her shoes, and he knew that because he saw the same thing as Chris Low.

"Where's Dale?" was the question that was often asked during the trial. I even saw a few WHERE'S DALE? T-shirts and buttons. Dale Edwards, I assumed, was back in Cleveland. Had he repeated his grand jury testimony at the trial, there was a strong likelihood he would have left the courtroom in a pair of handcuffs en route to jail for perjury.

McCoy Wagers, the night desk clerk, had also seen Dale Edwards that night. While Tyson was in Suite 606 with Desiree, Wagers talked to Edwards at the front desk, saw him make several phone calls from the front parlor, and watched him step out of the hotel briefly. While Tyson was six floors above, Edwards was making plane reservations to fly to Cleveland. Wagers also supported Low's observation that Tyson and Desiree walked into the Canterbury a few steps away from each other, and that Tyson was smiling and friendly. When Tyson departed, there were no smiles. He and Edwards left in haste, not even bothering to check out.

Contrary to most courtroom television shows and movies, liars are often effective witnesses. And two liars—Edwards and Tyson—are better than one. No matter how nonsensical the story, the more people who will say it, the more of a problem it creates for the prosecutor. Had Wagers and Low—and Virginia Foster, who also talked to Edwards while Tyson was in his suite with Desiree—not been able to provide a zone defense against Edwards, he probably would have testified. His testimony, even if it had been a lie, would have strengthened Tyson's position.

Building on Wager's and Low's testimony, we called Virginia Foster as our first major witness at a specially convened Saturday session Judge Gifford called for the benefit of the jurors, who had been sequestered since the start of the trial. We favored the decision. Our case was building momentum, and it was too cold outside to do much else except watch the Winter Olympics on television.

Virginia Foster had always told us the truth, but she had seldom told us everything she knew. What she saw, what she experienced, came out in drips. There was always new information, and it frustrated me because I wanted to get everything, right away. But that wasn't Virginia's style. Tyson and Edwards had sexually harassed her, grabbed her, propositioned her, and just talked dirty to her constantly during Tyson's visit to Black Expo, and she didn't like talking about it to a white prosecutor one bit. Most of what I knew I heard first from Darryl Pierce, the Indianapolis detective who had her confidence.

Virginia and I had had something of a meeting of minds a few weeks before the trial. It happened during one of our preparation sessions when I was doing a mock cross-examination of her. I had been picking on her a little, questioning and second-guessing everything she told me. "You keep saying that Desiree looked upset, how do you know she was upset?" "Well, I just know." "What kind of answer is that?" "I know what I'm talking about." "Why do you know what you're talking about?" She got angry and told me she knew because she had seen it dozens of times in her job as a guidance counselor. *Bingo.* "Then say that," I said.

That got us talking about what she did and how she could spot problems. She was a professional, trained in dealing with young girls who had been beaten, raped, and abused, kids who were disoriented, disheveled, confused. She knew there was something wrong with Desiree because she had seen women in trouble before. She then described exactly what she saw down to every nuance and facial expression.

It was that woman of professional competence who faced the jury. But she wasn't allowed to tell everything she knew about Tyson. Before Virginia testified, Williams & Connolly's gifted lawyer Lane Heard argued a motion to exclude any introduction of the sexual remarks or actions made toward Virginia, several of the Miss Black America contestants, and two local women. I argued that the experiences of Virginia Foster and several other contestants with Tyson demonstrated his "intention . . . to gratify himself irrespective of consent, irrespective of any kind of decency in his behavior, and clearly irrespective of the rule of law in criminal cases." Tyson's behavior during the time he was in Indianapolis was important; it established a pattern of behavior that circumstantially supported Desiree's account. It was important to our case that Tyson exposed his genitalia, made lewd comments, and lured Virginia Foster into a hotel room and assaulted her; in fact, he used the same line with Virginia—"I just want to talk"—that he would later use with Desiree. And it was also important that he physically assaulted Rosie Jones in a sexual manner at the opening ceremony. His conduct never changed. Heard responded that Virginia Foster had made at least four statements, and each time she had added a few details about Tyson's behavior. But he based his motion on case precedent rather than the facts, and Judge Gifford agreed, excluding any evidence of Tyson's "uncharged misconduct."

Ironically, our losing the motion may have made the state's case stronger. When Virginia testified, the jury saw a professional, articulate woman who, though it was never stated, clearly had only disdain for Tyson. But the defense could not explore the reasons for her bias; its hands were tied by its own successfully argued motion. By keeping the dirt out, Williams & Connolly robbed themselves of material for a good cross-examination. If Virginia had been allowed to testify about how crudely Tyson had treated her, the defense could have argued that that very treatment colored her account of the fateful night. Watching the cross-examination, I enjoyed the thought that Fuller might have outsmarted and outargued himself.

Watching Barb handle Virginia on the stand, I was sweating bullets, afraid that Virginia might be having a shy day. But though she was hoarse from a bout with the flu and occasionally spoke no louder than a whisper, she came across beautifully—quiet but confident, a self-made woman who was sure about what she had observed. Testifying on her wedding anniversary, she was as disarming as she was charming. She left no doubt in the jurors' minds that Desiree had changed during the hour she spent in Tyson's room.

Confirming Desiree's story, Virginia described how Tyson pleaded with Desiree on the phone to go out with him. "Please, please. I just want to talk to you," Virginia remembered him saying. He repeated the phrase several times, talking "like when a man is trying to get a woman to do something for him; so they beg and plead for it. They say, 'Please, please.' " She recalled that when Desiree finally arrived at the limousine, her hair was "fixed pretty." She did not observe any physical contact between Desiree and Tyson.

When Desiree walked out of the Canterbury, however, she seemed like a different person. She rushed into the limousine before Virginia could open the door. Her hair was messed up, and "she looked all frantic . . . like she might have been in a state of shock. . . . She seemed scared." Desiree appeared "dazed or disoriented" and kept repeating, "I don't believe him. I don't believe him. Who does he think he is?"

In his cross-examination, Fuller suggested that Virginia had been tired, that during Tyson's visit to Indianapolis she had gotten little sleep. Virginia agreed that she was exhausted, but not too tired to know what she saw. Fuller also implied that she had overcharged Tyson for the use of her limousine telephone, as if that charge—one Virginia denied—somehow raised questions about her character or vision. Throughout Fuller's cross-examination, Virginia remained unshakable about what she had seen: Desiree "came out in a hurry. She looked like she was disoriented. She was frantic. She looked scared." When we broke for a late lunch and Virginia was excused to go home for her anniversary celebration, I knew that she had added enormously to the credibility of Desiree Washington.

In the afternoon session the physicians took center stage. Dr. Thomas Richardson and Dr. James Akin explained what they knew about the nature of introital injuries and consensual sex. Simply put: introital injuries almost never happen during the kind of sexual encounter Tyson had described. Richardson had done between two and three thousand pelvic examinations and had seen the kind of abrasions Desiree had sustained only twice in women who said they had gotten them during consensual sex (and he had private doubts about those two). Akin had completed more than twenty thousand pelvic examinations and had never seen such abrasions in a woman who had voluntarily engaged in sex. Women do occasionally sustain vaginal injuries during sex, but they normally occur in the vaginal walls where, because of radiation treatment, venereal disease, infection, age, or general poor health, the condition of the tissue has deteriorated. In cases of rape, however, 10 to 20 percent of all victims suffer some kind of vaginal injury.

Richardson confirmed that in his examination of Desiree twenty-six hours after her sexual encounter with Tyson, he found two introital abrasions. Desiree, he testified, was in control of her emotions but visibly upset, and her voice had "a little quiver to it." Her demeanor was typical of a rape victim. As the examination continued, she became more and more distressed. She was in pain and emotional discomfort, and Richardson terminated the examination without performing a complete rape kit.

Akin, the reproductive endocrinologist and infertility specialist at the Indiana University School of Medicine, gave added perspective to Richardson's testimony. For a young man who had not been an expert witness before, he commanded the courtroom in a quiet, unassuming way. He treated the jury like an internal medicine class that was doing a rotation in ob/gyn, and he was a great teacher. He discussed the physiology of sexual intercourse and the nature of the injuries that a woman can sustain. Desiree's injuries, he believed, were "not consistent with consensual sex." The medical literature supported his opinion. After reviewing the findings of the literature and taking into account his own experience, Akin concluded, "I never say something can't happen one hundred percent. But the literature and my experience says [Desiree Washington's injuries] would be incredibly unlikely to have happened during consensual sex."

When a physician says "It sure looked like rape to me," jurors listen. In an effort to discredit Akin, Beggs turned her cross-examination into a long, involved discussion of the literature on sexual trauma and succeeded only in losing half the courtroom. As she went back and forth with Akin, I watched the jurors tune her out one by one. I tried to remain alert, but eventually even I was numbed silly by a discussion of the difference between "abrasion abrasions" and "micro abrasions."

Finally I objected: "This sophistry is wearing me out." The courtroom, noted a *Washington Post* reporter, "erupted in laughter," thankful, I suspect, for some break in the tedium. But I was serious. Someplace in the legal code there should be a sustainable objection based on severe and unusual boredom. It just shouldn't be tolerated beyond a certain point, and by five o'clock on Saturday afternoon, we had reached that point. Perhaps even Beggs agreed, for she soon concluded her cross-examination and we all retired for a one-day weekend.

On Sunday I read several out-of-town newspapers just to get a sense of how neutral journalists, many of them experienced jury watchers, had reacted to our case. It was like reading movie reviews. Personalities and performances more than issues dominated the coverage. I had become the country lawyer whose "colloquial style and down-home charm" had "drawn a chuckle from the stone-faced jury on occasion." Barb was the "down-to-earth and friendly," motherly figure who hugged Desiree after she finished testifying. Fuller was the "aloof professor," Beggs "impersonal and humorless." The trial had become a screenplay, replete with a heroic uphill struggle by the outgunned, outspent, beleaguered underdogs. David and Goliath, Valley Forge, the 1980 Olympic hockey team, the Hoosiers—we were the home team. After a week of the trial, journalists searching through their thesaurus of boxing metaphors reported that "Tyson was on the ropes." But Barb and I both knew that the trial was a long way from being over. We had expected a strong showing the first week, and the defense had yet to present its side.

On Monday we called a series of technical and character witnesses to corroborate aspects of Desiree's testimony. Stacy Murphy and Charrisse Nelson, two Miss Black America contestants, confirmed that Desiree was different after her encounter with Tyson. Murphy recalled a pageant function on the morning of July 19, with the contestants filming a dance number in front of Union Station. She and Desiree had a running joke that they were the only two contestants with no rhythm: "We used to say we were sisters under one rhythmless nation." But on that morning Desiree lacked her normal enthusiasm. When Murphy asked her what was wrong, Desiree confided that she had been raped by Mike Tyson. "She just didn't even look like herself, not the person I had grown to know," Murphy testified. "It wasn't her. . . . She was just like a zombie, like something had just totally taken over her."

Charrisse Nelson agreed. Desiree had told her about the rape, too. Nelson said Desiree looked around as she spoke, "holding herself. . . . She was just amazed." Nelson had told Desiree, "Press charges. Take him to jail."

In his cross-examination of both witnesses, Lane Heard sketched the outline of Tyson's defense. The idea was simple: demonstrate repeatedly that Tyson was so out of control that any woman who went out with him must have known what would happen. Heard's style was different from Fuller's or Beggs's. He was more relaxed and informal, with a southern drawl that seemed to say, *Let's sit down and talk awhile.* With the contestants he wanted to talk about Mike, about what a wild and crazy party animal the former champion was. The subtext ran, *You got some dirt on Mike? Let's hear it.* Just about every contestant who came in contact with him, regardless of how briefly, had at least one salacious tale.

Stacy Murphy remembered how Tyson had blown off Jesse Jackson at the opening ceremony. Black Expo was honoring a military leader, but Tyson ignored the show of respect and flirted with the contestants. Jackson tried to get Tyson's attention, but the boxer said he didn't want to be bothered. That's just the way he was: no respect for a major black leader, and certainly none for black women. Murphy remembered that when Tyson visited the contestants at the Omni, he was all hands: "Like an octopus. . . . He was feeling on one girl's behind and brushed up against one girl's breast and bringing another girl closer to him while touching another girl's body. He was pretty busy."

Nelson had seen Tyson in action even before Black Expo. She had met him in December 1990 at the Apollo Theater in Harlem. She was eighteen, and Tyson had asked for her phone number. "W-E-six, one-two-one-two," she had answered, giving him the telephone number for the local weather. When she posed for a picture with Tyson in Indianapolis, he rubbed her leg until she removed his hand. Later when he was standing behind her, he said, "Don't bend over like that. What I could do with you." Like Murphy, Nelson had no doubt that Tyson had sex on his mind.

Watching Barb and Lane Heard examine the beauty contestants, I sensed that the rest of the trial would provide copy for tabloid television. I could hear the come-on leads: "Mike on the Make," "Troubles with Tyson." The underlying message of the Tyson defense was, *Come on, Desiree was a mature woman. She knew what Mike wanted. He didn't force her into his room. We're all grown-ups here, and she got what she asked for—or at least, what she deserved.*

On Tuesday we concluded the state's case. A variety of voices had been heard in Criminal Court IV since the jury had listened to Desiree. The experts had spoken—physicians, lab technicians, police investigators. The limo driver, the desk clerk, the bellman had spoken. Beauty contestants had spoken. It was time to hear from Desiree again. Once more before we rested our case, we wanted the jurors to hear what Mike Tyson had done, not just to Desiree but to the whole Washington family. We wanted the jurors to remember that the scars of the victim had also disfigured her family.

Mary Bell Washington, Desiree's mother, was a soft-spoken, very beautiful woman in her forties. She had green eyes and a gentle temperament, and she and her husband, Donald, had reared three loving, independent children. From the first time I met her, it was clear that she suffered because she had not been able to prevent her daughter's terrible experience. It was that anguish, that palpable heartache, that I wanted the jurors to recognize.

Dressed in a blue suit with a pearl brooch, she spoke about the effect of Tyson's reckless actions. There was an eerie silence in the courtroom when she testified. As she spoke about her daughter, a note of loss could be heard in her voice, the grief that a parent would feel for a child who no longer existed. Although she was composed when she took the witness stand, several times during her testimony her voice cracked and tears ran down her cheeks. Her crying had a fragile quality—soft, quiet, unashamed.

Mary Bell Washington described her daughter when the family arrived in Indianapolis, almost a full day after the rape: "She just looked terrible when I saw her. She didn't look like the same girl that I sent down here. She was pale, and she was upset. . . . And I just ran through the door, and I just grabbed her and hugged her."

She told about Desiree's nightmares, about the nights her daughter crawled into bed with her because she saw Tyson's face in the dark and got scared. Desiree still called her from her college dorm when the nightmares recurred. One day Desiree said, "Mom, I'm not Desiree anymore. . . . Desiree is gone, and she's not going to come back." At the end of her testimony Washington said, "I just want my daughter back."

If I ever sympathized with the job Vince Fuller had undertaken, it was during his questioning of the witness. How do you cross-examine a shattered parent? Well,

> Q. Mrs. Washington—
> A. Yes.
> Q. —your daughter, Desiree, is a bright, intelligent young woman, is she not?
> A. I consider her to be intelligent.
> Q. And you love her very much?
> A. Of course I do.

Fuller concluded: "I have nothing further."

The court broke for lunch. Several jurors were crying. I think they realized that a mother wouldn't hurt that bad unless her daughter's pain was real.


Early that afternoon, with the playing of an edited version of Desiree's 911 tape, we completed the state's case. It was as if there was a ghost in the house, a disembodied voice full of pain drifting out of the machine in the front of the courtroom. The defense had attempted to block the playing of the tape, arguing that the call was not made until twenty-three hours after the incident. But Indiana law makes clear that these "excited utterances" are admissible even if a significant period of time goes by between the crime and when the actual statement is made. Judge Gifford ruled in our favor. The tape was a powerful piece of evidence; it was like bringing Desiree back, only this time without any opportunity for cross-examination.

Clear confusion registered in Desiree's voice. She told Esteen Smith, the 911 dispatcher, that she had been raped by "someone, like, famous." She described meeting the famous person, thinking he was a "nice person," being lured into his room, and raped. Like so many other victims of date rape, she feared "that people [would] think it is my fault for going to his room, that I was . . . naive to believe that he was . . . a nice person.'' She had conflicting emotions. She feared the publicity—that people would think she was after money—and the attacker's wealth and power, but she believed he should be punished for his actions: ''Part of me wants to do something, and part of me is just scared.''

After the recorder was cleared away, the state rested its case. It was a good case, a well-presented case. The confidence I felt would last about twelve hours.

# CHAPTER 15

# "PEOPLE EXPECT IT"

It was 3:00 A.M., and I had been asleep for less than two hours when I got the call and recognized Jeff Duhamell's voice.

"Greg, there's been a fire at the Athletic Club and a few people have died."

"Oh, shit."

Since the start of the trial, the twelve jurors and three alternates had been sequestered each night at the Indianapolis Athletic Club, a stately old brick building in the downtown. I feared that the flames that had engulfed the Athletic Club might also consume *State* v. *Tyson.*

The facts were these: at 12:08 on the morning of February 5, the Indianapolis Fire Department received a report of a fire at 350 North Meridian Street. Seventy-five firemen and twelve apparatus responded to the three-alarm fire. The first firemen at the scene were deceived by the blaze, which had started in the bar area on the third floor, because they saw no smoke. They discovered smoke on the third floor, however, and while they searched the lounge, a flashover—a spontaneous fireball created by heat in excess of 1,110 degrees—engulfed them, killing Captain Ellwood Gelenius and Private John Lorenzano. Thomas Mutz, a businessman from Illinois, also died in the fire. The blaze injured eleven other people, some critically.

Within hours after the fire was extinguished, Mayor Goldsmith announced that there was no evidence of arson, a finding that was reconfirmed by a later investigation.

But arson was all I could think about. It couldn't be a coincidence. I began to count the people who might profit if Tyson went free but quickly ran out of fingers. Some Tyson supporter, maybe one of the hundreds of well-wishers who waited every day outside the City-County Building in the early morning or late afternoon cold to catch a peek of him, or one of the people who packed the "Free Mike" rallies at local churches, could have started the fire. Perhaps someone who had something to gain if Tyson remained out of prison had paid an arsonist to start it. If I was paranoid, I believed that there was a logic behind my paranoia.

**W**ith news of the fire still burning in my mind, my thoughts returned to the previous morning in court. Tyson's defense team had attempted to introduce three new witnesses in the case. Allegedly, one of these women had seen Tyson and Desiree walk into the Canterbury on the night of the rape. She claimed that Tyson and Desiree were "all over each other," kissing and hugging and walking arm in arm. Although she was specific about the behavior of Tyson and Desiree, neither she nor her friends were very specific about anything else. Some claimed the limousine was white; it was gold. They remembered Desiree wearing a tight black miniskirt; she had on loose-fitting jams. Giving them the benefit of the doubt, I thought that they had probably simply gotten the date mixed up. The scene they described, down to the white limousine and heavy necking, fitted that of Tyson's arrival at the Canterbury with B Angie B on July 18, not his arrival with Desiree on July 19. Chris Low, the bellman on both nights, remembered both women quite clearly. Yes, B Angie B was on Tyson like an article of clothing. Desiree and Tyson, however, never touched as they walked into the Canterbury; instead, they were separated by several paces.

Our concern about the late-blooming witnesses centered on the timing of their introduction. All three were from Indianapolis, and the one who said she had seen the most had worked for Black Expo and was a friend of the Reverend Charles Williams, the president of Black Expo. In fact, it was Williams, a friend of Tyson's, who put the three women in contact with Tyson's lawyers. But why so late? we wondered. The Tyson case wasn't exactly a guarded secret in Indianapolis; it had only been the biggest story of the year. Why had the three women not come forward earlier? Why had they not appeared on any previous witness lists? Why had they waited until we were about to rest our case to get involved?

As Williams & Connolly's attorneys explained, the three women had first approached them at about four o'clock on the afternoon of Thursday, January 30. Concerned that the women might not be telling the truth, Tyson's lawyers decided to conduct their own independent investigation before informing the court or the prosecution of the surfacing of the witnesses. They wanted to examine the limousine to make sure a person could even see through its tinted windows, and they wanted the women to identify it. Not until late Sunday afternoon, February 2, were we told about the three new witnesses. By that time, of course, Desiree had testified and gone home and we were putting the finishing touches on our case.

We interpreted the appearance of the late bloomers as an attempt at trial by ambush, a tactic used more often in the federal than the county courts. We had no time to interview or depose the new witnesses. We had no time to investigate their allegations. With the jury sequestered, we could not ask for a lengthy continuance. Tyson's lawyers knew this, but when Lane Heard made a motion to add the witnesses, he aimed to give the impression that his motives were as pure as Rocky Mountain spring water: "We are here actually after the truth, and that is why it is imperative that these witnesses be allowed to come forward and give what is critical evidence."

When defense lawyers take shelter in talk of the truth, I get suspicious. Clothed in self-righteous indignation, Heard argued that it was an "absolutely false imputation" that he and his associates knew anything about the three witnesses before Thursday afternoon; to suggest as much was a "desperate insinuation." Jim Voyles and Vincent Fuller agreed. Voyles objected that the prosecution had attacked his credibility and integrity. Judge Gifford assured him that no one was questioning his integrity. Fuller also defended his integrity: "With my thirty-five years at the bar, no one in any court in the country has ever accused me of making misrepresentations to a court." He offered to make a statement under oath that he personally knew nothing about the latecomers before Saturday. Judge Gifford said that such a statement would not be necessary.

Who knew what, and when, was not really the issue. I didn't then nor do I now question the integrity of Fuller or Voyles. As I stated in court, however, I did believe that there was "something inherently distrustful or mistrustful or untrustworthy about a person who doesn't bother to come forward with . . . pivotal information until after a jury is sworn, opening statements have been heard, and the witnesses are on the stand." Based on a preliminary investigation, I also believed that it was physically impossible for the primary new witness to have seen what she alleged to have seen.

As Judge Gifford listened to Lane Heard argue for the motion, I watched her eyes harden into ice. Under Judge Gifford's intent gaze, Heard's sharp features seemed to soften; his hawkish nose and slicked-back hair didn't change, but his eyes became restless, as if he was looking for a place to hide. In a cold, controlled manner, the judge was becoming angrier by the second. She focused her anger on Heard, whose collar seemed to tighten in direct relationship to her mood. After he finished arguing his motion, Heard attempted to flee to his seat, but Judge Gifford prevented any tactical retreat. It was as though she had him on a line; every time he tried to scramble to his chair, she jerked the cord.

> HEARD (*concluding his motion*): And we urge Your Honor to let these late witnesses be heard.
> THE COURT: Mr. Heard (*pronounced* MISS-TER HEARD, *slowly, in three distinct syllables*), if you indicated that you had, in fact, first had knowledge of these witnesses on the first day that the State began the presentation of the evidence, why, in fact, was the State not advised at the time? (*The two "in facts" were like daggers thrown at Heard.*)
> HEARD (*squirming considerably*): Well, Your Honor, I guess the primary reason is that we have, as Your Honor might imagine, and it may be true of the Court as well as of our office and, I suspect, the Prosecutor's Office as well, we have gotten a lot of crank calls from people claiming to have evidence.

*Heard then launched into a story to prove how extreme crank calls can become and how he and his associates had not wanted to bother the court or the prosecutor's office with such trivia until they checked it out first. Satisfied with his answer, he made a move toward the safety of his chair.*

THE COURT (*unsatisfied with Heard's answer and with a quick jerk on the line*): Well, I can understand that prior to trial. I'm a little concerned about allowing a trial to proceed. My other question is that although you went out to examine the limo, did you, in fact, take the limo to the Canterbury and park it on the street the same as Mrs. Foster testified to?

HEARD (*by now as unctuous as Uriah Heap*): Your Honor, when we filed the motion on Saturday morning, we asked that the limousine be produced at the Canterbury, and that was the reason for suggesting that it be produced there. Your Honor had indicated that it should be produced elsewhere, and so we examined it elsewhere.

THE COURT (*this time jerking Heard back before he could even turn toward his chair*): But you didn't advise the Court as to why you wished to have it taken to the Canterbury, did you?

HEARD (*resigned to his fate*): No, Your Honor, we did not.

THE COURT: You did not advise the State as to why you wished to have it moved to the Canterbury?

HEARD: No, we did not.

George Horn prepared and argued our response to the motion to add the three witnesses. He asserted that adding witnesses of dubious credibility who had no new evidence to offer would both disrupt the rhythm of the state's presentation and prejudice the state's case. Judge Gifford concurred: "I feel that the Defendant's breach of the pretrial discovery order was not necessarily in bad faith, because I am presuming that you did not know of these people until the time that was indicated by counsel's filings. . . . However, I am of the opinion that not excluding the witnesses would result in substantial prejudice to the State of Indiana, and I believe that the State of Indiana is entitled to a fair trial the same as the Defendant in any case."

On one point, however, Judge Gifford wanted to be very clear. In case anyone missed her confrontation with Lane

Heard, she was angry. And the notion that the entire affair might have been a defense trick made her even angrier. "The Court does not appreciate being put in this position in the middle of a trial that's taken a great deal of effort if there is any possibility that it was done with the idea of causing some kind of a reversible error."

I had entertained the same conclusion. The pressure and the stakes of the case had in my mind bred ominous subtexts underlying everything that was said and done. I had begun to suspect that actions had meanings and interpretations that were not apparent on the surface. Tyson's lawyers must have sensed that their client was in trouble, that Desiree and Virginia Foster and Chris Low were credible witnesses, that the medical evidence spoke loudly of rape. Were they now establishing a record for an eventual appeal by forcing Judge Gifford to rule on slippery constitutional issues? The battles over the 911 tape and the new witnesses certainly fitted that interpretation of events. Even as I imagined the scenario, I thought that perhaps it was all simply a coincidence, and my fears the result of too little sleep and too much coffee. Perhaps I was just looking at sheets blowing in the wind and seeing ghosts.

Then Jeff Duhamell told me that the Athletic Club was on fire. And the sheets came off the line and began rummaging all over Indianapolis.


I wasn't the only person seeing ghosts. On Wednesday morning it seemed as if everyone connected with the case was jumpy. I heard reporters discuss not if the fire was set intentionally but rather who had started it. Outside Criminal Court IV, Judge Gifford ordered increased security. A metal detector similar to the type used in airports was placed in the hallway leading to the courtroom. Extra security officers and a bomb-sniffing Labrador retriever searched the building. Spectators were barred from the public area outside the court. Judge Gifford also postponed the trial for a day to allow her to ascertain what influence the fire had had on the jurors. Although none had been injured, they had all been awakened in the middle of the night by the fire alarms and escorted out of the Athletic Club, a few dressed only in their nightclothes or overcoats.

"The jurors are in good spirits under the circumstances," commented Joe Champion, a spokesman for Judge Gifford. Did he mean that they were happy to be alive? Or that they had been unaffected by the fire? Could they still sit in judgment of Tyson, or had the fire compromised their ability to reach a verdict? Would Tyson's attorneys ask for a mistrial? All day, members of the prosecution speculated about such questions. We sifted through a landfill of rumors searching for answers.

Later we learned that on the second floor of the City-County Building a drama was unfolding. The jurors knew that there had been a fire, but they had not been told how extensive it had been or how it had started. They were in the dark, alone with their own speculations. Outside the jury room a narrow window, maybe four feet high and six inches wide, threw some light on the matter. On his way to Judge Gifford's chambers, one juror glanced out the window and saw a flag flying at half-mast. Something had happened; someone had died. The information disturbed several jurors. Who had died? And how? What was going on? Their questions got no answers.

When Judge Gifford queried them, one juror, a thirty-six-year-old black man, said that he was too badly shaken to continue, and he was excused from the jury. From the prosecution's perspective, the change strengthened the jury. During the previous few days the juror had demonstrated clear signs that he was having trouble with the case. Judge Gifford advised Fuller and me that he had been a problem for the other jurors and for the courtroom staff as well. He was on edge, complaining to the other jurors and the bailiff about everything from the quality of the food and lodging to the demands of the jury assignment. Nothing was ever done to his satisfaction. His mood in the jury box seemed to range from bored to totally disaffected. Barb and I were particularly alarmed by reports that he was concerned about what his friends would think if he voted against Tyson. Since jurors are instructed to disregard all consideration of how the community might react to their verdict, his concern was inappropriate. Evidence, not any factor outside the case, should be a juror's only concern. For Barb and me, the juror's comments added up to one thing: a hung jury. He just didn't want to have to make a decision. The fire allowed him to avoid the difficult choice. When Judge Gifford asked if the fire would make it harder for him to render a verdict in the case, he said yes and took his free ticket home. The other jurors said no and remained in the box. Both Fuller and I were relieved.

The trial resumed on Thursday, February 6, as the defense presented a case that was like one of those syllogisms you learn in a logic course. It was simple, all nice and neat: major premise, minor premise, conclusion. Mike Tyson was a touching, grabbing, heat-seeking sex machine; all women knew this and avoided him if they didn't want to become part of his collection of sex toys; ergo, since Desiree Washington was a woman and didn't avoid him, she must have known what a "date" with Tyson entailed.

This defense, however, had several problems, the most important of which was that it forced Tyson's lawyers to completely raze the former champion's reputation, thereby alienating him from the jurors. Fuller and his associates had to present a Mike Tyson who was so insensitive and crude that no right-minded person could have any sympathy for him.

Running beneath the syllogism was another, even more disturbing, current. Tyson's defense trafficked in racial stereotyping; it drew on images and notions that many Americans, black and white, had been struggling against for more than three hundred years. The defense robbed Tyson of his individuality and turned him into a cardboard figure from a racist X-rated cartoon. He became not just a libidinous man, but a libidinous black man, a combination of Shakespeare's lusty Moor, Mandingo, and Superfly. After the trial Sonja Steptoe, a black writer for *Sports Illustrated,* called Fuller's tactics a "damnable defense." She insisted that by portraying Tyson as "your worst nightmare—a vulgar, socially inept, sex-obsessed black athlete"—Tyson's attorneys "fanned the fires of racism." I don't think that was Fuller's conscious intention. He had a client with a voracious sexual appetite and a bad habit of groping every woman who crossed his path. Given that set of facts, Fuller had to recognize his client's weaknesses and try to defuse their explosiveness. It just didn't work.

Fuller laid the groundwork for Tyson's case on the afternoon before the fire. As the first defense witness, John Horne, Tyson's friend and business associate, taught the Tyson 101 course to the jury. Tyson, Horne suggested, was something of a free spirit. A multimillionaire, he paid for everything in cash, possessed no credit cards, and was so forgetful that he needed a traveling companion to carry his driver's license and hotel keys. The point of Horne's short testimony was to alert the jurors that Tyson was something of a child. He bought on impulse, lost anything in his pockets, and needed a nanny to look after him.

On Thursday and Friday, Fuller and his team showcased the sexual dimension of Tyson's childish behavior. Tyson, they agreed, was very much the boxer, constantly on the move, with his eye toward scoring the big shot. Madeline Denise Whittington, Indiana's representative in the Miss Black America pageant and a student at Anderson University, a small, conservative, church-affiliated school, testified that Tyson lacked respect for both black leaders and black women. Engaged to the minister of music and associate pastor of the First Church of God in Toledo, Ohio, Whittington was sensitive to Tyson's slights. At the opening ceremony she watched Tyson mimic and poke fun at Jesse Jackson. "Down with dope; up with hope," Tyson mouthed while Jackson was delivering a speech. Whittington had never seen Jackson in person before, and she ignored Tyson's rude parody to listen to his speech. Sensing that she wasn't interested in him, Tyson commented, "Who does she think she is? That Catholic school motherfucker." But she did hear Tyson make sexual propositions to other contestants. "You want to come to my room? You want to party? I know I'm not going to get none from you, but I'm going to ask anyway."

South Carolina contestant Cecellia Alexander recalled that Tyson's constant efforts to get contestants to come to his room usually took the form of a joke, but he left no doubt that he was serious. Parquita Nassau, the Georgia contestant, was even more specific. Tyson told her that he liked "southern girls" because they liked to cook: "That's good, because I like to eat; and I'm not talking about food." When Nassau ignored him, Tyson said, "If you don't want to go out with me, I could move on, because I could have any one of those bitches out there." But he didn't leave immediately. Instead he felt her buttocks and said repeatedly, "I know you want me." She also overheard him tell another contestant, "I want to fuck you, and bring your roommate too, because I'm a celebrity, and, you know, we do that kind of thing."

And so it went. Witness after witness returned to the same muddy ground that Tyson had tried to drag them through. Disgust registered in their voices as they recounted Tyson's antics during the dance rehearsal and the opening ceremony.

Florida contestant Tonya Traylor was older than the other contestants, thirty at the time of the pageant, and more mature. Married, a college graduate, and co-owner of an insurance agency, she had moderated a weekly television game show called Varsity Brain Bowl, appeared in several commercials, and hosted a nightly radio talk show. She was also an experienced, successful beauty pageant contestant who spoke professionally about the need to stay focused during the contests.

Traylor saw enough of Tyson on the day of July 18 to reach a definite, mature judgment about him: "He—well, he wasn't my idea of really of—he wasn't a nice man." In fact, he was a crude, offensive, self-centered jerk who seemed concerned only with his own sexual gratification. "Everything he said had a sexual overtone to it," Traylor testified. "And most of the times he was just totally blunt. . . . He said . . . 'Do you want to go out?' . . . 'We can go here and then back to my room for sex or a kiss. A kiss will do. Sex would be better.' " When the contestants sat on Tyson's lap during the photo session, he made crude remarks about what he could do with his hands and touched them in a sexually suggestive manner. Traylor's roommate asked him why he acted "so sexual" and Tyson replied, "People expect it."


"In like Flynn"—the expression became part of the American argot in 1943 when actor Errol Flynn was tried, and acquitted, for the statutory rape of two teenage girls. Tyson was the new Flynn, acting as if he believed he was entitled to live by different rules, a self-styled code of conduct, and that all women should assume the position when he walked into the room. It was this arrogance, this sense that all privileges came with his status, that his defense lawyers underscored through their witnesses. Never had I seen a criminal case in which so many defense witnesses were lined up to attack the character of the defendant. Tyson's entire defense was reduced to three words: people expect it.

Fuller's point, of course, was that since people expected it, Desiree Washington also should have expected it. The Williams & Connelly lawyers labored to prove their defense by comments supposedly made by Desiree. Several witnesses also testified that they had heard, or overheard, Desiree talk about Tyson's wealth. When Whittington asked Desiree if she was going to go out with Tyson, Desiree supposedly replied, "Yes, of course I'm going. This is Mike Tyson. He's got money. He's dumb. You see what Robin Givens got out of him." Alexander testified that she overheard Desiree tell Whittington "that Mike wasn't the most intelligent man in the world, that he was dumb and that he was ignorant," but he was rich. And later, when another contestant called Tyson Desiree's husband and said that the boxer couldn't speak very well, Desiree shot back, "Mike doesn't have to know how to speak well. He'll make all the money, and I'll do all the talking."

Glancing occasionally at the jurors, I sensed that the gold-digger counterattack wasn't taking root. The jurors had seen and heard Desiree; her obvious innocence conflicted sharply with the notion that she was after Tyson's money. The jurors seemed more interested in the stories of Tyson's behavior. Several jurors stared at Tyson, as if they were struggling to get a fix on the fighter, but the boxer's face betrayed nothing. If he was embarrassed, if he was ashamed, if he regretted his boorish behavior, I never saw a hint of it in his face. He sat impassively, occasionally whispering something to Jim Voyles, and didn't seem much interested in what the witnesses had to say.

At 4:02 on Thursday afternoon, Fuller said the words that everyone had been waiting for since the start of the defense's case: "Your Honor, the defense calls Mike Tyson to the stand." Now we would have the classic courtroom clash: his story against hers, his credibility versus hers.

Dressed in an olive green double-breasted suit (one reporter who was up on color nomenclature described it as fern), the former heavyweight champion of the world walked slowly to the witness stand and promised to tell the whole truth and nothing but the truth. Then when he began to speak in his quiet, lispy voice, it was difficult to imagine that he had ever made the vulgar comments attributed to him. "Boxers are liars," José Torres had said.

Jim Voyles had prepared Tyson to testify, and he had done a great job. Tyson was sandpaper smooth—rehearsed, ready for every question Fuller asked him. But at times I thought I detected a slight shift in the tone of Fuller's voice, an indication of discomfort as he discussed Tyson's grabbing, feeling, aggressively sexual behavior. It was Lane Heard, not Fuller, who had examined most of the contestants, the witnesses who had discussed Tyson's sexual advances. Fuller's entire courtroom look and style, his brushed-back graying hair, expensive British-cut suits, eastern accent, and air of patrician charm, was at odds with the part he was now forced to play. I felt as though I was listening to Dean Acheson tell a filthy joke, and I hoped that the jurors would also feel awkward.

There was another problem, one I had half anticipated. Several of Tyson's biographers had observed that as a fighter Tyson was at his best when his opponent fought a predictable fight. He entered the ring with a plan, and he didn't like to vary much from that plan. A major problem early in his career, and one that had resurfaced in the previous two years, was his tendency to become frustrated and then turn passive. Seeing how carefully Tyson had been prepared for a father-son session with Fuller, I looked for spots to interject objections, which a series of leading questions made easier. I wanted to frustrate Tyson by forcing him to answer questions phrased slightly differently from those he had been asked during preparation. It worked. He didn't like changes in the script. During and after objections, I watched as he yawned, wrenched his hands, shifted his weight, and otherwise showed his discomfort.

He told the story of his life, which was that he had been trained to do one thing: knock people senseless in the ring. He had received most of his education on the streets and in the reformatories of Brooklyn, and had received his graduate degree in Cus D'Amato's gym. At an age when other boys were playing Little League baseball, he was training to be a professional boxer and had realistic expectations of winning the heavyweight championship. In his precocious, pedal-to-the-floor world, there was no time for formal education and finishing school. He was still a teenager when he turned professional, and he became the youngest heavyweight champion in the history of the sport. Between fights, he took his pleasures when and where he could with little thought of traditional behavior.

He asserted that when he met Desiree, he bluntly explained that his interest in her was entirely sexual. That was his style: get in a woman's face and proposition her; if she said yes, fine; if she said no, "I'd just move on. I'd say, 'Excuse me, I'm out of here, I'm gone.' " No wasted time, no misunderstandings; he was a man for the disposable age.

He admitted there was a small misconception when he first asked Desiree for a date. When she accepted she said, "We can go to a movie or dinner or something." That wasn't what Tyson had in mind. "I explained to her that I wanted to fuck her," he testified. She answered, "Sure, just give me a call," and "That's kind of bold." "That's the way I am, I just want to know what I'm getting before I get into it," Tyson added.

As expected, Tyson denied that he had raped Desiree, suggesting that she was as sexually aggressive as he. As soon as Desiree was in the limousine, the two began kissing and touching. Within minutes, they were inside Suite 606. Sitting on his bed, they talked for about ten minutes. Then they got down to business. They kissed some more. She undressed. He undressed. He continued to kiss her—"on the neck and around the ears, back of the neck and chest and nipples, the stomach." He performed oral sex until she indicated that she wanted to have sexual intercourse. Fifteen, maybe twenty, minutes later it was all over.

Desiree went to the bathroom. "I was watching her. She had her underwear on, they were polka dot. . . . She was in the mirror doing her hair, a little dance, like *shoo, shoo, shoo,* doing her hair." A nice piece of domestic staging, although Virginia Foster had testified earlier that Desiree's hair was a mess when she had arrived at the limousine. Since they both had early appointments, Tyson asked her to stay the night, but she decided to return to her room.

That decision, Tyson claimed, had culminated in his appearance in court. She wanted him to walk her to the limousine. He was too tired and refused. She left in a huff, irritated at his lack of chivalry.

Seventy-seven minutes after he began his questions, Fuller ended by asking, "Mr. Tyson, at any time did you force Desiree Washington to engage in sexual intercourse with you?"

A.  No, I didn't. I didn't violate her in any way, sir.
Q.  Did she at any time tell you to stop what you were doing?
A.  Never, she never told me to stop, and she never said I was hurting her. She never said no, nothing.

The jury had now heard both versions of what happened in Suite 606. The two participants were 180 degrees apart on every important issue. One charged rape, the other claimed consensual sex. The jurors had the night to weigh the stories and compare.


If this had been a movie, if Perry Mason had been a prosecutor, the classic formula for courtroom drama would have dictated the finale. "Isn't it true, Mr. Tyson, that in the early hours of July 19, you lured that innocent eighteen-year-old girl up to your expensive hotel suite, locked the door, and raped her?" "Yes, yes, it's all true. How I wish it were otherwise. I did it. I did it. Take me away."

But this wasn't fiction, and I didn't expect any surprise confessions. Tyson had a story, most of which only Desiree could contest. At several important points it conflicted with his earlier grand jury testimony, and I could use that to show a pattern of deceit. But I suspected that I would not be able to shake the main outline of what he said. In fact, the problems I faced as I prepared my cross-examination had less to do with what Tyson would say than how the jurors would perceive him. If I turned up the heat, would it burn him or me?

This was a subject George Horn, Barb, and I had discussed often during the weeks preceding the trial. How hard should I press him in cross-examination? How would he react? For more than a week, all the jurors had seen was a passive, polite Tyson. They had not seen the rage that had accounted for his success inside the ring and his failures outside. They had not seen what Desiree had seen, the sudden, frightening personality change, one second playfully talking about his pigeons, the next throwing her on the bed and raping her. In my cross, I wanted to get under Tyson's skin, make him uneasy, maybe provoke a sudden flash of anger. But that tactic carried certain risks. Tyson was unpredictable. Jerking his emotional wires was dangerous.

I talked with several psychological experts in an attempt to anticipate how Tyson would respond to different situations. José Torres had provided a few clues. I could confuse Tyson, get him to lie, and ultimately confess "bad things" about himself. Torres even believed that put under enough emotional pressure, Tyson would break down and cry. I'm sure that Torres wanted that to happen, but the specter frightened me. If Tyson cried, it was likely to engender sympathy from the jurors, something that Tyson's impoverished background would already have raised. I didn't want that to happen.

George Horn had put me in contact with Jim Wright, a brilliant behavioral specialist who worked for the FBI out of Quantico, Virginia. Wright's job entailed, among other things, producing psychological profiles of unknown mass murderers. He was the real-life equivalent of the FBI psychologist in *The Silence of the Lambs*. Working with fragments of evidence, often no more extensive than details of the crime scene, he drew the faces of the faceless, filled in the personalities of the anonymous. He had worked on the Hinckley case and, more recently, the case of Charles Ng, the Asian-American mass murderer deported to the United States from Canada in the early 1990s. George had fed Wright information about Tyson ranging from the fighter's background, boxing style, relationships with women, and the smallest nuances of his relationship with Desiree. Wright then ran it through whatever computer he had for a brain and arrived at certain conclusions. For two hours on the night before my cross-examination of Tyson, George and I talked with Wright on the telephone.

The thing that concerned me also bothered Wright: Tyson's unpredictability. Wright believed his personality was dangerously weak. He might get angry and go after me. He might cry. He might turn completely passive, even to the point of assuming a fetal position. Wright said that there were two types of serial rapists: one who raped so as to reinforce his power, the other who sought reassurance of his power. The power reinforcement rapist seeks to demonstrate his strength and virility to someone else (the victim); the power reassurance rapist attempts to validate his masculinity to himself. Of the two, the power reassurance rapist has the weaker personality, and Wright believed that Tyson belonged to this group.

Wright's profile fitted what we knew about Tyson, including the information provided by the other women who had come forward during the investigation to tell us that they too had been sexually assaulted by Tyson. Their claims were old and unsubstantiated, as well as inadmissible as evidence, but at least one of them described a rape that bore eerie similarities to Desiree's. The women said that Tyson seemed to thrive on their fear. That conformed to the pattern of the power reassurance rapist, Wright claimed. If a woman fought back, hit the man and told him to get in line, the weaker personality would often abort the assault. When Virginia Foster had found herself alone in a hotel room with the sexually aggressive Tyson, she hit him in the chest and told him to behave himself. And he did. Desiree had become afraid and cried. He didn't.

My cross-examination, Wright believed, would mostly be damage control. He doubted that Tyson would confess. More likely, he would break down in the manner of a persecuted man, which would hurt the state's case. "Don't push him too hard," he cautioned. I should show the jurors his other lies, make him answer questions he had not anticipated, make him work without a script. But I should be careful not to go after him full-bore.

The last person I talked to that night was Mike Beaver, a lie detector specialist and an old friend. Mike had been my skull man for years; his insights into the minds of criminals had in the past been uncanny, transcending textbook explanations. "You've got to show the jury the bad Mike," he advised. "Push him. Hard, if necessary. He won't crack. He won't cry. But he'll probably get mad. And that's what you want those nice jurors to see. They need to see that that man with the soft demeanor and quiet, little-kid voice can be a mean son of a bitch in a real hurry." He also said I should get Tyson to lie, make him admit that he would lie if it suited his purposes.

Less than ten minutes after I started to cross-examine him, I realized that getting anything out of Mike Tyson would not be easy. Jim Voyles had appealed to Tyson's professionalism, I learned later. The courtroom was a ring, and Tyson had to know his limits, what he could and could not do, what he could and could not say. You couldn't go beyond your limits; you couldn't get sucked outside your safety zone. Voyles later commented that Tyson had never failed to do what he asked, that he had prepared for his courtroom appearance as though he was getting ready for a fight.

Tyson, I'm sure, understood that I would try to trap him. But his success was based on avoiding traps and setting his own. As we talked, I sensed a confident witness. I also sensed an intelligent man who may have had little formal education but possessed a street I.Q. of about 300.

We began by discussing his career. Tyson recalled his early months with D'Amato, when the crafty trainer had ignored the physical aspects of the sport and concentrated instead on mental preparation. But the longer we talked about his sport, the more I was aware that he was searching my face, as if he was asking, *Where are you coming from? Where are you going with these questions? What does boxing have to do with this business here?* He didn't like the loss of control. Several times he gave answers that attempted to make me clarify my intentions: "I don't understand what you mean"; "I don't understand what you are saying." He wouldn't allow me to move at my own pace; he insisted on slowing me down to give him time to think through the ramifications of his answers. Slowly I circled in on José Torres's insight into the boxer's mind: that his great skill in the ring was based on deception. Tyson at last admitted that his success was the result of cunning, the ability to feint—in a word, to lie.

He also confessed that the story he had told the grand jury was different from the one he told the previous afternoon. Before the grand jury he had testified that when he made the date with Desiree, he said, "I want to be alone with you. I want you." He claimed that Desiree answered, "Okay. Just call me." "I don't like to come straight on and say, 'Want to screw?'" Tyson told the grand jury; he didn't like being so blunt. Since September, however, his story had changed. Now he said he told Desiree, "I want to fuck you," and she answered, "Sure, give me a call. That's kind of bold."

Caught in the discrepancy, Tyson tried to lie his way out. He suggested that the transcript of his grand jury testimony was inaccurate; it was not. He said that Dave Dreyer had cut him off during his grand jury testimony; the tape of his testimony demonstrated that Dreyer had not. Finally he claimed that he was embarrassed to use the four-letter word in front of the grand jury because "there was no younger kids in there my age or anything." It was only the pressure of the trial, he said, that permitted him to overcome his embarrassment over using the word.

There were other changes in Tyson's two sworn testimonies. In September Tyson had claimed that Desiree wore tight pink hot pants that showed her thighs and a blouse "cut off to her stomach" for their date; in fact, she wore loose-fitting, knee-length jams, a bustier, and a jacket. Tyson admitted the error and tried to use humor to cover his mistake. "I'm not a professional at women's attire," he said. And besides, he was more interested in what was beneath the clothes.

On a more important matter, he said that he had not told the truth to the grand jury about where Dale Edwards had been during his liaison with Desiree. In September he had testified that Edwards was in the parlor of his suite during the entire time he was in the bedroom with Desiree. But Chris Low, McCoy Wagers, and Virginia Foster testified that Edwards was many other places during that time, but never in Tyson's room. Faced with the obvious, Tyson recanted: "I know he should have been in that parlor room. That's where he was supposed to be."

To keep this point from being lost on the jury, I tried to demonstrate that Tyson's "mistake" concerning Edwards's whereabouts was part of a larger pattern of mistakes.

> Q. So when you answered the question in the grand jury, you were supposing where he was, but you didn't really know?
>
> A. I didn't know, really know. I was to believe that he was in the parlor.
>
> Q. Kind of like supposing that somebody wants to have sex with you but you don't really know, isn't it?
>
> A. Excuse me, sir?
>
> Q. I'll withdraw the question.

After eighty minutes, Tyson left the witness stand. Confronted with the discrepancies between his grand jury testimony and his trial testimony, he had not become rattled. He admitted that he had made a mistake about what Desiree was wearing and where Edwards had been. He affirmed that he had lied to Jesse Jackson about going on a prison visit. He agreed that his professional success was based on deception. But he had not come unglued. On the witness stand he demonstrated his professional discipline.

He slipped just one time. At one point, the cross-examination became mildly heated. I was close to Tyson, asking him about what he had said to Desiree and why his story had changed. I could see he was getting angry. Then I turned around, walked back toward the prosecution table, and changed the topic. As George Horn and Barb told me later, when I turned, Tyson saw a piece of Desiree's clothing that I had placed near him. In one quick, short, violent swipe of his hand, he flicked it away. There was rage in that movement. George immediately looked at the jury. The brief moment was not lost.

More witnesses followed Tyson, but they weren't important to either side's case. Tyson's friend Johnny Gill claimed that he recalled Tyson saying "I want to fuck you" to Desiree. "Mike was just being Mike," Gill said. But under cross-examination, Barb pointed out that Gill had not reported the remark to the police in the summer or in his deposition the previous month. It appeared that he remembered the comment at about the same time Tyson had, although Gill testified that the comment was the only part of the conversation he remembered.

An Illinois contestant, Tanya Levette St. Clair-Gills, took the stand and told simply unbelievable stories about Desiree. According to her, Desiree talked like a prostitute. Although she and Desiree had not become particularly close friends, she reported that Desiree remarked about Tyson, "Wow, he's really built. Wow, oh, his butt. Oh, it's something to hold on to. It's something really cool to hold on to." And later, comparing Tyson with the taller and heavier Dale Edwards: "Did you hear what they said about the chubby man and the not so chubby man? You know, they say the big man don't have nothing. Their things are real little. I bet Tyson got some." I watched jurors openly shake their heads while she testified. They weren't buying her fantasies.

The saddest case for me, however, was the testimony of Pasha Oliver, Desiree's roommate who had been so supportive after the rape and during the grand jury phase. I don't know for sure what happened to Pasha, but at some point between her grand jury testimony and the trial her story changed dramatically. In her grand jury testimony she had said Tyson was a gentleman, that he was polite, that he had not talked dirty, and that he had not touched her. By the time of the trial she was claiming that Tyson had said nasty things to her and fondled her buttocks, and she had retained a lawyer who filed a civil suit against the fighter. One thing was certain; in one of her sworn testimonies she committed perjury. In my cross-examination of her, I put on my best pissed-off Daddy face and just flat went after her. Point by point, I went over her grand jury testimony. She squirmed and tried to back into a corner and told more lies to cover the first ones. It left me feeling sick.

We had heard enough rumors of money changing hands to suspect that someone might have gotten to some of the contestants. But whatever the reasons for the contestants' lies, they were obvious and they probably hurt Tyson more than they helped him.

The bottom line was that the defense's case lacked credibility. Tyson's lawyers called only one expert witness, Dr. Margaret Watanabe, who said that vaginal abrasions like the ones Desiree suffered could have resulted from consensual sex but admitted under cross-examination, as she had during her deposition, that she had only seen three such cases in more than ten thousand pelvic examinations. With that statement her testimony supported the prosecution more than the defense. The other witnesses simply tried to smear Desiree with charges of money grubbing and lust.

The defense rested its case late Sunday morning. The jurors had heard twenty-five prosecution and twenty-five defense witnesses. The most respected reporters had all but pronounced Tyson guilty. Writing for the *New York Times*, Anna Quindlen wondered what sort of person could consider Tyson a role model after hearing his own witnesses testify: "Why in the world should Mike Tyson, a man who apparently can't pass a ladies room without grabbing the doorknob, be a role model? Whether he raped anybody or not, it's clear he has disrespected black women from one end of this country to the other, as though they were hamburger and he were hungry." Tyson's only message was that "if you're rich and dress well, you can do what you want. At least until you go to jail. Or until you're washed up. . . . In all the ways that truly matter, Mike Tyson already is."

Neither Anna Quindlen nor any of her colleagues, however, was seated in the jury box. And the jurors were not primarily concerned with whether Tyson was a lout or whether he was washed up. They had to decide if he had raped Desiree Washington.

At one-thirty on Sunday afternoon, Judge Gifford called the lawyers from both sides into her chambers and asked when we would be ready to go with final argument. I had given it some thought, and said I'd be ready that afternoon. Fuller turned ashen and resisted going forward that day. I didn't blame him; for the last week he had been focused on presenting his case and probably had not had time to prepare his final argument. Judge Gifford gave us both an ice queen smirk and said, "All right. Nine o'clock tomorrow morning."

# C H A P T E R  16

---

# THEY ALWAYS KNOW

**F**inal argument is high drama. It is life frozen in place, and it is what every person who ever dreamed of being a trial lawyer lives to do. I have never felt closer to death than at that moment, that second of silence, before it is my turn to start. I have never been more exhilarated than those times when I have had the evidence, the metaphysics, God, motherhood, John Wayne, and the American flag on my side while I stormed through an argument.

When Vince Fuller rested his case, the evidence phase of the trial concluded. The victim, the accused, the witnesses—they had all said their piece. It was now time for the lawyers to talk.

As I left the City-County Building on Sunday afternoon, I saw the sun for the first time in two weeks. Actually, it wasn't so much the sun as a clear indication that there was a sun somewhere above the dense cloud cover. It reminded me that there was a world beyond Criminal Court IV, beyond the tunnel that had become my life, and also how totally engrossed in the case I had become. I think the police could have informed me that the IRS was auditing me, my kids had been kidnaped, my house had burned down, and the governor was traveling around the state calling me a commie and I would have said, "Is that right?

Well, I guess I'll deal with it next week." My life was the case; everything else was white noise.

Walking out of the building, the ever-present journalists reminded me that the next day I would be speaking not just to the jury, or even to the spectators jammed into the courtroom, but through them to about one hundred million people around the world. "Good luck," many shouted. Or, "Kick ass."

More pressure—just what I needed. I knew they meant well, but their encouragement made me feel as though I was on an airplane that had just taken a sudden five-thousand-foot plunge.

Final argument had always made me feel sick. I remembered my first murder case, the one I lost. I rehearsed all night in my basement, stomping and yelling. I recalled my first death penalty case. For hours I walked up and down Meridian Street, repeating what I planned to say, so absorbed that occasionally I noticed other pedestrians cross to the other side of the street to avoid me. I practiced and rehearsed and then forgot everything when the time came and went from the gut.

Before organizing our Tyson arguments, Barb and I ate pizza at my house, and I got a chance to see my wife and kids. During the second week of the trial I had begun to realize that the pressure of the trial—the media attention, the death threats, the security precautions, and my own inattention—had unbalanced an already shaky marriage. Sometimes at night when I couldn't sleep I would creep into my young son's bedroom and curl up on the floor and listen to him breathe while I considered what had gone wrong. There was no answer, or maybe too many answers. The Tyson trial had not caused the problems; it only intensified them. I told myself that when the trial ended my life and my marriage would return to normal. I might have believed my little fiction if I had been able to remember what "normal" was. It certainly wasn't the silence, the lack of interest, the bruised egos. As I lay there, I was comforted by the soft sound of my son's breathing, but the only conclusion I reached was that I had a job to do.

From the house, Barb and I went to my office to begin work. In Indiana and many other states, final argument is a three-act play. First the state presents its summation, which reviews and interprets the evidence; then the defense gives its final argument; finally the state presents its rebuttal of the defense's claims. Although more than a few defendants have complained about the balance of the procedure, it is fair because the state carries the burden of proof. From the first, Barb and I had planned that she would present the summation and I would deliver the rebuttal.

As we worked we tried out different ideas on each other, sharing thoughts, arguing back and forth over what would or would not work, and trying to anticipate what Fuller would argue. Several months before, it had occurred to me that Tyson had used his status as a celebrity to lure Desiree into his bedroom and rape her. He used his fame as adroitly as another rapist might employ a gun or a knife. Barb took up the idea and worked it beautifully into her final argument, which would show that the evidence pointed toward Tyson's guilt. I labored to develop an argument that would achieve two additional results: first, get rid of the Palm Beach atmosphere and the glitz and focus the jurors on midwestern values; and second, convince them that they should not punish Desiree for her own imprudence. She had made a mistake in following Tyson to his room, but that mistake did not mitigate or excuse his actions. I thought about Bobby Knight, the Indiana University basketball coach, and how he referred to his players as his "kids." He called them that for a reason; they might all be six-foot-eight, but emotionally as well as chronologically they were still kids, capable of looking like all-Americans one night and not able to find the door to the gymnasium the next. The difference between Knight's players and Desiree was that her mistake didn't get her fouled out of a game; it had ruined her life.

Our work session broke up about half past midnight, and I went home, passing by a Chevy Astro van parked at the end of my driveway, seven hundred feet from the house. Bob Simms, a policeman who was watching my family, informed me when I walked through the door that the van had been there too long and that someone was inside it. Bob looked out the window, then I looked. He looked, I looked. Finally he said, "Well, I guess I better go out and talk with him." "I'll go with you," I said. We got in his surveillance car, an old piece-of-shit Pontiac Fiero, and inched closer to the van.

When we were about twenty feet away the van's driver turned on his lights and took off. We followed him north at a speed slightly faster than the Fiero wanted to go. Bob needed both hands, so I handled the radio, giving our directions to IPD dispatch. We followed him north of Indianapolis, north of Noblesville, when suddenly all hell broke loose. On a road surrounded by cornfields, two Hamilton County sheriff's cars and two State Police cars blocked the highway. There were lights and noise and nearly a dozen uniformed officers. The driver was pulled out of his van, turned upside down, and frisked.

They ran his name through the crime computers and didn't find anything. Evidently he was just some mope who had gotten lost and stopped outside my house for a brief nap before moving on. On that particular night he couldn't have picked a worse address. I had to smile as I heard him describe how he had awakened from his nap by a wild Fiero bearing down on him.

It was almost three o'clock when I finally got to bed. I was up again at four-thirty, reviewing my final argument outlines. The first was long and detailed; the second was a shorter, more organized version; the third was fragmentary, a brief, one-page selection of main ideas. I read them again and again—detailed, well organized, fragmentary—beating them into my simple head so I wouldn't forget anything important. Shortly before seven, Jack Geilker, my driver, arrived and we headed for the City-County Building and one more morning lit by sun guns and awakened by the reporters' first questions: "Are you ready? Will you win?"

**W**aiting for the call to court before final argument is the distilled essence of being a trial lawyer. It's a perfect pain: you have a knot in your stomach so tight that you feel as though you swallowed a baseball; a tension so great that when you smell coffee your gut wants to let go, and you race to the bathroom; a pressure so complete that you have to remind yourself to take a deep breath. I sat in the war room, reviewing the outlines and looking at the clock every fifteen seconds. Finally it was nine o'clock. A court official knocked on the door and said it was time to go.

Our entourage took another sojourn down the six flights of steps between the fifth and second floors, came out into the lights blasting us in the face, turned left toward Criminal Court IV, and opened the door to the courtroom. I thought of every hackneyed expression I had ever heard about such a moment—there was tension you could cut with a knife, atmosphere that was palpable, drama you could taste—and they all seemed to fit. Fuller's head was down as the chief defense lawyer prepared to make his argument, but everyone else at the defense table cast a hawkish glance in our direction. For them the trial was over; all that was left were a few speeches and a vote count. I think the eyes of every reporter snapped to the door when it opened. A few reporters spoke to us; the locals gave us knowing grins. Desiree was sitting next to my daughter Betsy.

I had insisted that Desiree return to Indianapolis for the final argument. She was my corpus delicti, and I wanted the jurors to see her before they began their deliberations. She looked nervous. I walked over and whispered to her, "The fight's over for you; just loosen up. You did your part. You kicked his ass. We'll handle the rest." I should have known some reporters would overhear my comment—and several did—but I wanted to reaffirm what a good job she had done and how brave she had been for telling her awful story to the world. She had been humiliated, treated like a freak in a sideshow, but she had shown strength and character.

Barb began her summation by quickly introducing the theme that Tyson had "used his fame and his reputation in the same identical manner that a thug in an alley uses a knife or a gun in order to accomplish his purpose." Nervous at first and tied to her notes, she soon moved away from her papers and tore into Tyson's case. Date rape was rape, she told the jurors; it wasn't half a crime, it was a full crime, just as the statute described it. That Tyson used religion and his own status among African Americans to win Desiree's confidence only made the crime more sordid.

Moving closer to the jury, Barb carefully reviewed the evidence—Donald Washington's idolization of Tyson, the boxer's innocent advances at the rehearsal, the late-night "date." She reviewed the findings and opinions of the medical experts, evaluated the testimony of the key witnesses, and compared the testimony and characters of Desiree and Tyson. "The statement 'I want to fuck you' that the Defendant claims to have made directly to the face of this eighteen-year-old high school graduate, the honors student here, that he just slams into her face, and she supposedly just kind of laughs and responds, 'Yeah, sure, give me a call,' . . . that's what the Defendant is asking you to accept. . . . " That statement, recalled months after his grand jury testimony, was the heart of Tyson's defense, and Barb demonstrated that it was ludicrous.

The longer she spoke, the more she ripped and tore. She discussed the faulty memories of the defense's witnesses, how so many of them had changed their stories. Pasha Oliver, Johnny Gill, Frank Valentine, Tanya St. Claire-Gills: consider the credibility of their stories, she asked the jurors. Compare them to those of Virginia Foster, Chris Low, and McCoy Wagers, witnesses with no personal stake in the outcome of the trial.

Barb's summation was incisive, aggressive, and convincing. Leaving Vince Fuller standing in a hole, she renewed my flagging energies. As she finished, I looked at Fuller and Tyson to gauge their reactions. Tyson, as always, was emotionless and seemingly uninterested. He was bent over the defense table writing something—I later learned that throughout the trial his writing had really been only copying. Fuller also looked preoccupied, which was to be expected. He had one last chance to keep Tyson out of prison.

The podium returned. Banished from the courtroom by Fuller after the bad press it had received during the first few days of the trial, the podium was placed in front of me so that as Fuller delivered his final argument I was looking into his right earlobe. For the next hour I listened to him, although I wished I had not.

Afterward the press would pan Fuller's final argument. The criticism, I believe, was based on his delivery. He tended to speak in spurts, and his voice was too big and his style too formal for the small courtroom. The reporters who had to listen to his argument on closed-circuit television in the basement media room had an especially difficult time following him. But I heard nearly every word, and the content was overwhelming. Since I had started arguing cases in 1972, there had never been a lawyer who so undressed my case, who so intimidated me, and who made me want to wet my pants and run away until Vincent J. Fuller went to work on our case. One item at a time, he picked out the elements of our argument, tore them up, and pitched them over his shoulder, so that by the time he finished, the prosecution's case lay in litter around his feet. His elocution may not have been right for that courtroom and he may have not communicated well with the jurors, but what he said was brilliant.

He began with a short lecture on the nature of criminal law, from the presumption of innocence and the burden of proof to reasonable doubt and the need for a unanimous vote for a guilty verdict. I sensed that his argument was intended to get a hung jury. "Why is it that a criminal process verdict must be unanimous?" he asked. "I think this answer is simple; that our society is terrorized by the thought of convicting an innocent man." When he said this, I looked at the jurors. Was he talking to a particular one or two? Did he sense that one or more of the jurors would be paralyzed by the decision-making process? If so, who were they? If he swayed them, I would have to fight to get them back.

Attempting to raise doubts, he compared Tyson to Desiree. The boxer was a high school dropout who was weak in intellectual and analytical skills. Desiree Washington, however, was schooled and poised beyond her years. She had met world leaders, won academic honors. She was nobody's fool, no wide-eyed child. Looking directly at one juror but speaking to them all, Fuller said, "I submit to you, it insults your intelligence to be led to believe that a young woman of this woman's background, her sophistication, would get into the back of a limousine, be hugged and be kissed on the mouth and not leave that car forthwith unless she knew what was coming."

He continued, raising questions about the state's case. Pointing to a floor plan of Suite 606, he argued that Desiree could have left if she had wanted to. He said that Desiree's statements to other contestants demonstrated an interest in Tyson's money. He claimed that she had given slightly different versions of the rape to different people. He suggested that Tyson was a considerate lover, engaging in foreplay and ejaculating on the sheets as a form of birth control. He speculated about the meaning of Dr. Richardson's medical report: several small introital abrasions were found but "no lacerations and no contusions." The idea, one that was a throwback to another legal era, was that if a woman did not have serious bruises and injuries, she had not resisted to her fullest ability and therefore had not been raped. All Fuller had to do was create a reasonable doubt and all our work would go down the drain; Desiree Washington's courageous stand would be for nothing.

Fuller moved on to the conclusion of his final argument by advancing a possible motive for Desiree's charges. Backing off from the gold-digger defense, which had gone nowhere during the trial, he argued that Desiree was offended by Tyson's treatment of her after they had had sex. "I submit Miss Washington suddenly realized that she's been treated like a one-night stand or worse, and her dignity is offended. . . . Mr. Tyson's behavior, no doubt, was rude in his treatment of Miss Washington after their sexual encounter. She is a woman of great pride, of great achievement. And now she feels she's been treated like a one-night stand." Fuller described Desiree as an "embarrassed and humiliated" woman, and one bent on revenge.

For all the intellectual dazzle of Fuller's final argument, it was not a crafted piece of theater. It went on too long. In the middle of it, juror number 5 raised his hand and indicated that he had to go to the bathroom. In over twenty years of trying cases I had never seen that happen, but the guy couldn't wait.

In his final few seconds before the jury, Fuller returned to his lecture on the nature of American law. "I want to remind you once again, the State's burden to prove to each and every one of you is guilt beyond a reasonable doubt and that your verdict must be unanimous. If one of you alone has a reasonable doubt, no verdict can be returned." Translation: *Give us one "not guilty" and we'll be happy.*

By the time he finished I was sick inside. Browbeaten and fearful, I remember thinking, *Okay, meathead, how are you going to follow that?*

I told Tommy Kuzmik that I wanted the podium disposed of in four-tenths of a second after Vince's shadow was gone. Kuzmik followed the instructions. Judge Gifford looked at me and said, "Mr. Garrison." It was the last swing, the final word in the most publicized case of any career.

When I was younger my style was to come smoking out of my seat as soon as my opponent sat down and snatch the moment away from him. This time I waited a few seconds, composed my thoughts, and started quietly. I felt awkward, self-conscious, as if my face was flushed, my eyes squinty, and my cheeks puffed.

To combat the feeling of disorientation, I decided to do what had worked for me in the past. Working under the old courtroom assumption that the last person who gets mad wins, I got mad. And the more I thought about the smoke and mirrors that Fuller had brought into the courtroom along with his podium, the madder I became.

"You know," I addressed the jurors, "I find it curious that as parents the very things that we try to inculcate in our kids—ingenuity, self-motivation, honest integrity and honest ambition, achievement—are turned around on their ear in this case and used as your proof that you can't believe that this young lady tells the truth. We need to open the doors and turn on those big fans and blow all of Mr. Fuller's smoke out of this room. Then we need a hose so that we can wash the mud off of all these people, particularly [Desiree Washington], who for the last hour, or for the last seven days, has been the victim of an assassination of her character and her honor by those people."

I told the jurors that there was only one victim in this case, and that the former heavyweight champion was not that person; the victim was a young woman whose biggest sin "was to have the unmitigated gall to stand up to [Tyson] and his resources and his defense team." I wanted the jurors to look at Desiree and to compare what they saw with the portrait Fuller had painted.

I also asked them to consider the medical evidence, the most important information in the case. All the doctors agreed—theirs as well as ours—that women do not or only on exceedingly rare occasions sustain introital injuries during consensual sex.

The most important factor they had to consider, however, was the victim herself. Sure, she had made a mistake and used poor judgment, but she was young and immature. Why did Bobby Knight call his players kids? I asked. "Which person in this room, in this community, that's ever raised a kid can't write a book about being inconsistent, hitting home runs one moment and not being able to find your way home the next?"

As I talked, I watched the faces of the jurors. I looked into the eyes of each one of them. Nobody blinked, nobody slept, and nobody had to go to the bathroom. I knew they were with me, that they believed in our case. It was just as Leroy New, an early mentor of mine, had told me years ago: "They'll believe in your case if they believe in you. Your credibility is far more important than the credibility of any of your witnesses." On that day, in that courtroom, the jurors believed that Barb and I were not blowing smoke, that we had complete faith in our case. And I think Fuller and Voyles realized it.

Fuller's delivery was seamless. Mine was not. Speaking without notes, I felt I was herky-jerky, hopping from one point to the next without smooth transitions. But I was communicating, and once I found my way to the narrative of the events, my transitions became more logical.

In the main body of my argument I sought to show that the gold-digger defense was absurd. Desiree had wanted her roommate to accompany her on the date; she wore her pajama bottoms under her jams; she took a camera to record the night's events. Where was the gold digger? If the jurors were to believe the defense's story, they would have to assume that Desiree was a sexual athlete who made love until she was injured; then popped out of bed, fluffed up her hair, and became offended when Tyson didn't offer to walk her to the limousine.

"There's the fatal flaw in this ridiculous fairy tale," I asserted. According to Tyson, he had said, "Stay the night. You got to get up early. I got to get up early. Come to bed with me." Pausing, giving the jury a second to think about what Tyson had testified he said, I then continued, "Guys, that's a home run. If you want in Mike Tyson's life and he makes love to you and invites you to sleep with him, how are you rejected? . . . If you are the little weasel here who wants Mike Tyson's . . . money and wants to be the next Robin Givens, you have just kicked one through the uprights. You are going to sleep with him. . . . You are going to snuggle. You are going to kiss him and keep him all warm for two or three hours and do anything he wants you to do and ingratiate yourself to him like the naughty little person you really are. And when he gets up in the morning, he's going to take you back to your hotel, and he's going to leave town with your phone number and your address, and you're going to have his along with a promise of a return engagement."

A few jurors shook their heads, as if to say, *Yeah, that makes sense.* Barb told me later that she was looking at the defense table when I made the comment about the home run. She said that Beggs and Voyles dropped their hands to their laps and seemed to deflate, as though they had considered the argument and hoped we had not.

The jurors looked convinced, and I didn't want to stretch my final argument out to the point where I began to lose them. I finished the narrative of events, then I suggested how they should evaluate the different witnesses and evidence. I was ready for my conclusion. But then I realized that I had forgotten something. I had planned to read a passage from *United States* v. *Wade*, a 1967 Supreme Court decision. As soon as I began to introduce the case, Fuller erupted from his chair like a legal Mount Vesuvius.

> MR. FULLER: Your Honor, I object to Mr. Garrison reading case law to the jury. I believe that's the Court's province, not—
>
> MR. GARRISON: I believe he doesn't know the law of Indiana, because that has been the law for years. You may read from the law books.
>
> THE COURT: He may read.

Fuller later told me that he was upset with Voyles for not telling him that I could read the text of earlier cases; if he had known it was a possibility, he would have read the passage from *Wade* himself to lessen its effect.

The section I read dealt with the roles of the prosecution and the defense in a criminal trial:

> Law enforcement officers have the obligation to convict the guilty and to make sure that they do not convict the innocent. They must be dedicated to making the criminal trial a procedure for the ascertainment of the true facts surrounding the commission of a crime. . . . But defense counsel has no comparable obligation to ascertain or present the truth. . . . We insist that he defend his client whether he is innocent or guilty. . . . If he can confuse a witness, even a truthful one, or make him appear at a disadvantage, unsure or indecisive, that will be the normal course. Our interest in not convicting the innocent permits counsel to put . . . the State's case in the worst possible light, regardless of what he thinks or knows to be the truth. . . . In this respect, as part of our modified adversary system and as part of the duty imposed upon the most honorable defense

counsel, we countenance or require conduct which in many instances has little, if any, relation to the search for the truth.

I believed every word of that statement. I believed Tyson was guilty; I believed that Fuller had an obligation to his client and a duty to the Constitution to cloud the issues to such an extent that the jury would find Tyson not guilty. That was the system, and my job was to prevent the injustice of a verdict of not guilty.

Finishing my final argument, I returned to where I had begun two weeks earlier during voir dire: "If when we're done here you don't think he did it, then send him out of here. I'll tell you the truth; I don't care, if that's what you feel. But don't let any other pressure, the smoke, the mirrors, the mud fight with this little kid, obscure the fact that the evidence is almost mathematically clear that this man raped this girl."

I left them with one thought—that we were in Indianapolis, Indiana, not Palm Beach or Washington, D.C.: "The world's eyes are on us. [People everywhere] want to know if the citizens of Marion County have got the courage to do a hard thing. I don't want this man convicted because the world watches. I want him convicted if you believe the evidence proves beyond a reasonable doubt that this beautiful, honest kid came to town, got deceived by a professional deceiver, got lied to, schmoozed and romanced, isolated and defeated, raped and made the subject of deviant behavior. If that's what you believe, and the evidence is so, then that must be your judgment. That's all."

"That's all." It was the only closing I could muster. I had stolen it from *Patton*, George C. Scott's movie where the gravel-voiced, tight-jawed general, wearing a shiny chrome-plated helmet liner and ivory-handled revolvers, addresses a division-size encampment of troops. With the American flag as a backdrop, he rails and rages and whispers and breathes fire. Then he says that no matter what happens, he will be damned proud to lead those fine men into battle. Silence. He looks left; he looks right. Then: "That's all." Why that fragment of show business entered my mind, why I shamelessly copied it, I don't know. It just did. I could think of no "therefore find him guilty as charged" bullshit. All I could do was sit on the edge of the prosecution's table, shoulders stooped over, feeling as though I was sixty years old, and say, "That's all." At that moment it expressed everything I had left to say about *State* v. *Tyson*.

I sat down, exhausted, and had what I can only describe as an out-of-body experience. The lack of sleep, the family problems, the death threats, the end of my participation in the case: for the past two weeks all I had known was down the steps, up the steps, *State* v. *Tyson*. My family had become those people; my life had become a tunnel.

In the back of my head a little voice said, *It's over*. I heard the slow wheels of justice turn. Judge Gifford's voice droned in the background as she read a lengthy set of instructions to the jury. It all ran together, all the talk about reasonable doubt, presumption of innocence, credibility of witnesses, expert testimony, *blah, blah, blah*. All a bunch of nonsense syllables to me at that point. I felt as if I was a kid again and was falling asleep on my parents' couch; I could hear a voice speaking, but it sounded muffled, as though it was coming from another room. There was a peaceful, reassuring quality to Judge Gifford's instructions, almost like that of a monastic chant, or like a priest's pronouncing a benediction. I heard, but I didn't listen.

Then I remembered that I had said nothing about Tyson's TOGETHER IN CHRIST button. I had several made up especially for the trial, and I had planned to hold one during my final argument, but I had forgotten. It seemed so important, and I had forgotten. I felt stupid, and I was pissed. I had let Desiree down. I thought I should have presented a blowout ending that would have knocked the jurors out of their chairs, set them on fire, and sent them out ready to convict, just *because*. But I didn't have the strength. I felt like just another worn-out, beat-up, half-dead, punch drunk, down-at-the-heels lawyer who just didn't have enough energy to finish the job right. I was so disappointed.

Jeff Modisett, the man who had picked me to prosecute the case, revived me. Sitting behind me, he passed me a brief note: A+ WORK. THANKS A LOT. Dave Dreyer passed up another message of praise. I looked behind me and saw Desiree; she smiled. Beside her Betsy gave me a "that's my daddy" grin. I saw other faces looking at me. They did not turn away in embarrassment;

in fact, several looked as though I had just cured cancer, slain a dragon, and hit the sixty-second home run. It was incredible because I was sure I had done a chopped-up, half-assed job.

The droning came to an end. The judge swore the bailiff and said, "The jury is now in the charge of the bailiff." The jurors rose and shuffle-footed between the seats as if they had bowling balls fastened to their ankles. I could see the weight pulling at them as they trudged out the door to begin their deliberations. The lawyers looked at each other. In a corporate civil suit I would have shaken Fuller's hand, but we couldn't do so in a case like this, in front of his client. I'm not sure we even spoke. Later, in the judge's chambers, we did shake hands and exchange a few words. I think he knew that we had won the fight, that we had won on the basis of the evidence and won the debate. But none of us knew who had won the trial. Sometimes in the alchemy of a trial the result is more than the sum of the evidence and the words with which the contest is waged. The personalities of the jurors, where they were attentive and where they were not, have to be factored into the outcome.

The entire prosecution team went to Iaria's, an Italian bar and restaurant on the south side, to eat pizza and salad, drink beer, and await the verdict. It was cold and nasty outside; a light rain fell, and the morning weatherman had promised snow by nightfall. Inside Iaria's it was warm, and after two or three beers I started to relax. I felt as though someone had removed an ice pick that had been sticking between my shoulders for the past two weeks. The tension began to ease out of my muscles. A television was tuned to CNN, which had a reporter talking about the case. The volume was turned low, or maybe the noise inside the bar drowned it out. I watched footage taken only that morning: I saw myself going into court, coming out of the courtroom, going to the john. Everyone became quiet and we listened to the television commentators talk about the trial as if they were doing half-time analysis of the Super Bowl. It was the same thing on ESPN and the local channels. I wondered if I had been at the same trial as a few of the commentators, who didn't seem to have a clue about what had taken place. Every so often there would be a live update about the jury—deliberations had broken off for lunch; the jurors were doing this or that. Watching your life on television almost as it was happening only extended my out-of-body feeling.

Lunch came and went. I had slept so little that I got buzzed on my few beers and slowed down drinking. Day turned to afternoon, afternoon turned to news time, and news time turned into time to drink some more. On every station it was the same thing; we saw ourselves go in and out of court half a dozen times. A few people got silly; a few got philosophical. The evening crowd drifted in and Iaria's began to fill up. There was nobody in Indianapolis who didn't know who we were, so we answered questions while we ate dinner. After dinner Jeff Modisett and I had a quiet talk, probably the closest one we had had during the entire case. He generously said that he was proud of my effort and that regardless of the verdict he had gotten his money's worth. He even told me that he wanted to try a major case with me, at which point I felt like choking him. The idea of ever trying another criminal jury made me want to vomit.

The evening crowd drifted out. Time rolled by in half-hour segments—eight-thirty, nine, nine-thirty. We had been in Iaria's for seven or eight hours. Ten, ten-thirty. A local newscaster speculated that Judge Gifford would soon send the jurors back to their hotel for the night. Unlike some other judges, she wasn't the type who played hard ball with juries; she wouldn't make them stay in the jury room until three or four in the morning.

Everyone had left Iaria's except a few regulars and us. Tommy Kuzmik got a page, and he called the courthouse from a pay telephone on the wall of the bar. I expected him to return with the news that Judge Gifford had dismissed the jurors for the night. But when he came back he had a sort of dramatic young buck look on his face. He looked around, and from across the room I could see the knot in his stomach. "We got a verdict. Let's go."

By the time we reached City-County the rumors of a verdict had electrified the place. Cameras were going crazy and reporters screamed questions that were impossible to answer. "What's going to happen?" "Has he been found guilty?" I got tired of saying "no comment" and stopped commenting altogether.

Everyone on our team gathered one last time in the war room: cops, victim assistance aides, paralegals, young lawyers, research assistants—they were all there. "Listen up," I said. "Somebody is going to win this thing and somebody is going to lose. Whatever the result, whatever happens, your heads are held up. We did the right thing. We done our damnedest and we put them through it. If we win, we behave with dignity. We don't act like a bunch of mopes on 'Let's Make a Deal.' I don't want any grins or smiles or celebrations. If we lose, same thing. No grumbles, nobody says shit. Pack it up and go home."

I was the first one in our group to walk into the courtroom. I looked at the defense table. Tyson was sitting alone; the Williams & Connolly attorneys had not yet arrived. For a second, Tyson and I looked at each other, and of course, like the sphinx he was, he revealed nothing. But over the years I have become acutely aware of one thing: defendants always know when they have been had. I can go back through death penalty verdicts and murder cases and liquor store holdups and burglaries and it is always the same; I know if I won or not because the defendant knows. One of them even said to me before the verdict, "You got me." I began to say "I don't know," but he interrupted, asserting, "No, you got me."

Looking at Tyson, I felt sorry for him. I didn't pity him; he was too strong a man to pity. But I felt compassion for a man who had won a world's title, had money in his pocket, women hanging all over him, an opportunity to influence people who idolized him, and was sitting alone in a criminal courtroom in old Indianapolis late at night about to head for the slammer. Once again I asked myself why he had to do it.

When Fuller and his team arrived, they looked subdued. The jury had been out for almost ten hours, which, according to popular courtroom theory, was too long for a not guilty verdict and not long enough for a hung jury. When a jury returns a verdict in the three- to ten-hour range, it has been my experience that the verdict is usually guilty.

When all the lawyers were present we a had brief meeting in Judge Gifford's chambers and then returned to the courtroom to hear the verdict. The room was jammed with reporters. A few seemed ready to sprint for the telephones once the verdict was announced.

The jurors trudged back to their seats. None of them smiled or looked at Tyson, another indication of an impending guilty verdict. Then we listened to a replay of an old melodrama that I had often heard before. Judge Gifford asked if the jury had reached a verdict. The jury foreman, the IBM marketing manager and ex-marine, said, "Yes, we have." He handed verdicts on the three charges against Tyson to the bailiff, who passed the forms on to Judge Gifford.

For what seemed like a minute, I held my breath. My heart was pounding, and my only thought was that no matter what the judge read, I would not betray any emotion. I sat with my eyes locked on a legal pad.

Finally, Judge Gifford began to read the verdict:

"As to count I [rape], we the jury find the defendant, Michael Tyson, guilty.

"As to count II [deviate sexual conduct, forced insertion of finger into a sex organ], we the jury find the defendant, Michael Tyson, guilty.

"As to count III [deviate sexual conduct, forced oral sex], we the jury find the defendant, Michael Tyson, guilty."

Someone later told me that Tyson's head jerked slightly and he whispered, "Oh, man," when he heard the first verdict. At the time, I was concentrating all my attention on writing a note on his file. I heard the verdict, but I didn't see anything.

Judge Gifford set sentencing for March 6. I argued that Tyson's bond should be revoked and that he should be remanded into the custody of the sheriff. The judge refused, although she did require him to surrender his passport. King, who sat behind Tyson holding a Bible during the reading of the verdict, stepped forward and gave her the document. Surrendering his passport meant nothing; Tyson could buy one in Chicago for a hundred dollars and slap in any picture he wanted. It was ludicrous to believe that there was anything keeping Tyson in the United States. This was a man who by conservative estimates had ten million dollars left in his pocket. He could buy a Lear jet, pay a pilot fifty thousand dollars to fly below radar, and be in Argentina the next day. And he could probably fight again— in South America, Asia, Africa. King could undoubtedly get his fights sanctioned by one of the boxing organizations, and perhaps he could even arrange cable coverage. His supporters could attribute all his problems to American racism, and he would be even more of a draw for being a fugitive. Jack Johnson, after all, had fled the country after a conviction and continued to defend his title, eventually losing it in Cuba. But Judge Gifford disagreed, and the proceedings ended.

I don't know what happened when I walked out of the courtroom, but I felt as though I stepped onto one of those moving sidewalks they have in airports, one set at about a hundred miles an hour. It snatched me up and from then on, for the next thirty-six hours, everything blurred together. I remember certain events but have little awareness of continuity. There were the smiles and handshakes in the war room. Cops slapping each other on the back, whooping and hollering, and swearing a blue streak. A few quiet moments with Barb, who expressed her sadness for Tyson and her joy that we hadn't let Desiree down.

Someone led the entire prosecution team down to the media room in the basement for a press conference. Stepping out of the prisoners' elevator, we were met by a crush of people. There were sun guns alight, flash guns going crazy, cameras whirling, people trying to out-shout each other. I looked at Tommy Kuzmik, Jack Geilker, Jeff Duhamell, Darryl Pierce, Charlie Briley, Steve Ogle, Cary Forrestal, and the other security policemen and saw concern. They formed a human wedge and pushed through the wall of humanity into the media room. The sound was deafening, screaming and screeching and hollering and every other sort of racket. Tripods were set up pellmell around the room, and cords criss-crossed every which way. The place smelled of cigarette smoke, discarded butts, and bodies mashed together. I thought to myself that nobody was going to be able to hear a thing. We were placed in front of twenty or thirty microphones that looked as if they had been taped together. ABC, NBC, CBS, CNN, ESPN, local stations, stations I had never heard of, stations I wasn't sure even existed. Other reporters pressed toward us holding recorder microphones.

Someone cried for order, although it had little effect. Jeff Modisett spoke for a few minutes. "We're very thankful for the verdict of guilty," Modisett said. "But I don't think we should lose sight of the fact that this is in some ways a tragic moment because two young people's lives have been dramatically affected." Jeff was exhausted. For two weeks he had sat on the sidelines, wringing his hands like a coach who had turned the game over to his players. If something had gone wrong, if Barb or I had made an embarrassing mistake, Modisett would have had to share the blame. Although he never second-guessed us during the trial, he had assembled the team, and he was the only member of that team who would have to stand for reelection.

After a few comments he turned the press conference over to me. I thought I was just talking to a gathering of reporters. I had no idea, not the faintest hint, that I was speaking live to people around the world. CNN had a live feed, ESPN had a live feed, all three networks had live feeds, and the international media were on satellite hookup. John Ostby, an old friend, watched the press conference live at seven in the morning on the island of Malta. I might have choked and fallen over on my side as though I had been shot if I had known what was happening. Instead I was just tired, sensorially deprived from fatigue and stress and too many beers. I had a nagging suspicion of what was happening to my marriage, I hadn't slept in twenty-four hours, I had been involved the night before in a high-speed car chase, and that morning I had delivered the final argument in the highest-profile case I ever tried. And now, as I started to speak, the reporters wouldn't quiet down. A fight had broken out over a problem with someone's sound equipment, and between the yelling of the combatants and everyone else screaming for them to be quiet I couldn't hear anything. At that point I reached my limit. I wasn't a politician, I wasn't planning to run for any office, I had finished my job, and I just didn't need this shit. And I told them so. I said I wasn't going to shout for them. I was going to talk quietly, and if they didn't quiet down, I was going to leave.

They got quiet. During the trial I had met many of the reporters. I liked most of them, and I respected many of them. They too put in long hours and worked under pressure. But they had been kind to Barb and me, and in their own way, gentle. They had paid attention and had been sensitive to nuance. Their reports had generally been accurate. Now they wanted to talk. Fine, we talked. Their questions were purposeful and made sense, and after it got started I enjoyed the press conference.

I said what I believed: "Professional athletics have become such a megagod that it is sometimes unresponsive to the morals of a community. Sometimes it just doesn't matter what a super-star does: It's okay. Tonight, at least this once, that type of behavior has not been tolerated." I had no sense of what the case meant to the rest of the nation or to future date rape cases. But I did know that Marion County had signaled that in its jurisdiction, date rape was a crime.

After the press conference, Rob Smith, the press liaison for the prosecutor's office, led Barb and me to the first floor for one-on-one media interviews. The activity on the first floor made the basement scene seem tame—almost like an open ba-zaar in Calcutta or Bombay, vibrating with humanity, people shouting to each other in a dozen or more languages. The floor was a maze of wires and cords. Everyone was transmitting live. I remember doing interviews with reporters from Australia, England, France, Italy, and Germany. I talked with reporters from the local stations as well as CNN, ESPN, and the major networks. Each station had a "studio," which amounted to a three-by-six-foot patch of floor that the station reporters had taped off for themselves, and Rob ushered me from one to the next until I lost track of time and place.

The interviews continued most of that night and for the next few days. Again and again the reporters asked the same ques-tions. Repeatedly I gave the same answers. It was all very sim-ple: eventually criminals convict themselves. Tyson's mistake was that he had raped a woman who refused to shrink quietly into some corner and who refused to be bought off or intimi-dated. He had raped a very special person, a sweet, gentle, kind, courageous, strong, determined woman. And he had raped her in the wrong city.

---

# ALAN
# IN WONDERLAND

*Men should be required to take a woman's verbal re-*
*fusal at face value. "No" must be understood to mean*
*precisely that. Old cultural patterns—no matter how*
*entrenched—must adapt to developing concepts of*
*equality.*

ALAN M. DERSHOWITZ, *1985*

**H**e should have answered no when Judge Patricia Gifford asked, "Mr. Tyson, do you have anything you would like to say at this time?" Six weeks before, Tyson had been found guilty of rape, and on this blustery day at the end of March 1992, Judge Gifford would determine his sentence.

Vincent Fuller had made a plea for leniency, describing Tyson as a "sensitive, thoughtful, caring, gentle man" who had emerged from an impoverished background to win world acclaim. Along the way, however, Tyson's managers had ignored his education and socialization. It was a failure that had left Tyson incomplete as a person, and that had led to this appearance in court. Fuller said Tyson needed counseling, he needed ther-apy, but he did not need to go to prison.

Then Tyson spoke for himself. He admitted that he had been "kind of crass" during his stay in Indianapolis and that the "situation . . . just got way out of hand." He said he was sorry that Desiree Washington "took it personally," but that he had not "hurt nobody. Nobody [had] a black eye or broken ribs. . . . They showed no bruises, no scars. Emotional, which she's saying. I'm not a psychiatrist. . . . I don't know what emotional disturbance is."

Tyson said he was sorry for many things, but he had not raped anyone. He was the real victim. "My personal life has been incarcerated. . . . I've been hurt. . . . I've been crucified. I've been humiliated. . . . I've been humiliated socially. . . ."

When he finished his eleven-minute statement, Tyson an-swered several questions, then seemed to withdraw emotionally from the proceeding. In his hand he held a small piece of white paper that a court reporter said had a Muslim prayer and a series of boxes printed on it. He focused on the paper as Judge Gifford considered his sentence.

After hearing all the recommendations, Judge Gifford made her decision. She sentenced Tyson to ten years for each of the three felony convictions and fined him $30,000. She then an-nounced that the sentences would run concurrently and be-cause of mitigating circumstances, she suspended four years. Bottom line: six years. Even with good behavior, Tyson would spend the next three years of his life in prison.

Until the end of the proceeding I hardly even noticed the new-est member of the Tyson entourage. Sitting behind Vincent Fuller, the back of his chair pressed against the wall, was a shortish, balding man with a fringe of frizzy auburn hair. He looked intently at Judge Gifford, barely moving except to jot down a note to himself occasionally. Another lawyer from Wil-liams & Connolly, I assumed.

My attention was fixed forward, to where Judge Gifford sat, not to the defense table at my left. Only minutes before, Fuller had asked that Tyson be released on bail pending the outcome of his appeal. He stressed that his client had never failed to meet the conditions of his earlier bail, that he had appeared promptly for all proceedings. Again, Fuller emphasized the three excluded witnesses, suggesting that their stories would have supported part of Tyson's testimony. I had argued against the granting of the appeal bond. The defense's case, I maintained, demonstrated a pattern of sexual aggression on Tyson's part. The witnesses who had testified for the defense had recounted instance after instance of his unwarranted and unwelcome sexual advances, ranging from suggestive statements to physical assaults. Tyson knew how to rape, he had done it at least once and been convicted, and he did not deserve to be free pending appeal. It was simple: the court had an obligation to protect the public by sending guilty, convicted rapists to prison.

Judge Gifford cleared her throat and, addressing Fuller, got straight to the point: "I am going to deny your petition for bail." She counted off the reasons for her decision: the seriousness of the crime, the potential for flight, and the unlikelihood of reversible errors in the record. If the Court of Appeals believed that there was a strong possibility of reversal, then it could grant bail. But on this day, March 26, 1992, the court denied the petition and remanded Mike Tyson to the Department of Corrections. With that, she started to rise.

The solemn finale was shattered by a loud racket to my left. A quick glance was enough to ascertain the source of the commotion. Stretched out on the floor, face down as if he was inspecting the fibers of the wall-to-wall carpeting, or perhaps performing some exotic religious rite, was the man I had noticed earlier sitting behind Fuller. Evidently he had tripped as he hurriedly got out of his chair. My first thought was that his head was going to explode; embarrassed, his bald spot glowed three shades of red brighter than his hair. As he lifted his head, adjusting his glasses with his left hand, he struggled unsuccessfully to regain his dignity. His face stiffened into a stern scowl. He seemed to be looking around for someone to blame, but finding nobody, simply shook his head as a general reproof to everyone in the courtroom. With his right hand he clutched a stack of papers tightly to his chest. "I'm off to see justice is done," a reporter sitting to his right heard him mutter.

Breaking every rule of courtroom decorum, he lumbered to his feet and darted for the door. I thought he must have the runs. Several reporters later told me that he took a sharp right as he exited the courtroom, an equally sharp left when he reached the stairs, raced straight out the north exit of the City-County Building, across Market Street, and into the City Market. He was apparently working under the assumption that the City Market, an all-purpose quick food center where you can buy everything from gyros and pizza to collard greens and fudge—doubled as the Indiana Court of Appeals, and that he could file a bond appeal somewhere between the fruit stand and the Chinese take-out place. When he realized his mistake, he hustled into a waiting van that took him the four blocks to the Court of Appeals, where he filed Tyson's bond motion.

That was my introduction to the techniques and methods of Alan M. Dershowitz, Harvard professor and appellate lawyer for the rich and guilty. At the time I thought he was a buffoon, a Falstaff of the legal world; only later would I comprehend the issues he raised about the American justice system.


Alan Dershowitz, as he likes to tell his lecture and television audiences, has chutzpah. He likes the role of the pushy outsider on the inside, the shtetl Jew who has forced his way into the Boston Brahmin house party, and in his book *Chutzpah* he encourages all Jews to follow his teaching, to renounce their fear of *shande far di goyim*—"being 'lightning rods' for anti-Semitism"—and assert themselves. His autobiographical writings enshrine this idea of himself as the outsider, the "Brooklyn street kid, a street fighter in a three-piece suit." The most salient feature of his life, Dershowitz seems to say, was not his Yale Law School degree, not his clerkship with Supreme Court justice Arthur Goldberg, not his full professorship at Harvard Law School—not any of these hard-won confirmations of status. Rather, the key to his psychological makeup was his upbringing in Borough Park, the Jewish enclave in Brooklyn where he read comic books, played basketball on driveway courts and stickball in the street, and fought for turf against outside gangs.

Although he eventually left Borough Park for Yale and Harvard, he struggled to keep Borough Park from leaving him. He rebelled against the straitlaced traditions of the Ivy League—not at first, to be sure, but rather when his position became secure. Initially he was what the Ivy law establishment expected—*Law Review* at Yale, budding scholar at Harvard, committed to the politically correct liberal issues. "He was a very different person back then, a much quieter man," Derrick Bell, a black professor at Harvard Law, remembered. He had not yet developed that special heat-seeking sense that would allow him to lock in on camera flashbulbs and television lights. He was an academic, not a celebrity.

All that changed, and the rebellion started, in the early 1970s. Some journalists suggest that personal trouble activated the transformation, that his son's brain tumor and the breakup of his Orthodox Jewish marriage made him rethink his career. Other Dershowitz watchers believe it was all the result of the Sheldon Seigel case. Seigel was a follower of Rabbi Meir Kahane, a thug for the Jewish Defense League, and a part-time police informer. In 1972 one of Seigel's bombs exploded in the midtown Manhattan office of the Columbia Artists Management Company, a booking agency that had recently brought Soviet performers to the United States. The bomb killed Iris Kones, a Jewish woman who worked in the office. It was a big case, a political case that attracted the attention of the White House and the Kremlin as well as that of New York authorities. A federal grand jury indicted three members of the JDL. Sheldon Seigel was from Borough Park, and hometown connections brought Dershowitz onto the case. Although he was criticized for defending a murderer *and* an informer, Dershowitz won the case, but not before he used several suspect— "totally improper," remarked the judge in the case—tactics, including reading from a transcript of a tape that in fact didn't exist. Of course, Seigel was guilty; that was never in doubt. Dershowitz won because the detective who cracked the case had stepped on a few toes in the process. The Seigel case, noted the journalist Paul Keegan, "brought together the major themes that would dominate his career: representing a despicable villain who was clearly culpable . . . and justifying his defense by claiming that the constitutional issues at stake were of greater importance than the crime. . . ."

The Seigel case made Dershowitz into a minor legal luminary. Coupled with his Harvard professorship, he had the credentials for the late-night talk shows. Within a decade he began to appear frequently on "Nightline," answering questions and arguing constitutional niceties. He liked the publicity and became involved in other notorious cases. Dershowitz defended F. Lee Bailey of mail fraud, then helped him on the Patty Hearst case; he appealed *Deep Throat* star Harry Reems's obscenity conviction; he came to the defense of the Soviet political prisoner Anatoly Shcharansky; he defended Bernard Bergman, "the meanest man in New York," and convict-turned-writer-turned-killer Jack Henry Abbott. It seemed as if Dershowitz was either holding court at the center or passing judgment on the periphery of half the sensational trials of the late 1970s and 1980s.

Then came the Claus von Bülow case, which shoved Dershowitz into the middle of American popular culture. In 1981 von Bülow, a European aristocrat, member of Newport high society, and international jet-setter, was charged, tried, and convicted of injecting his wife, Sunny, with insulin in an attempt to murder her. Although Sunny lived, the injection resulted in an irreversible coma. The trial was a media free-for-all. Hundreds of reporters crowded into the Newport courthouse while outside striking-looking women wore T-shirts announcing their support of the aloof Dane. Money, mistresses, a touch of madness, and rumors of kinky sex—the trial had everything that makes tabloid television successful. It was Agatha Christie meets Jackie Collins—old money, older passions, and modern glitz. It made Claus von Bülow a cult figure.

Faced with the likelihood of spending the rest of his life in prison, von Bülow asked Dershowitz to handle his appeal. For Dershowitz, it was a supremely satisfying moment: von Bülow, the ultimate WASP whose father had been tried as a Nazi collaborator, turned at his time of greatest need to Harry Dershowitz's son Alan von Borough Park. At his first meeting with Dershowitz, von Bülow announced, "I need the best lawyer I can get. I am absolutely innocent and my civil liberties have been egregiously violated." After making von Bülow squirm awhile, Dershowitz accepted the case. He constructed an appeal that won von Bülow a new trial, in which he was ultimately acquitted.

Dershowitz followed up his success by writing a book on the case, *Reversal of Fortune: Inside the von Bülow Case*, which, like

Dershowitz's other books, is marvelously entertaining and self-revealing. It languished in hardcover but became a paperback best-seller after Jeremy Irons won an Academy Award for his portrayal of von Bülow in the film based on Dershowitz's book. Dershowitz's stock rose with each paperback sale. He became as famous as von Bülow—and much more adroit at capitalizing on that fame.

Fame and failure became the primary bonds that linked him with his clients. As Keegan remarked, "more than anything, what Dershowitz's clients had in common was their celebrity. Each case temporarily satisfied his craving for attention. As an appellate lawyer, he had only a slim chance of overturning a conviction. 'I'm like a brain surgeon brought in after the tumor's been discovered,' he says. . . . So while his client usually loses, Dershowitz rarely does." Perhaps Keegan's characterization is overdrawn, for Dershowitz continued to defend poor, noncelebrity clients. But in the public's mind, he became known as the defender of the hawks of American society, the arrogant privileged few who believed that the laws of the land did not apply to them. And even stranger than his defense of them, he seemed to like them and often characterized them as decent, albeit misunderstood, people.

Since 1990 his list of celebrity clients has grown to include the biggest hitters on the tabloid crime scene—Park Avenue's Leona Helmsley and Wall Street's Michael Milken, as well as Marlon Brando's son Christian, family murderer Dr. Jeffrey MacDonald, Senate influence peddler Alan Cranston, religious influence peddler Jim Bakker, and Woody Allen's accuser Mia Farrow. How Jeffrey Dahmer and Amy Fisher have remained off the list is a mystery, for Dershowitz traffics in the rehabilitation of lost reputations. Leona Helmsley, he claimed, was a victim of anti-Semitism; Michael Milken, not only a warm, dedicated family man and an "incredible person" but also a man like himself, one with chutzpah, was also a victim of anti-Semitism. Anti-Semitism looms large in his explanation of American judicial behavior, and he drags out his tired and well-traveled charges in shabby attempts to counter the justified decisions of the courts. Paul Keegan asserts that Dershowitz "has traded his most valuable legacy—the proud Jewish heritage—for his own fame and glory." And, Keegan speculates, by invoking the Holocaust he has created the "ultimate sin": us-ing "the greatest horror in the history of humankind to get his sleazy clients out of jail."

It made sense for Don King to turn to Alan Dershowitz. Tyson was a perfect Dershowitz client: rich, famous, and guilty. Added to these qualifications, Tyson was black, which allowed Dershowitz to substitute the race card for his more familiar line on anti-Semitism. Although I played no active role in the appeal process, I followed Dershowitz's legal and theatrical maneuverings with growing unrest and disgust. Make no mis-take, Dershowitz had a complete right to accept Tyson's appeal. My dispute was not with his taking the job; it was with what I believed to be his abuse of the judicial process, and the manner in which he and his supporters resorted to racial arguments in an effort to overturn decisions.

Successful lawyers are creatures of habit. Once I learned that Dershowitz was handling Tyson's appeal, I began to study his life, just as I had Tyson's and Fuller's. To understand Dersho-witz, and to ascertain what approach he would take in the Ty-son appeal, I turned first to his writings. What I discovered was a thoughtfully candid discussion of his attitude toward the cli-ents he defended and the tactics he employed to win their re-lease. Reading Dershowitz's books was intriguing because they had the pace and charm of the best kind of courtroom novel and frightening because they threw light on what I fear may be the future of American justice, a future in which the legal sys-tem will be the slave of public opinion as manufactured by tab-loid television.

Before I read his books, and six weeks before I saw him at Tyson's sentencing, I got a feel for Dershowitz the man. Two days after the end of the trial, he called me at my office. He was soft-spoken and friendly—more amicable than I expected from the youngest man to be appointed full professor in the history of Harvard Law School. I was immediately certain he wanted something from me. The editor of *Penthouse*, he told me, was interested in doing one of the magazine's monthly in-terviews with me. It was a fair request. My refusal to do the interview had nothing to do with Dershowitz and everything to do with my mother and my own general opinion of such magazines. Dershowitz mentioned that he sometimes wrote for *Penthouse,* and I wondered briefly what his colleagues at Harvard thought about his literary outlets. But we had fought on different sides of the pornography issue, so it wasn't surprising that he penned articles designed for the filler pages between pictures of naked women.

Dershowitz's books and newspaper articles gave me a better understanding of his attitude toward his profession. Time and again he states that his central interest is in protecting individual constitutional rights. He is moved by abstractions more than by people, and he readily admits that almost all of his clients are in truth guilty. As an appellate lawyer, he is a lawyer of last resort. Criminals come to him only after they have been convicted; juries have already heard their cases and judged them guilty. "The criminal system," Dershowitz wrote in *Reversal of Fortune,* "is like an isosceles triangle: at the base is the large number of arrests; near the middle is the smaller number of trials; above that are the convictions. As you climb from the broad base to the tiny pinnacle, the system filters out the vast majority of innocents. By the time you get to appeals, you are near the narrow top, and there are few innocents left."

There is an old story in the legal profession. A lawyer wins an important case and wires his client, JUSTICE HAS PREVAILED. His client shoots back a return telegram: APPEAL IMMEDIATELY. The tale, which Dershowitz used in one of his books, underscores his own relationship with his clients. They are not interested in justice, and certainly not in any abstract conception of truth. They are guilty and convicted, and look to Dershowitz to work his sleight-of-hand legal magic to get the decision overturned. At that point, Dershowitz turns to the Constitution in search of an area, a technicality, to ground his appeal. He usually fails, not because he is bad lawyer—he is a very good, incredibly imaginative one—but because the vast majority of convictions are free of reversible error.

Not only are the people whom Dershowitz represents almost all guilty; they are also, as he notes, "guilty defendants who lie." They avoid the truth, hide from the truth, cover up the truth, and ignore the truth for the simple reason that the truth is what got them convicted in the first place. Truth be damned—they want their freedom. Dershowitz knows this, of course, so he seldom argues that his clients are factually innocent. Instead he tries to shade the truth, making it seem more complex and more subject to interpretation than it really is. In his world, truth loses its objectivity and becomes subjective, capable of multiple interpretations. Reality becomes vague and impersonal.

It is no coincidence, I believe, that Dershowitz was captivated by Akira Kurosawa's *Rashomon,* a film about the impossibility of discovering objective truth. The film revolves around four separate tales—or versions—of a rape. The truth of what happened is chimerical. Each person attempts to shift the blame away from him- or herself. Who is lying? Who is telling the truth? Is there any such thing as truth? *Rashomon* offers more questions than answers. "Men are only men," says the rapist and murderer. "That's why they lie. They can't tell the truth, even to themselves. . . . Because they are weak, they lie . . . to deceive others."

That an appellate lawyer would take such a position and attempt to muddy the judicial waters is logical. In my opinion, however, Dershowitz goes beyond throwing a fistful of dirt into the waters. As part of his appellate strategy, he takes a liberal interpretation of the canon of professional ethics. The American Bar Association has strict rules governing the scope of pretrial publicity and just what a lawyer can and cannot tell reporters. Dershowitz evidently doesn't believe that the same dictates govern pre-appeal publicity, for he has treated his life as an attorney like a movie career. Hype is his forte; he plays more to the television cameras and reporters than to the judges on the appeals bench.

For Dershowitz, the first battle in the appellate process is with public opinion. Most of his recent clients have shared two things: fame and guilt. Newspapers and magazines have printed and television has broadcast reports, and often sensational stories, of their activities and trials. The public rightly views them as guilty. Enter Alan Dershowitz with "new evidence" and a novel twist on reality. Segments of the media are anxious to aid Dershowitz in his crusade for "justice." *Penthouse* and other magazines willingly print his articles. But television is far more important in the battle for public opinion.

Dershowitz's rise to fame has paralleled the emergence of tabloid television. "A Current Affair," originally hosted by Maury Povich, was the first and most successful of the tabloid "news" shows. Premiering in 1986 on Rupert Murdock's Fox television network, the show was patterned after Murdock's tabloid newspapers and magazines. "A Current Affair" featured episodes on palimony suits, scandalous divorces, problems of the rich and famous, sensational crimes, and beautiful half-dressed women. Intellectually, it emphasized gossip; visually, it highlighted skin. As a nightly show, its producers were constantly searching for new stories, and they quickly discovered that lurid trials provided material for multiple episodes stretching over weeks or even months. The Robert Chambers case involving murder and "rough sex" and Rob Lowe's sexual activities in Atlanta during the 1988 Democratic Convention provided grist for dozens of stories in 1988 and 1989. The success of "A Current Affair" led to others of the same genre broadcast by rival networks. In 1989, both "Inside Edition" and "Hard Copy" went into syndication. By the early 1990s, three or more tabloid shows were broadcast each evening.

Dershowitz's clients soon became the darlings of the format. Claus von Bülow, Michael Milken, Leona Helmsley, Christian Brando, Mia Farrow—each dramatized tabloid television's most popular theme: the fall from grace of the rich and famous. All had hired Dershowitz, of course, after their fall was complete. His job was rehabilitation. Once again tabloid television cooperated, for in its soap opera world a tearful resurrection drew ratings almost as high as a juicy crucifixion. Although Dershowitz's clients were playing for real-life stakes, their performances for tabloid television were pure show business, and Dershowitz was their booking agent and director. The object was to gain sympathy and give their slanted version of the facts. As for truth, no one was interested—not the producers or consumers of the shows, and certainly not Dershowitz or his clients.

"Not only is it perfectly proper for a lawyer to go public in an effort to influence a prosecutor to drop the charges against his client, but it is, at least in my view, improper to neglect this important forum of advocacy," Dershowitz candidly admitted. For him, law was a branch of public relations. He used the media to argue his case out of the range of prosecutors who could challenge the "facts" and interpretations he presented. Dershowitz arranged for von Bülow to appear on "Nightline"; he put a weeping, humbled Helmsley on "The Joan Rivers Show"; the Mia Farrow–Woody Allen case played itself out on one tabloid television show or another. When he took on Mike Tyson, it was more of the same.

According to Vincent Fuller, the decision to hire Dershowitz to handle Tyson's appeal was Don King's call. It wasn't a decision that pleased Williams & Connolly, who expected to work the appeal. Following the tradition of Edward Bennett Williams, the lawyers at Williams & Connolly did not discuss their cases with journalists or show business gossip columnists. "We make our arguments in the courtroom, not on the courthouse steps," remarked Brendan Sullivan, Jr., who, like Fuller, had been a protégé of Williams's and was a member of the firm's executive committee.

Once before a convicted Williams & Connolly client had turned to Dershowitz. In 1989, Leona Helmsley had dumped the Washington, D.C., firm in favor of Dershowitz, who failed to overturn her income tax evasion conviction or reduce her sentence.

Throughout the trial I had watched Fuller struggle both to win an acquittal for Tyson and, failing that, to establish a record for appeal. The dual effort was a Williams & Connolly trademark. A lawyer establishes a record for appeal by questioning every possible judicial ruling. For instance, Williams & Connolly lawyers questioned sixty-one rulings by U.S. District judge Gerhard Gesell in the Oliver North case, which set up the eventual appellate victory. I knew that Fuller was constructing a similar paper trail, but the media and King cut him off before he could reveal his strategy.

Dershowitz attempted to ignore the facts that had been established in the trial. In his view Tyson, not Desiree, was the true victim. Tyson had been "railroaded," he claimed, a victim of a "stacked deck" and an unfair judicial system. In place of facts, Dershowitz advanced sound bites. His arguments spun together an assorted collection of half-truths and statements taken out of context, which he presented to the public with the air of a man coming off a mountain holding stone tablets.

Dershowitz's basic approach was to take the offensive. He attacked Judge Gifford, Jeff Modisett, Desiree Washington, and me. He claimed that Judge Patricia Gifford, a former prosecutor, had been hand-picked by Modisett, and that her rulings and instructions to the jury prejudiced Tyson's case. Several times he called press conferences to announce some new smoking gun. But each time, what he claimed was fresh evidence that justice in Tyson's trial had miscarried was just another tired, recycled argument; his smoking guns were more like broken peashooters. But by making his points loud enough and long enough, he was able to confuse the public and blur the central issues of the case.

I got my first close look at Dershowitz's methods in early June 1992. I foolishly agreed to be interviewed by Harold Dow, a staff reporter for Ed Bradley's "Street Stories." I had always been impressed with Bradley's work on "60 Minutes," and I was led to believe that he planned to do an unbiased report on the Tyson case. I talked with Dow for an hour, carefully going over the facts concerning the three late witnesses for the defense and Desiree's legal arrangements with Ed Gerstein. The three witnesses, I explained, might have seen Tyson with B Angie B, but not with Desiree. Everything they described—the color of the limousine, how the woman was dressed, how Tyson and the woman were holding on to each other and kissing—accurately depicted Tyson's arrival with B Angie B at the Canterbury in the early morning of July 18 but not the scene with Desiree twenty-four hours later. As for Gerstein, the facts about his role as the Washingtons' civil lawyer were well known to everyone involved in the trial, and it was Fuller's decision not to go into them in any great detail. Dow seemed interested in what I had to say, asked all the right questions, and assured me that the story would be impartial.

A few days later I agreed to another interview, this one with a woman from the Fox network who was compiling an investigative piece on Don King. As we made small talk at the end of the formal interview, I mentioned the "Street Stories" show. Oh, yes, she said, she knew all about it. It was going to be a "Tyson piece." King had demanded that over half the hour-long show feature a prison interview with Tyson. With full confidence in the integrity of Ed Bradley and Harold Dow and the news department of CBS, I insisted that she must be mistaken. "Right, it'll be *real* impartial! Sorry, but impartiality isn't part of Don King's and Alan Dershowitz's style. They go for the sure thing. But believe whatever you want. And oh, yeah, the check's in the mail."

I have no idea what deal the producers of "Street Stories" made with Tyson or King, but the Fox reporter's predictions were dead on the money. At least half the show focused on Tyson's protestations of innocence. He painted himself as a young, single, wealthy victim, an easy mark for a fortune-hunting woman. He had never raped anyone, he said; in fact, he described Desiree as the sexual aggressor. If he made a mistake, it was refusing to walk Desiree down to the limousine. If only he had been more of a gentleman, he would not be locked away in prison with inmates who called him a "tree jumper" and guards who were addicted to power.

Dershowitz agreed that Tyson was unjustly incarcerated because of a "terrible misunderstanding." Desiree "acted like a groupie, behaved like a groupie, [went] to [Tyson's] room like a groupie," and then pressed charges after Tyson treated her like a groupie.

Interestingly enough, Dershowitz had earlier discussed just this sort of misunderstanding. In 1985 he wrote an article about a rape that occurred in a Hmong community in California. The Hmong, members of a mountain tribe in Laos who relocated to the United States after the Vietnam War, practiced a form of ritualized rape as part of their courtship customs. In "marriage by capture," a Hmong man takes a woman from his community to his family's house to consummate their union. As part of the ritual, the woman is expected to protest the consummation to demonstrate her virtue, while the man is expected to force the act to show his strength. In one case, a woman who said no meant no, and she filed rape charges against the man. Who was wrong? Dershowitz deplored the ritual and asserted that regardless of different cultural norms, no means no: "Men should be required to take a woman's verbal refusal at face value. 'No' must be understood to mean precisely that. Old cultural patterns—no matter how entrenched —must adapt to developing concepts of equality."

Perhaps by 1992 Dershowitz had flip-flopped on the issue. More likely, however, he now found it convenient to argue that a misunderstanding by one of his own clients canceled all bets. Tyson had thought Desiree was a groupie; therefore their having sex, no matter how much she protested, had to be consensual. And if it wasn't—well, who could blame Tyson for the misunderstanding?

It wasn't the first time Dershowitz had allowed the current needs of his client to govern his philosophical position. Before Michael Milken became one of his clients, Dershowitz had written articles criticizing the federal court that had tried him for going easy on the financier. Then Milken hired him, and Dershowitz had an abrupt change of heart. Milken was suddenly a Wall Street saint, the good guy in the white hat who drove a station wagon, was loyal to his wife, and took care of business—and who was little more than a scapegoat for a government that wanted to punish the very greed it had fostered.

In Dershowitz's argument, Desiree was insignificant, her suffering, her nightmares, her mangled dreams meaningless. But Dershowitz was a lawyer fighting for his client. There was no excuse for "Street Stories." Ed Bradley came across as a glorified emcee. If CBS had wanted a story rather than a biographical profile, the network should have turned Mike Wallace and his "60 Minutes" staff loose on Tyson. But then, I doubt that CBS would have obtained the exclusive "first prison interview" with Tyson.

The "Street Stories" mess convinced me to stay away from the taped and edited television format. The issues at stake were too important to allow some producer to bend and shape my words. I had no interest in the battle of sound bites. Besides, once the foreman read the guilty verdict in *State* v. *Tyson,* the case belonged to the state attorney general's office. During the next eight months I refused half a dozen requests to "debate" or "discuss" the case on television with Dershowitz. For almost half a year I had lived the case, and during that time one essential fact became obvious: the State of Indiana sent Mike Tyson to prison because he had raped Desiree Washington. I didn't send him there, nor did Barb Trathen, Jeff Modisett, or anyone else from the prosecutor's office. Judge Gifford's rulings played no part, nor did Vincent Fuller's legal strategy. The system worked, and Tyson was held accountable for his actions. Paul Wolff, a partner with Williams & Connolly, said, "You fight hard, and you do the best you can. Cases are dictated by the facts. Nobody wins them all."

**D**ershowitz fought as hard as anyone. From the moment he fell on his face at the sentencing hearing, he scrambled to win

Tyson a new trial. He ratcheted up the level of media hype a few notches and kept it there. Seldom did a week pass without Dershowitz firing a charge at the prosecutor's office. He dealt in sensational absolutes—the "worst injustice," the "greatest crime." He saw more smoking guns than a sightseer at the O.K. Corral. But when he filed Tyson's appeal, he failed to add any new twists to the case. The grounds for the appeal were the very ones that had been anticipated by journalists and lawyers since the final verdict.

Dershowitz questioned the legal relationship Desiree and her parents had had with Ed Gerstein. Desiree, Dershowitz suggested, had hired Gerstein to negotiate a book and movie deal based on her experiences and to file a civil suit against Tyson as soon as the trial was successfully completed. From the start her motive was simply to capitalize on her brief link with Tyson, and she lied on the witness stand about her true legal connection with Gerstein. Based on her alleged perjury, Dershowitz petitioned Judge Gifford for a new trial in August 1992.

The facts concerning this ridiculous charge are simple. To begin with, only a fool would file criminal charges in order to set up a subsequent civil suit. The burden of proof in a criminal case is more severe than in a civil case, and the chance of winning an acquaintance rape case is less than fifty-fifty. Dershowitz would have his public believe that Desiree was involved in an elaborate, Machiavellian crapshoot; that she had risked everything on a criminal action just to make her civil suit look better, and that she had endured the pain and criticism of a bitter, nationally spotlighted trial to enhance her chances of signing a book and movie contract. The entire scenario reads like a cheap novel. If Desiree wanted money from a civil suit, she could have simply filed one and avoided the nightmare of the trial. For that matter, if all she wanted was money, she could have dropped the case and accepted the million-dollar bribe she was offered. She wanted not wealth but justice; she wanted to prevent Tyson from raping another woman.

The trial record demonstrates for anyone who cares to read it that Desiree did not lie about her legal relationship with Gerstein. On January 31, toward the end of his cross examination of Desiree, Vincent Fuller had raised the issue of the Washingtons' legal representation. Desiree said her family had hired a lawyer to "help with all the media." Fuller asked, "Do you think he has some retainer arrangement with your parents?" The precise legal definition of "retainer" would not likely be known by the average teenager. I had instructed Desiree that if she didn't understand a question to say so. With this in mind, she answered, "I don't know what 'retainer' means." Fuller continued his cross-examination, asking Desiree about contingent fees and other financial arrangements. She replied that she knew very little about her family's contract with Gerstein.

Fuller then changed the direction of his questioning. For Dershowitz, however, Desiree's admission that she was not familiar with certain legal terms somehow "proved" that she committed perjury.

In her eight-page ruling, Judge Gifford stated that the fee agreement was not "newly discovered evidence" that could win Tyson a new trial. Furthermore, she accused Dershowitz of attempting to "perpetrate a fraud upon the court," citing an interview broadcast on ESPN radio on June 28 in which Dershowitz said that Donald Washington had referred to movie rights as "where the money is." After reading a transcript of the interview, Gifford concluded that Dershowitz had misrepresented Washington's statement. Washington had quoted Gerstein's opinion on movie rights; he hadn't made the statement himself.

In the next few months Dershowitz shifted his attack to Judge Gifford herself, accusing her, in essence, of being a stooge for the prosecution, favoring the prosecution in her rulings and her instructions to the jury. It was a wild idea. During the trial Judge Gifford ruled against the prosecution as well as the defense, and she was coldly intolerant of any courtroom tricks.

Dershowitz then went after the jurors. His public relations campaign to smear Desiree, second-guess Judge Gifford, and achieve sainthood for Tyson convinced several jurors that they had not heard all the evidence. Although most of the jurors said that the Washingtons' legal arrangements with Gerstein would not have influenced their decision—"If she was so greedy, why didn't she take the million and run, instead of taking the chance with the trial?" asked one—two jurors said they now questioned Desiree's motives. Deval L. Patrick, Desiree's lawyer, commented that there was no book or movie deal—not then, not ever. The reassessment of the case was based not on new evidence, just Dershowitz's "public relations effort to besmirch [Desiree] Washington and to influence the people who will sit in judgment of the appeal and the civil suit."

But Dershowitz continued his assault. In January 1993, the month before the oral arguments on Tyson's appeal, Dershowitz appeared on CBS's "Maury Povich Show" with three jurors from the trial. The jurors maintained that they believed that Tyson was guilty as charged. "Rape is rape," one asserted. Desiree "was taken advantage of, she said no, [Tyson] forced himself on her." The show, however, gave Dershowitz valuable airtime.

Dershowitz's involving jurors in his media carnival has set a dangerous precedent. Jurors hear what the court and the rules of evidence decide they should hear. During a trial they are told not to discuss the case and sometimes are even sequestered from the public to prevent them from being influenced by outside forces or information. Jurors should not be encouraged to second-guess their decision after a trial is over, especially by a lawyer representing the very person they convicted.

In mid-January, Jeffrey Modisett finally spoke out against Dershowitz's tactics. Modisett said he had tried to keep a low profile but was tired of Dershowitz's attacks on "the judge, the jury, [the prosecutor's] office, the court of appeals and the victim," whom Dershowitz had branded as "a liar, perjurer, and even a racist." "We did not put Mike Tyson in prison," he continued. "Mike Tyson's actions did." Ignoring Modisett's criticism, Dershowitz followed his own script, repeating the same charges that had caused Modisett to take a stand. Modisett's appeal for decency was lost in Dershowitz's public relations blitz.

Modisett's concerns were primarily professional. Desiree Washington's concerns were personal. The campaign undertaken by Dershowitz to free Mike Tyson, which by now had taken on the trappings of a crusade, made it impossible for Desiree to recover from the rape. Her nightmares continued, made worse by Dershowitz's charges. "I was attacked once, and now I'm attacked over and over again," she told an Indianapolis reporter. "I can't heal, and I can't get better. . . . I basically lost my life."

It was her first public statement in almost a year. Dershowitz interpreted Desiree's plea that "enough is enough" as another sign that she planned to profit from the case. "I think it's in her financial interest to come forward now," he told reporters.

"Maybe she thinks . . . she'll have a better opportunity to get book and movie rights."

When I read Dershowitz's statement, I thought of Joseph Welch, the counsel for the U.S. Army in the Army–McCarthy hearings of 1954. Toward the end of the hearings, McCarthy attempted to assassinate the character of a young member of Welch's law firm. Welch implored him to desist. McCarthy, bit in his teeth, refused. Finally, exasperated, Welch said, "Have you no sense of decency, sir, at long last? Have you left no sense of decency?"

On a bitter cold Monday, February 15, 1993, in a 125-year-old courtroom with heavy oak paneling and stained-glass windows, Dershowitz officially argued Tyson's appeal. An enormous chandelier hung high above his head; photographs and daguerreotypes of dead judges lined the walls. Three robed appellate judges, Jonathan S. Robertson, Patrick D. Sullivan, and V. Sue Shields, sat behind a raised bench. Almost two hundred fifty spectators and reporters filled every seat in the Indiana Supreme Court chambers in the State Capitol. Some had lined up before dawn for tickets to the proceedings. Others were friends of the accused, state officials, or guests of the court, mostly law clerks and lawyers with a little pull. Rubbernecking like witnesses at a bad traffic accident, they had come to see if Alan Dershowitz was as good as he claimed.

Dershowitz outlined the main issues of the appeal: the three excluded witnesses, the selection of Judge Gifford, her final instructions to the jury, the admittance of the 911 tape, and the Washingtons' contract with Gerstein. Restraint marked Dershowitz's arguments. His television swagger and bombast were gone; he had turned down the volume a notch. He argued technicalities and judicial judgment calls: the three witnesses, although late arriving and even tardily reported, should have been allowed to testify; the 911 tape was not a "spontaneous utterance"; the selection of Judge Gifford to try the case was made "wisely, if not fairly"; Desiree's true motive in the case was financial gain.

Dershowitz's most dubious contention was that Judge Gifford gave the wrong instructions to the jury. Judge Gifford, he said, should have instructed the jury to consider Tyson's "state of mind." He argued that the case was not simply about who had lied and who had told the truth; there might have been a middle ground of ambiguity and moral uncertainty. Tyson might have believed that Desiree's no really meant yes. Tyson might have misinterpreted Desiree's no, but misinterpreting a command hardly constituted rape. "A mistaken fact negates the crime," Dershowitz insisted. And Judge Gifford should have instructed the jury to that effect.

The argument boggles the imagination. "No harm, no foul," as a defender in a basketball game might plead after a brush foul. But in Desiree's case there was real physical and lasting psychological harm, and still Dershowitz cried no foul. It is akin to insisting that one *thought* the shooter wanted to be stripped, tripped, and knocked to the floor. Innocent by virtue of incorrect thought.

Larry M. Reuben, chief counsel for the Indiana attorney general, and Deputy Attorney General Matthew Gutwein disputed all of Dershowitz's contentions. They defended the selection of Judge Gifford, her rulings on the three witnesses and the 911 tape, and her instructions to the jury. There was no moral ambiguity in the case, Reuben said. Tyson testified that Desiree consented to have sex with him. "Either he raped her or she consented."

Some two hours after it began, the oral argument ended. The Court of Appeals adjourned, and the lawyers, reporters, and spectators filed out of the courtroom. Before heading out into the cold, the major players in the drama spoke to the reporters and television cameras. King repeated how great it was to live in America and that Tyson was the victim of a lying woman, and then with a quick "Ciao baby" was out the door. Reuben and Gutwein said they were pleased with the proceedings. Dershowitz agreed. Maintaining his best solemn, "we only want to be treated fairly" face, Dershowitz told reporters he didn't have time for lengthy statements or involved questions: "I'm off to see Mike Tyson and hope that justice prevails."

On August 6, 1993, a cool summer day more than two years after the rape, justice did again prevail. By a vote of two to one, the Indiana Court of Appeals upheld Tyson's rape conviction.

Dershowitz had a short conversation with the former world's champion, then appealed immediately.

# E P I L O G U E

———

Inside the Indiana Youth Center in Plainfield, a short drive from Indianapolis, Mike Tyson waited, not so much for his release, but for the end of each day, each week, each month. Sentenced to serve six years, he knew that if he stayed out of trouble he would be released in three. But staying out of trouble was never Tyson's strong suit. On March 15, 1993, he clashed with a prison guard over his phone privileges. The imbroglio tacked an additional thirty days onto his sentence—his good-behavior release moved back to May 9, 1995. Alan Dershowitz casually brushed off the episode: "There are misunderstandings in prison—this was one of them."

The following month there was another misunderstanding, at least according to Dershowitz. The *New York Post* reported that Tyson had converted to Islam and taken the name Malik Abdul Aziz. Not so, said Dershowitz. "Someone is circulating false stories. [Tyson] told me, 'When my Islamic teacher comes to me, I talk about Islam; when you come to me, we sometimes talk about the Jewish faith.' "

But more often the two talked about the chances of Tyson's being released before May 9, 1995. Dershowitz remained optimistic, even after the Indiana Court of Appeals denied his appeal for a new trial. He filed motions requesting that the

Indiana Supreme Court review the case, which, he asserted, stands "as a textbook of errors—both legal and factual."

Before any review could take place, however, a majority of the five-justice Supreme Court had to agree to consider the review. And Tyson's odds had been shortened the previous November when Chief Justice Randall T. Shepard had preemptively disqualified himself from considering the case. On September 22, 1993, Tyson once again fell short by a single vote. The Supreme Court deadlocked 2–2 and issued a brief statement saying that it would not review the Court of Appeals decision. The justices were not required to give a reason for their decision, and they didn't.

During the week after the announcement, reporters focused their attention on Chief Justice Shepard. Why had he disqualified himself? Ugly rumors bubbled to the surface; wild conspiracies were spun out of thin air. Some dark and mysterious secret, it was thought, linked the judge and the boxer together. The truth, as it turned out, was as weird as the rumors but strangely poetic in its justice. A year earlier, on October 3, 1992, Dershowitz had attended his Yale Law School thirty-year class reunion. He was the center of attention. An Australian camera crew filmed him in the University commons, and classmates greeted him warmly. Then a stranger pushed her way up to Dershowitz and began intently discussing the Tyson appeal. "In the neighborhood I grew up in, they would have called her a yenta," he later recalled. She lectured one of the country's leading appellate attorneys on the niceties of appeal work in Indiana. The conversation was well advanced by the time Dershowitz asked the woman's name and discovered she was Amy W. MacDonell, not a lawyer herself but married to Randall T. Shepard, Yale Law School, class of 1972—and the Chief Justice of Indiana.

The conversation had compromised Shepard, and he correctly withdrew from any consideration of the case. Although Dershowitz assumed that Shepard would have voted in favor of reviewing Tyson's appeal, his conclusion was hardly warranted. Shepard had in fact written the opinion in *Welshart* v. *State*, the very case dealing with late-blooming witnesses that Judge Patricia Gifford had used in her decision not to allow Tyson's three eleventh-hour witnesses to testify. It seems unlikely that Shepard would have found fault with his own opinion. The central irony remained: Dershowitz had been bitten in the ass by his own celebrity.

*Time* magazine listed the Supreme Court decision in its "Milestones" section, right below the announcement that Woody Allen would not be charged with sexually molesting his daughter and above Nolan Ryan's decision to retire from baseball. Tyson, the brief note concluded, "has virtually no legal options remaining." Wrong. As long as Tyson had money he had legal options.

The most obvious option, and the least likely to succeed, was appealing to the United States Supreme Court. Dershowitz knew that he would have to couch an appeal to the Court in constitutional terms. In his petition for writ of certiorari, he asked the Court to review the case, arguing that rape shield laws violated the Sixth Amendment to the Constitution, which gives the accused the right to confront his accuser. Rape shield laws prevent defense attorneys from exploring aspects of the accuser's past; they protect innocent victims from being dragged through the mud. Dershowitz sought a return to an outdated system where a woman's past was fair game. The chances were remote that the Supreme Court would move against rape shield laws or even decide to hear the case. Dershowitz also continued to work legal avenues in Indianapolis by filing two Post Conviction Relief (PCR) petitions. One was based on the Washington family's financial relationship with Ed Gerstein, the other on alleged aspects of Desiree's sexual history. Both promised to keep the case in the news; neither offered much hope of overturning Tyson's conviction.

Ironically, Jim Voyles, Tyson's capable Indianapolis attorney who had been largely ignored during the trial, offered the best chance for Tyson's early release. Like any good attorney, he continued to work for his client outside of the glare of publicity. His best chance for any modification of the sentence was to convince Judge Gifford that Tyson had been rehabilitated, an unlikely scenario unless Tyson admitted that he had terribly wronged an innocent young woman.

"They won't allow me to heal," Desiree told me the last time I spoke with her. I thought about other victims, other crimes, about the people and families I knew who would never recover fully from some act of violence. I wanted to tell her that justice can never be complete and that the criminal process can never take away the hurt. Instead, I said simply, "I know."

# I N D E X

10/20/94

J. K. Hosier